Capitalism, Socialism and Technology

Charles Edquist

To Lena, Harald and Holger

Capitalism, Socialism and Technology

A Comparative Study of Cuba and Jamaica

Charles Edquist

Zed Books Ltd.

Capitalism, Socialism and Technology was first published by
Zed Books Ltd., 57 Caledonian Road, London N1 9BU,
in 1985.

Copyedited by Anne Beech
Typeset by Forest Photosetting
Proofread by Gordon Willis
Cover design by Ian Hawkins
Printed at The Bath Press, Avon

British Library Cataloguing in Publication Data

Edquist, Charles
    Capitalism, socialism and technology : a comparative
    study of Cuba and Jamaica.
    1. Sugarcane — Cuba — Harvesting   2. Sugarcane —
    Jamaica — Harvesting   3. Agricultural innovations —
    Cuba   4. Agricultural innovations — Jamaica
    I. Title
    633.6'15'097291   SB229.C9

    ISBN 0-86232-393-2
    ISBN 0-86232-394-0 Pbk

US Distributor
Biblio Distribution Center, 81 Adams Drive,
Totowa, New Jersey 07512.

Contents

Figures

Tables

Preface

I have been studying the relations between technology and socio-economic conditions since the mid-1970s. My earlier theoretical studies indicated that it would be interesting to continue this work by comparing technical change in societies characterized by different socio-economic systems. I believe that the present study is one of the first attempts to investigate in detail the differences between a capitalist and a socialist country in relation to causes and consequences of technical change in a specific economic sector. However, one of the main reasons for carrying out the study was to highlight various issues of significance for other countries also, particularly Third World ones. Examples of such general issues addressed in this book are listed in Chapter 1.

The present study is based on data collected during field work in Cuba and Jamaica. Altogether I spent about 7 months in the two countries at various occasions during the 1979-83 period. In Cuba I was happy to collaborate with Centro de Estudios de Historia y Organizacion de la Ciencia "Carlos J. Finlay" (CEHOC), an institute within the Cuban Academy of Sciences, where I was invited to be a visiting research follow. I also co-operated with the Ministry of the Sugar Industry as well as with the Ministry of Metallurgical and Mechanical Industry. In Jamaica I co-operated with the Institute of Social and Economic Research (ISER) at the University of the West Indies in Kingston and with the Sugar Industry Research Institute (SIRI) in Mandeville. These organizations very generously provided support that was important in several respects. They were of invaluable assistance in data collection as well as in organizing visits to sugar cane production units and to factories producing equipment for sugar cane agriculture. Last, but not least, they helped me to arrange interviews with researchers and decision-makers concerned with sugar cane production in both countries.

In regard to Cuba I want to thank, in particular, Tirso W. Saenz, Vice President of the Academy of Sciences and P.M. Pruna at CEHOC. In Jamaica I was greatly assisted by Mike Shaw, Reginald Burgess and Colin Lee at SIRI and Vaughn Lewis, Eddie Greene and Omar Davies at ISER. In addition a large number of persons in both countries have made themselves available for interviews and discussions, some of which will be referred to in the text. Others have assisted me in collecting information in libraries, government agencies, private sugar organizations and labour unions.

However, in spite of all this assistance, the data base is somewhat weak in certain places. This is partly explained by the fact that the technical changes in sugar cane agriculture during the last 25 years are insufficiently documented. This is the case more for Jamaica than for Cuba and more for the earlier part of the period studied than for the latter. All in all, however, the documentation is more satisfactory in the case of Cuba than in Jamaica, probably because sugar cane mechanization has been a bigger issue in Cuba. However, this applies primarily to information on a technical level. In regard to economic information – e.g. costs and prices – the data problems have been particularly severe for Cuba. This led to certain problems in the analysis. In particular my attempts to move from the technological to the economic and social level in the analysis have partly been constrained by the unavailability of essential economic data.

In my attempts to collect economic information with regard to sugar cane harvesting, secrecy on the part of the Cuban authorities was a severe obstacle. In spite of having accepted my project and invited me as a guest researcher, they gradually became more sensitive during the research process. The more pieces of the puzzle I managed to find, the more reluctant they became to provide additional information, although I asked specifically for data which I had very good reasons to believe the relevant authorities themselves had access to. Perhaps my efforts to make the puzzle as complete as possible conflicted with the strategic interests of a small country subject to the threat of economic and military warfare. Hence, my understanding of technical change in a very important economic sector may have become too comprehensive for the Cuban authorities. An alternative reason for their reluctance to assist me is the fact that the result of my puzzling does not, in certain respects, accord with the official Cuban picture of the process of sugar cane harvest mechanization.

The pictures of the processes of sugar cane harvest mechanization in Cuba and Jamaica presented in this study are based on all relevant published material which I have been able to find, a large number of unpublished papers and reports, and numerous interviews with people involved in the process of mechanization. Some of the empirical material has not been previously available and most of it has not been presented in a systematic form.

I have worked part-time on this study for several years. Therefore a large number of colleagues have criticized earlier versions of it or commented upon different sections presented at conferences.[1] During the work I have acquired many personal and intellectual debts as well as many friends, and a few enemies, in Cuba, Jamaica and elsewhere. I will express my sincere gratitude to those who have assisted me simply by listing them in alphabetical order: Lino E. Abreu, Oscar Almazán, Erik Baark, Richard Baum, M.R. Bhagavan, George Beckford, Claes Brundenius, Reginald

Burgess, Rolf Carlman, Daniel Chudnovsky, Charles Cooper, Omar Davies, Olle Edqvist, Juan Ferrán, Martin Fransman,Luis Galvez, Emilio Garcia Capote, Christer Gunnarsson, Hans Gustavsson, Bo Göransson, Jack Hackett, G.B. Hagelberg, C-H. Hermansson, Staffan Jacobsson, Andy Jamison, Bard Jögensen, Ulla Kinnberg, Colin O. Lee, Kent Lindkvist, Mr Loeser, Carmelo Mesa-Lago, Thandika Mkandawire, Manuel Moreno Fraginals, Camilla Odhnoff, Jan Odhnoff, Lesley Palmer, Gunnar Paulsson, Brian Pollitt, P.M. Pruna, Sergio Roca, Nathan Rosenberg, Tirso W. Sáenz, Anders Sandström, Chris Scott, Mike E.A. Shaw, Jon Sigurdson, Mr Stephenson, Frances Stewart, Yael Tagerud, Hans Vallentin, Susumu Watanabe, Hakan Wiberg, Stefan de Vylder. I am particularly grateful to Charles, Olle, Bo, Staffan and Kent who have given detailed comments on the manuscript in various stages of completion.

The project from which this study emanates has been carried out at the Research Policy Institute, University of Lund, Sweden, where it is part of the research programme, "Technology and Development". The project has been financially supported by the Swedish Agency for Research Cooperation with Developing Countries (SAREC). I gratefully acknowledge this support. Last, but not least, I want to thank the Sisters at the Convent of Rögle, just outside Lund, for providing stillness during various critical periods of the work with this book.

Charles Edquist
Lund

Research Policy Institute
University of Lund
Box 2017
S-220 OQ Lund
Sweden

Notes

1. Earlier versions of parts of the present study have previously appeared in Edquist (1982a, 1982b, 1983 and 1984).

Part 1: Introduction

1. Scope and Outline

This study deals with socio-economic aspects of technical change in sugar cane harvesting in Cuba and Jamaica. Socio-economic aspects refer both to the determinants as well as the consquences of the choice of technique. The time period encompassed by the study stretches from the late 1950s to the early 1980s. By examining and comparing the choice of techique to do the same tasks (cane cutting and loading) in two countries with different socio-economic systems, I am attempting to contribute to our knowledge about the driving forces behind, and the effects of, technical change.

The idea was to carry out a comparative economic systems study which could illuminate issues of general importance for Third World countries. Examples of such general questions addressed in this study are:

Which are the most important determinants and obstacles to technical change under capitalism and socialism?

What effect did the transition to socialism in Cuba have on technical change?

Which social and economic factors influenced the performance of various technologies?

How can a technical capability be developed in Third World countries?

Which role does the capital goods industry play in the generation of such a capability?

What is the relation between technical capability, technical dependency and the technology gap?

What are the consequences for various social classes of different choices of technology?

What is the relation between technical change and employment?

Why are the interests and strategies of workers and labour unions in relation to technical change, different in a capitalist and a socialist context?

Why does the strategy of using "appropriate technologies" contribute to the perpetuation of underdevelopment?

The comparative case study was used to highlight general issues of this kind and the cases studied were chosen with this in mind. Cuba was chosen because it is one of the few Third World countries with a sufficiently long history of socialism. Jamaica was chosen because it is a capitalist country located in the same area of the world and since it was at a level of development comparable to that of Cuba in the 1950s. Sugar cane harvesting was chosen because it is a substantial sector in the economies. The sugar sector has for a long time been a major employer of labour and quite a significant foreign exchange earner in both countries. With regard to mechanization of sugar cane cutting and loading, both Cuba and Jamaica were at the same level in the late 1950s. At present both countries are relatively advanced in this respect compared to other Third World countries.

In this study the choice of technique in sugar cane harvesting is examined in four situations, as shown in Figure 1.1, where the socio-economic systems are also indicated. However, due attention is also paid to the transition from one period to another in the same country.

Figure 1.1
Basic Design of the Study

	Late 1950s	*Early 1980s*
Cuba	(1) capitalism	(2) socialism
Jamaica	(3) capitalism	(4) capitalism

The story of sugar cane harvest mechanization is strikingly dissimilar in the two cases. In the 1950s, the cutting as well as the loading of cane were exclusively manual tasks in both countries. The mechanization of cane loading started in Jamaica in 1961 and in Cuba in 1964. At the present time, practically all cane is loaded mechanically in both countries, but the dynamics of the mechanization processes were quite different. As regards cane-cutting, efforts to mechanize were initiated in Cuba in 1967, but these attempts did not succeed until a breakthrough came in the early 1970s. In the late 1960s the Cubans had designed an efficient harvester, but the Cuban mechanical industry was not capable of producing it. It was therefore manufactured in West Germany. In 1981, 50 per cent of the cane – 33.3 million tonnes – was harvested by combine harvester in Cuba. This means that more cane was mechanically cut in Cuba than in any other country. All harvesters for Cuban needs are now designed and produced in Cuba, and Cuba has become the largest producer of cane combine harvesters in the world. However, these machines are considerably less productive than some of those produced in capitalist countries, including the machine mentioned above, which was designed in Cuba but produced in West Germany. In Jamaica trials with combine harvesters were carried out in the early 1970s, without resulting in their introduction, and all cane-cutting is still carried out manually with machetes.

The processes of mechanization in Cuba and Jamaica are closely related to socio-economic conditions. Cuba was gradually transformed into a socialist society during the 1960s while Jamaica remained capitalist.

Traditionally, the most important actors in sugar cane agriculture in both countries were plantations, small cane farmers, sugar workers and unions, and the state and its agencies. During the agricultural reforms in Cuba in the early 1960s, the plantations were transformed into state farms. Unemployment was high in Jamaica during the whole period studied: almost 30 per cent in 1980. In Cuba, open unemployment gradually decreased from 12 per cent in 1960 to 1.3 per cent in 1970, but thereafter it grew again and stabilized at around 5 per cent in the late 1970s. In the early 1980s it decreased somewhat again.

The first objective of this study is to describe the processes of technical change in sugar cane harvesting in two countries with different socio-economic systems and thereby give substance and specificity to the picture outlined above. The second objective is to analyse the determinants and consequences of these processes, which means that neither the techniques nor the socio-economic and political conditions as such, but the relationship between the two, are placed at the centre of focus.

The third objective is to compare, in an explicit way, parallel phenomena in the two countries. The way in which the study has been designed gives ample opportunity for comparing the processes of the choice of technique for the same task (cane harvesting) in societies with different socio-economic systems. Hence it is a comparative socio-economic systems study, and the comparisons are probably more interesting and illuminating than the analyses of the two cases as such. However, the descriptive and analytical elements are preconditions for the comparative analysis.

The study is organized in the following way. In Part 1 an analytical framework for studying socio-economic aspects of choice and transfer of technique is presented (Chapter 2). This framework is a combination of a structural perspective and an actor-oriented one, based upon my previous work on the relations between techniques and social conditions. In Chapter 3 the reader is introduced to the various techniques in sugar cane harvesting.

Part 2 examines two cases: Cuba (Chapter 4) and Jamaica (Chapter 5). The structure of the sugar industries is outlined and the actors in the field of sugar cane harvesting are identified and discussed. On this basis, the actual choice of technique in sugar cane harvesting from the late 1950s to the early 1980s is described in some detail. The source of supply of equipment for cane harvesting – i.e. whether it is domestically produced or imported – is also addressed. Part 2 is essentialy descriptive.

Analysis and Comparison follows in Part 3, Chapter 6 examines the determinants or causes of the actual choice of technique in sugar cane harvesting in Cuba and Jamaica. In order to make this analysis detailed and specific some conceptual and theoretical specifications are required. Therefore comparative methodology is addressed and some general characteristics of various kinds of comparative studies are discussed. The concept of *social carriers of techniques* is also introduced and defined. A social carrier of a technique is a social entity which chooses and implements a technique; it "carries" it into the society. The carrier may be, for example, a private company, an agricultural co-operative or a government agency. More specifically, the concept is defined in terms of six conditions (interest, power, organization, information, access and knowledge) which are all necessary and, when taken together, sufficient for the implementation of a specific technique to take place. It is an "actor concept" related specifically to the choice of technique; a social concept that is technique-centred. The reason for developing the concept was to make possible a more specific analysis of the determinants of technical change.

On the basis of these theoretical specifications, the socio-economic and political determinants of the choice of technique are treated in some detail for the cases of Cuba and Jamaica. An investigation is made of those actors that have the interest, power, organization, information, access and knowledge to choose and implement various cane harvesting techniques. The structural constraints to which these social carriers of techniques are subject when making a choice are also analysed. Finally the determinants identified in the two cases are compared to each other.

Chapter 7 analyses and compares some socio-economic consequences of the actual choice of technique in the two countries – the performance of various cane harvester models, the generation of technological capability, technical dependency, consequences for employment and work conditions, etc. The role that actors such as workers and unions play in relation to technical change is strikingly different in capitalist Jamaica and socialist Cuba. These differences are examined and related to the phenomenon of Luddite machine destruction and the concept of "appropriate technology". The latter concept has been in fashion during the last decade as the basis for a strategy to solve the huge unemployment problem in many developing countries by using more labour-intensive technologies. An empirically-based critique of this strategy is presented as part of the discussion about the consequences of the choice of cane harvesting techniques on employment in the two countries.

In Chapter 7 I also address the relation between choice of technique and supply of equipment on the one hand, and the generation of an indigenous technological capability on the other. This leads to a discussion of such issues as technology transfer and the role of an indigenous capability to design and produce capital goods in processes of technical change. Several arguments are presented as to why such a domestic capability in the capital goods industry is crucial to facilitate comprehensive technical change in other economic sectors – i.e. where the capital goods are used. Finally, technological dependence and the technology gap in regard to the design and production of cane harvesting equipment are discussed. The relation between technological capability, technology gap and technological dependence is quite complicated. All three of them may well increase simultaneously for a certain country, if, for example, the global technology frontier moves faster than the rate of capability generation in the country.

In Chapter 8 some implications of this study for other Third World countries are discussed.

Policy implications of the analysis as well as conclusions of relevance for theories about technical change are presented in various contexts in Part 3. It would be fruitless to draw any conclusions of relevance for policy from the analysis without taking into account the socio-economic and political environment within which the technical change takes place. This environment is therefore given a central role in the analysis, which means that a fairly wide political-economic and also partly sociological approach is used, particularly in Chapter 6. However, it is supplemented by a narrower and more detailed economic analysis of various issues – such as employment and generation of technological capability – especially in Chapter 7. In other words, the study as a whole is a combined political-economic and economic analysis and the relative emphasis given to these different approaches is determined by the inherent requirements of the various specific problems analysed. On the whole, the study is interdisciplinary in character, rather than a work in economics or sociology.

2. Methodological Approach and Conceptual Framework

METHODOLOGICAL POINT OF DEPARTURE

I have earlier treated theoretical aspects of and methodological approaches to the study of socio-economic aspects – i.e. social and economic determinants and consequences – of techniques and technical change in various publications (Edquist 1977; Edquist and Edqvist 1979; Edquist 1980). This chapter is to a considerable extent based upon these studies. The theoretical point of departure for the present study was formulated in the earlier studies and they are thus parts of a long-term research programme within which the present study is an empirical continuation. The empirical part of the research programme was planned on the basis of explicit theoretical considerations. Therefore I will present the earlier work in some detail – partly here and partly on pp.76-8. I will also discuss the relation between the theoretical and the empirical work.

Social and historical research involves an interplay between theoretical and empirical work and neither of them can be considered primary. However, these two elements can be given different relative weight in various stages of the research process.

Where theoretical work is emphasized, the theoretical discussions are normally illustrated with reference to reality by means of examples. Such references to data and observations may be occasional or more systematic, and are normally based on secondary material of various kinds which may, of course, be more or less defective. Such referring through illustrations is a way to try to ensure that concepts and theories actually have a relation or analogy to the real world and are thus useful for empirical work.

Where empirical work is given a large relative weight, it must, of course, be carried out in a systematic manner and often be based on primary material. In practice, theoretical and empirical work are interwoven for most researchers and it cannot be postulated that one of them should always be given priority.

Attempts to explain social processes are the only way to improve our knowledge about causes and consequences in the social sciences. When attempting to explain a social process, all researchers use some sort of conceptual and theoretical framework – explicitly or implicitly, consciously or unconsciously. This has consequences for how reality is perceived and interpreted. In other words, data, observations and experiments are not independent of concepts and theories. I personally prefer to relate explicitly explanatory attempts to theoretical considerations, since an explicit theoretical or analytical framework is helpful in formulating questions and in looking for relevant data. It also facilitates generalizations and theoretical progress by means of feedback from the empirical work.

A Structural Approach

In my long-term research programme on the relations between techniques and socio-economic conditions, I therefore chose to start by concentrating on theoretical work, and in doing so, I used other authors' theories and results as a point of departure. For example, many of the structure-oriented concepts and ideas were taken from the historical materialist tradition. They were "processed" in a rationalistic manner but simultaneously with frequent references to the relevant section of reality.[1]

Edquist (1977) is an attempt to structure and discuss, mainly theoretically, the very comprehensive problem complex of relations between techniques and social conditions. First, an attempt is made to formulate a holistic perspective on the relations between nature, techniques and social conditions. Partial aspects of this totality are then dealt with separately. For example, I discuss social and economic conditions as driving forces behind technical change, which is regarded as a logical and temporal sequence encompassing invention, innovation and diffusion. I also discuss the effects of techniques and technical change on socio-economic conditions in rather general terms (Edquist 1977: part I).

The general discussion is then applied to the economic history of energy techniques. I concentrate upon the social and economic aspects of five technical "breakthroughs" in this development: the water wheel, the steam engine, the combustion engine, the electric motor and the nuclear reactor. Each of the five techniques is dealt with in a separate chapter which focuses on the social preconditions for, and social consequences of, the different techniques (Edquist 1977: part II).

The development and implementation of the energy techniques are explictly related to different modes of production or socio-economic systems, such as ancient slave society, feudalism, simple commodity production, capitalism and post-capitalist or socialist societies. The water wheel and its use for milling was known during antiquity and spread rapidly during feudalism, when it was one of the means whereby the feudal lords could appropriate part of the produce from the serfs. The steam engine was structurally incompatible with simple commodity production but not with private capitalism. The general use of electricity and the combustion engine coincided with the maturing of capitalism. But electricity also necessitated state intervention in the economies of many countries and this tendency was later strengthened with the development and implementation of nuclear energy. The two latter energy techniques are incompatible with the "pure" private capitalist mode of production but compatible with the structure of socialist societies and of capitalist societies with state intervention in the economy. Alternative energy techniques are also dealt with in a similar perspective. As suggested above, technical changes arising in societies dominated by specific modes of production may necessitate changes of these same socio-economic systems (Edquist 1977: part II).

The relations between techniques and organization of work in the units of production are also investigated. Distinctions are made between socially and technically conditioned, between horizontal and vertical, and between functional and personal division of labour, respectively. These analytical tools are used in an economic–historical discussion of the division of labour in pre-industrial handicraft, in the putting-out system, in manufacture and in modern industry (Edquist 1977: part III).

The approach in the book can, on the whole, be characterized as a structural one, and empirical observations are used mainly for illustrative purposes; examples and data are presented to illustrate the theoretical discussion of concepts and relations between them. The structural approach is also combined with a long economic–historical perspective which makes it possible and necessary to deal with societies with different modes of production or socio-economic systems.

Hence, a largely synchronic discussion is supplemented by applications to two more specific fields – energy and division of labour – where a long-term historical perspective provides a diachronic element. In this way, the theoretical work was related to different spheres of reality, and in this process the exclusively structural approach – with its genesis in the historical materialist tradition – proved to be increasingly insufficient. Such an approach, by itself, can explain change only in a broad and sweeping way, and the "distance" between structural theory and reality is quite great. There is a need for concepts and theories at an intermediate level of abstraction that can function as a bridge between structural theory and empirical studies.

At the very last stage of the work with the book, these problems made the need for a supplementary actor-oriented approach increasingly obvious. In the discussion of alternative energy techniques, it was mentioned that every technique must have a "social carrier" in order to be implemented. However, the concept remained undeveloped and was not really used in Edquist (1977).

Edquist and Edqvist (1979) is a continuation of the attempts to develop a theoretical framework for the study of social and economic aspects of the choice of technique. The objective of the long-term research programme was a theory-based empirical study, and it was decided that such a study would be carried out in the specific field of socio-economic aspects of choice of technique in developing countries. Therefore the study is partly a transformation of the previous structural approach into a direction that can make it applicable to a study of choice of technique in such countries.

The structural determinants of the choice of technique were first focused in the booklet. They were discussed in relation to societies with different socio-economic systems and with particular emphasis on developing countries, capitalist as well as socialist. Socio-economic transformations were also dealt with in an economic–historical perspective. The theoretical perspective employed took its point of departure in the historical materialist tradition. A discussion of the shortcomings of neoclassical economic theory in this context was also presented (Edquist and Edqvist 1979: ch.3).

The implications for the choice of technique of the internal dynamics of different kinds of societies were discussed. We looked in some detail at the determinants of the choice of technique in different kinds of agricultural production units at the micro level – such as peasant ownership farms, co-operative farms, private capitalist farms and state-owned farms (Edquist and Edqvist 1979: ch.3).

A Supplementary Actor-oriented Approach

In Edquist and Edqvist (1979) we concluded that the structure of the socio-economic and political systems strongly conditions the choice of technique. Thus, the choice is not only, or even primarily, a matter of conscious policy-making by decision-makers who function as actors. Yet social entities and institutions actually do make decisions to implement some techniques rather than others, and they do often have some freedom of action. Their degree of freedom of action is determined by structural factors. Therefore, if the relations between social and technical change are to be properly understood, an actor-oriented approach is necessary as a supplement to the structural one. Hence, a structural and an actor-oriented approach should be combined. If one starts out with only one of them, it might be impossible to perceive the complex character of reality in this respect. Therefore, the actor concept "social carriers of techniques" was developed and defined (Edquist and Edqvist 1979: ch.4). It will be presented in Chapter 6, where it will actually be used.

Thus we attempted to integrate structural and actor-oriented approaches instead of regarding them as mutually exclusive and contradictory. By combining these two approaches, two fallacies can be avoided. One is an extreme deterministic attitude to technique, implying that the structure determines everything, and that there is no scope at all for actors to influence the choice of technique. The other fallacy is a pure actor-oriented, "agent" approach: i.e. a voluntaristic attitude implying that the actors exclusively determine the choice of technique without being subject to any structural constraints at all. In order to avoid the latter fallacy, the actor concept should be intrinsically based on the structural theory; it should be defined, in part, from a structural point of view (Edquist and Edqvist 1979: ch.4).

When studying and trying to explain social, economic or technical change over time, this methodological problem of the relations between structural constraints and possibilities on the one hand, and acting subjects on the other is always present, implicitly or explicitly.

An important question concerns the relative weight that should be given to structural factors and actors, respectively. In the subject at issue here, the choice of technique is never free from restrictions, and the constraints are more or less severe in different particular cases. For example, a poor farmer in Tanzania, working his soil at his small family farm, does not have much of a choice but to use his hoe. Oxen and ploughs or tractors are simply not accessible to him and his farm would, in any case, be too small for these alternative techniques. His "choice" is almost completely conditioned by the structure. For a large electric power producing company in Sweden, the situation is very different. The scope of choice includes everything from small water turbines in tiny rivers to nuclear reactors or large power plants fired by oil or coal. Here the freedom of action is quite substantial (Edquist 1980: 22-3).

Accordingly, structural and actor-oriented approaches should normally be combined in an analysis of the socio-economic aspects of techniques. However, it is not possible to determine in general or *a priori* the relative weight that should be given to each of the perspectives. Such a judgement can only be made on an empirical basis and for specific cases, since the structural constraints vary, to a considerable extent, in different particular instances (Edquist 1980: 23).

All processes of social, economic and technical change are multicausally determined. Therefore it is always incorrect to talk about *the* cause of technical change. Hence, a study of determinants of a certain choice of technique is a question of identifying all – or the most important – factors which result in a certain choice of technique, i.e. causally to explain a multicausally determined process.

A study of consequences of a certain choice of technique is a question of examining a few out of the many effects of the process. And these effects are normally simultaneously influenced by a number of other factors which are not the object of study. It is not a question of (multi)causal explanation. For example, the employment situation is certainly affected by the choice of techniques. However, it is not exclusively determined by this factor. Social and economic conditions and policies are other important determinants.

For the above reasons, there is a basic difference in studying determinants and consequences of, for example, technical change. The need for theory is larger in the former case since the ambitions are higher. As a consequence, the theoretical framework – partly presented here and partly on pp.76-8 – is primarily developed for the study of determinants of the choice of technique and it will be extensively used in Chapter 6.

However, it is not always possible to distinguish sharply between determinants and consequences of the actual choice of technique, since perceived or estimated consequences do influence the choice of technique made by various actors. Therefore, the theoretical framework presented here has some relevance also for the study of socio-economic consequences of the choice of cane harvesting techniques in Cuba and Jamaica (Chapter 7).

The theoretical point of departure for this study directly influenced the design of the empirical study. The time periods and countries were chosen to compare societies with different structural characteristics, with various kinds of actors, and with differing relations between them. The theoretical framework presented above also served as a guide for formulating the questions to ask. Thereby it also partly influenced what type of data and other information to collect and present.[2]

SOME DEFINITIONS

In many studies *technology* is used in a very comprehensive sense and the term often includes many important phenomena of a social character such as knowledge, management, organization of work, other elements of social organization, etc. The same is true, of course, when transfer of technology is discussed. It then becomes problematic to study the relations between technology and social conditions, because the relation between the two phenomena cannot be satisfactorily investigated if they are not conceptually distinguished from each other. If we want to study the relations between two phenomena or aspects, we must have concepts for them, and these concepts should overlap each other as little as possible.

Therefore, I will use the term *technique* to denote only the material or physical elements of what is often called technology. Thus by techniques is meant tools, implements, instruments and machines that are produced by man and which in turn are used to bring forth products and services. Technical change, then, means simply that new techniques are used for productive purposes.

Regarding technology, on the other hand, I follow the tradition of using it in a more general and comprehensive sense, including techniques but also non-material aspects, such as technical know-how, management, organization of work, etc. I am aware that a strict separation between technique and such non-material elements can sometimes be problematic. Such a distinction is methodologically advantageous, however. As will be evident in this study, my choice of a narrow and strictly material definition of techniques certainly does *not* imply that I consider the non-material elements of technology as being of minor importance for choice, implementation and transfer of techniques.

In the present study, "actors" means all organized social entities with a stake in sugar cane agriculture, which can be considered to have some interest with respect to, and some influence on, choice of technique in this sector. The "actors" are, of course, the subjects which directly influence the decisions to implement some techniques rather than others. But such choices are – as argued above – not merely a matter of conscious decision-making by actors. For example, the structure of the socio-economic and political systems strongly conditions the behaviour of actors and thereby the choice of technique.

"Structure" is here defined as the overall character of the socio-economic system and the general employment situation in a certain country at a specific point in time. In the context of this study, the character of the socio-economic system may be either capitalist or socialist. The employment situation may be one of unemployment, shortage of labour or one of balance on the labour market.

It could perhaps be considered controversial to include the employment situation as a part of structure and thereby place it in the same basket as the character of the socio-economic system. However, the employment situation is a very important determinant of choice of technique, since it partly determines the interests of at least some of the actors. In addition, there is a strong empirical relation between socialism and low open unemployment and between underdeveloped capitalism and high unemployment, at least in the two countries under investigation here. For these reasons it is appropriate to include the employment situation in "structure".[3] This inclusion implies that factor endowment and relative factor prices are included in the concept of structure.

It would, of course, be methodologically advantageous to make a strict separation between actors and structures. However, this is even more difficult than in the case of technique and the non-material elements normally included in the concept of technology, because the actors actually are *parts* of the socio-economic system, i.e. of the structure. Simultaneously, however, I have argued earlier that the actors are strongly affected by the structure.[4] At the same time they do often have some freedom of action. Therefore it is useful to employ a combined structural and actor-oriented approach, although it is impossible to make a strict separation between structures and actors.

Notes

1. Edquist (1977) is an example of this.
2. There is a risk that relevant data are excluded because they do not fit the theoretical framework. The risk is, however, at least as large if the framework is implicit and unconscious as if it is explicit and conscious. I am aware that my analytical framework – like all others – cannot cope with everything and solve all problems. In Chapter 7, therefore, I will discuss matters of interest which cannot be handled by my theoretical framework.
3. This does not exclude the possibility that certain actors may influence the employment situation.
4. They can, of course, also influence the socio-economic system and thereby contribute to a process of structural change, e.g. a social revolution. However, this

aspect is addressed only marginally in this study. What is at issue here is rather how actors – in a structural context – influence another process, i.e. technical change.

3. Techniques in Sugar Cane Harvesting – Some Introductory Remarks

Field operations in sugar cane agriculture cover a whole range of tasks, of which the most important are land preparation, cane planting, cultivation (weed control), fertilizer application and harvesting. In terms of labour requirements, harvesting has traditionally overshadowed all other stages of cane agriculture.[1]

The optimum harvest period is from December through April–July in both Cuba and Jamaica, depending on the area. The harvest lasting, for example, from December 1965 until May 1966 is called the 1966 harvest or *zafra*. Sugar cane yields may vary between roughly 30 and 300 tons per hectare in different parts of the world. In both Cuba and Jamaica, yields are at the lower end of this spectrum. From the harvest, the cane stalks should be as "clean" as possible at the factory gate. The four tasks which have to be executed to achieve this are to cut, clean, load and transport the cane.[2] All these operations can be carried out in many different ways, i.e. by different combinations of labour and equipment. In other words, both labour and techniques can be of different types or qualities. The four most common types of harvesting method are:

i)   the cane is cut and loaded manually;
ii)   the cane is cut manually and lifted by mechanical loaders;
iii)   the cane is cut and loaded mechanically, but by different machines;
iv)   the cane is cut, cleaned and loaded mechanically by means of combine harvesters.

Traditionally, the harvest in all countries was executed primarily by means of manual human labour and animal power in combination with very simple techniques. Around 1950 the Cuban *zafra* (i.e. the sugar harvest) was described in the following terms:

> Thousands of Cubans throng the highways, the railroads, and the byways to get to the mills, to the colonias, for the zafra. Millions and tens of millions of tons of cane have to be cut. A hundred thousand machetes in the hands of a hundred thousand men will do the cutting. Millions of stalks of cane – each one held in a human hand for a few seconds while the machete in the other

hand cuts it at the bottom and deftly trims the leaves before it is thrown on a pile of other stalks. Then these millions of stalks must be lifted by sweating human bodies into the large, two-wheeled carts which patient, sturdy oxen will draw to the mill or to the railroad spur. The power exerted by men and oxen in the zafra is stupendous. One wonders what the equivalent in kilowatts would be! It is hard work, often grueling for both man and beast, for Cuba has taken few steps to relegate this burden to machines.
(Nelson 1951: 58)

At present, half of the cane-cutting in Cuba is mechanized. Combine harvesters cut the cane at ground level, chop the cane stalks into pieces, clean the cane, and load it into a truck or tractor cart running alongside the harvester. Thus the combine harvester accomplishes three of the tasks necessary in the harvest: it cuts, cleans and loads the cane.

Cane is more difficult to harvest mechanically than most other crops, e.g. cereals. It has to be cut close to the ground in order to retain the part that has the highest sugar content. At the same time, however, the root must not be damaged, since the next crop will normally grow from it.[3] The top of the cane stalk must also be cut and the leaves separated from the stalks. In addition, the weight of the crop is, as we saw, extraordinary. Finally there are many types and varieties of cane: they may grow erect or inclined, the stalks may be thick or thin, etc. Therefore, a sugar cane combine harvester is quite a complex machine, weighing more than 10 tons. A combine harvester can replace 30–50 manual harvest workers.

Both in Jamaica and in Cuba, mechanical loading was introduced during the first half of the 1960s. Mechanical loaders can be of two types. A "push-pile" loader pushes the cane along the ground until enough has piled up so that it may be gathered with a front-mounted grabber and loaded into in-field trailers. A "grab-type" loader, which is attached to a tractor, grabs bundles of cane and loads them into the means of transport. The loaders may be used in combination with hand cutting or with mechanical cane-cutters which only cut the cane at ground level and leave it in heaps. A mechanical loader can replace about 10 manual loaders.

A serious problem for the sugar mills is the extraneous matter that accompanies the cane stalks into the factory. Extraneous matter is everything except clean millable cane stalks, such as trash, weeds, dead cane, green tops, earth and stones. Extraneous matter can cause operational difficulties in the factories and decrease the sugar yield per ton of cane. This problem is always present, but its magnitude often increases when mechanical cutting and loading are introduced.

In order to reduce this problem, the cane has to be cleaned; among other things, the leaves have to be separated from the cane stalks. This separation can be done manually by the hand-cutters or mechanically as one of the operations in combine harvesters. Another method is to burn the cane fields before harvesting. Such controlled burning destroys the dry, dead cane leaves and some of the green leaves and weeds. Burning considerably increases the productivity of the manual cane-cutters. It also facilitates the work of loading machines and – in particular – of combine harvesters. On the other hand, burning has negative consequences for the recovery of the fields and the quality of burnt cane deteriorates rapidly if it is not promptly taken to the factories for processing.

Burning has long been practised in, for example, Hawaii. In Jamaica it was introduced in 1961; by 1969 nearly 70 per cent was burnt before the harvest (Shillingford 1974: 86). In Cuba, however, the general policy was to cut the cane "green" (unburnt) until the 1971 harvest. In most cane-producing countries, burning is highly controversial and it is an intensively debated issue.

The cleaning of the cane can also be done at special cleaning "plants", where extraneous matter is eliminated using air or water. These plants can be used as a complement both to manual and to mechanical cutting and loading.

As regards the transport of cane from field to factory, ox carts, railroads, tractors or trucks – and various combinations thereof – can be used.

These examples clearly illustrate that for all the four tasks constituting the harvest, there is a spectrum of techniques which can be used. The "choice of technique" is actually a choice within such spectra. The number of available techniques, however, may increase over time because of technical progress. In the case of cane harvesting, such technical change has been particularly rapid during the last two decades.

An actor making a choice of technique may also try to widen the spectra by means of inventing, developing and designing new techniques. Adaptations are particularly important in agriculture, since machines normally have to be adapted to local soils, varieties, topography and climate. In addition, a crop like sugar cane grows very differently under various conditions. It sometimes stands erect and sometimes it sprawls or lies down, badly lodged and tangled. Accordingly, cane harvesting machinery differs in various cane-producing areas, and local adaptation is often necessary. In reality, therefore, the choice among existing techniques can sometimes not be separated from the process of technical development and technical adaptation to local conditions.

In a recent survey carried out by R. Fauconnier the degree of mechanization of cane harvesting around 1980 was established for 35 cane-growing areas. Cuba and Jamaica were not included. The 35 regions were grouped in 6 categories:

1. In two regions – Hawaii and Australia – both cutting and loading of cane are now completely mechanized. These are also two of the regions where cane harvesting machinery started to be developed. The third important area in this respect is Louisiana. In Hawaii very high agricultural yields (200 to 300 tons per hectare) are obtained over two-year cycles. There, push-rakes, i.e. bulldozers fitted with heavy cane rakes, are used to remove the whole crop in bulk. Grabs then load the cane onto large trucks. In Louisiana, the straight-stemmed, low-yielding cane (60-90 tons per hectare) has proved suitable for whole-cane cutting with the cane left in

windrows by the cutting machines. These windrows are then picked up by loaders. In Australia the yield is 80-120 tons per hectare and the cane is sometimes lodged and tangled. This has required the development of a cutter–chopper–loader which harvests the crop in one single operation. Use of this type of combine harvester is expanding most rapidly internationally at present.

2. The second category consists of regions where harvesting is highly mechanized with a high proportion of mechanical cutting. Among the seven regions in this category are Puerto Rica, Florida and Venezuela. Cuba would also belong to this group.

3. In the next category all or most of the loading, but practically no cutting, is mechanized. Here we find, for example, Kenya, Zambia and some regions in Brazil. Jamaica would also belong to this category.

4. In the fourth group we find areas with practically no mechanical cutting and high degrees of both mechanized and manual loading. Examples are Reunion, Belize and some regions in Brazil.

5. The fifth category is composed of areas with mainly manual work and only some mechanization. Examples are the Philippines, Guadeloupe and Mauritius.

6. In the last group harvesting is completely manual. Examples are Morocco, Thailand and Pakistan (Fauconnier 1983: 787, 789, 800).

In the late 1950s sugar cane cutting and loading were completely manual tasks in both Cuba and Jamaica, i.e. they were at the same level in this respect. Since that time there has been a global tendency towards increasing degrees of mechanization; various countries have gradually transformed themselves into more advanced categories in the classification above. Today Cuba is the most mechanized countries among the – relatively few – developing socialist cane-producing countries and Jamaica is among the more mechanized developing capitalist cane-producing countries. Accordingly, both these countries are relatively advanced with regard to the degree of mechanization of the sugar cane harvest, in comparison to other developing countries.

As late as in the beginning of the 1970s, only Australia, Louisiana and Hawaii were advanced in mechanical cane-cutting and in Hawaii the conditions were quite different from those found in the Caribbean. This limited the availability for Cuba and Jamaica of possibly suitable machines, but also of experience and know-how with regard to the use of cane-cutting machines.

Notes

1. A sugar factory consists of two main parts. In the mechanical part, the cane stalks are crushed and the juice extracted. The rest of sugar processing resembles a chemical plant. There, the juice is cleaned, the water evaporated, the sugar crystallized, etc.

2. However, transport of sugar cane from field to factory will not be dealt with in this study: the main emphasis will be on cutting and loading.

3. Such a crop is called a "ratoon crop". When cane is replanted, the crop is called the "plant crop". Replanting is done every three to seven years.

Part 2: Two Case Studies
Cuba 1958-83;
Jamaica 1958-83

4. Cuba: 1958-83

STRUCTURE AND ACTORS IN THE SUGAR SECTOR

Until 1959, Cuba was a capitalist country heavily dependent upon the USA economically, politically and technologically. According to Mesa-Lago, the five most serious socio-economic problems in Cuba in the late 1950s were the slow rate of economic growth, the excessive significance of sugar in the generation of GNP and exports, the overwhelming dependence on the USA in regard to investment and trade, the high rates of unemployment and underemployment, and the significant inequalities in living standards, particularly between urban and rural areas (Mesa-Lago 1981: 7). As shown in Table 4.1, unemployment was high in the 1950s and fluctuated seasonally between cane harvest time and "dead season" (non-harvest time).

Main Actors in the Cuban Sugar Sector in the late 1950s

As will be described below, the most important actors in the sugar sector in the 1950s were the sugar mill (estate) owners, the cane farmers, the sugar workers and unions, and the government.

Sugar Mill Owners
The sugar mills in Cuba were very large enterprises representing investments of several million dollars, controlled in most cases by a corporation rather than by an individual, and with many thousand hectares of land at their disposal. The workers were both industrial and agricultural, the former representing the labour force for the maintenance and operation of the mill itself, the latter for the cultivation and harvesting of the cane. That cane which was produced by the sugar mills themselves was called "administration cane". In 1958 there were 161 sugar mills in Cuba, about one fourth of which were owned from abroad, mainly by US citizens (Nelson 1951: 45, 122; Nelson 1972: 61; CERP 1965: 523). The foreign-owned mills were the giants, controlling 40 per cent of all sugar up to 1959 (Morgan 1962: 94).

Table 4.1
Open Unemployment in Cuba Selected Years, 1943-81
(per cent of labour force)

1943[a]	21.1	1967	5.3
1953[b]	8.4	1968	4.3
1956[a]	20.7	1969	2.9
1957[b]	9.1	1970	1.3
1956-7 [c]	16.4	1971	2.1
1957	12.4	1972	2.8
1958	11.8	1973	3.4
1959	13.6	1974	3.9
1960	11.8	1975	4.5
1961	10.3	1976	4.8
1962	9.0	1977	5.1
1963	8.1	1978	5.3
1964	7.5	1979	5.4
1965	6.5	1980	4.1
1966	6.2	1981	3.4

[a] During dead season
[b] During harvest
[c] The figure for 1956-7, and all the following years, refers to annual averages.

Sources: 1943-56/57, Dominguez (1978: 91); 1957-71, Mesa-Lago (1981: 122); 1970-80, Brundenius (1983: table 4); 1981, Brundenius (1984: table 1).

Note: The figures in Table 4.1 are based on censuses and samples up to 1961. In 1970 a new census was made and in March 1979 rather detailed demographic surveys were taken in Cuba. In 1981 a new census was made. These are the only unemployment figures that are empirically based on direct data. For the other years the table is based on estimates made by Mesa-Lago (1962-9) and by Brundenius (1971-8 and 1980).

In the 1950s the mill owners (*hacendados*) were organized in the National Association of Sugar Mill Owners (Asociación Nacional de Hacendados de Cuba), founded when the mill owners reorganized in 1934.[1] By a 1935 law it was officially recognized as the legal representative for the industrial sector of sugar production. A compulsory fee was also established. The Sugar Mill Owners' Association had a very strong influence over the sugar sector during the entire pre-revolutionary period (CERP 1965: 337).

Cane Farmers
A key figure in the production of sugar cane was the cane farmer (*colono*) who was often a renter of company-owned land, but who could also be

"independent" in the sense of owning his own land. However, the "independent" cane farmers remained dependent upon the sugar companies for credit, transportation of cane and cane-processing (Nelson 1951: 122).

In January 1934 the Cane Farmers Association of Cuba (Asociación de Colonos de Cuba) was created by an act of law, organizing all the cane planters in Cuba until 1961. All cane planters were required to belong to the association whether they owned, leased, rented or were share-croppers on the land. The main activity of the association was to protect the interests of its members (CERP 1965: 336).[2]

The heterogeneity among the *colonos* was extreme. In 1952, 94.39 per cent of all the cane was produced by *colonos* and about 6 per cent was administration cane. Some 61.2 per cent (about 38,000 in number) of the smallest *colonias* (cane plantations) produced only 8.6 per cent of the total amount of cane and 1.2 per cent (or 730 in number) of the largest *colonias* produced 29.0 per cent of all cane (CERP 1965: 523).

While the number of mills remained constant over a long period, cane plantations experienced a substantial increase in number during the 1941-58 period. This increase was due to the subdivision of existing *colonias*, the formation of new ones, and the recognition of sub-*colonos* as full *colonos* by a law of 1953. From 30,020 *colonias* in 1939, the number increased to 62,298 in 1952 (CERP 1965: 522).

Sugar Workers
The scarce data available does not make it easy to analyse the level of employment in the sugar industry in Cuba. However, estimates of the maximum employment for each year have been presented for the crops of 1928-40. According to these between 250,000 and 350,000 field workers were employed. A large part – perhaps as many as 100,000 – were either Haitians or Jamaicans imported for the harvest work (CERP 1965: 349-52).[3] The harvesting of sugar cane was characterized during this period by a complete absence of mechanization. In 1958 there were approximately 370,000 professional cane-cutters (see Table 4.3). According to another source, nearly half a million people were employed in the sugar industry during the harvesting season in the late 1950s; about 300,000 of these were employed on plantations, some 180,000 in factories and 6,000 in the refineries (Morgan 1962: 96). In 1956-7 the total Cuban labour force was 2.2 million persons (Mesa-Lago 1981: 113). Hence almost one fourth of the labour force was employed in the sugar sector in the late 1950s.

In December 1932, the National Syndicate of Workers of the Sugar Industry (SNOIA) was formed. Delegates from 32 mills attended. It was the first labour organization of importance within the sugar industry and it was to become the country's most important labour union. At the formation of this syndicate, a programme of minimum improvements was agreed upon, which included, among other things, the extension of the maximum 8-hour day to all workers, wage increases and improvement of sanitary conditions in the sugar mills. After the fall of President Machado, a wave of strikes during August and September 1933 spread through the sugar industry, and 36 mills were occupied by the striking workers (Nelson 1951: 148; CERP 1965: 383).

The SNOIA was just one example of labour union organization in Cuba in the first decades of the century. In January 1939 the First National Labour Congress of Cuba took place in Havana. A total of 567 unions attended, and the Cuban Confederation of Labour (CTC) was organized. The CTC was to be the only central labour organization in Cuba, bringing together all organized workers. The Secretary General of the CTC elected in 1939 was the Communist leader Lazaro Pena and Cuba's labour movement was until 1947 strongly dominated by the Partido Socialista Popular, i.e. the Communist Party (CERP 1965: 384). By the 1950s the Sugar Workers' Union included practically all workers in the sugar industry and, with its 500,000 members, was the biggest sugar workers' organization in the world (Morgan 1962: 96).

In 1958 CTC was composed of 33 national federations of industries –for example, the Sugar Workers' Federation – and six provincial federations. These federations had a membership of 2,490 individual unions and more than one million members (Nelson 1972: 150).

Government

From the early years of the Republic until the outbreak of the First World War, the Cuban government abstained from interfering with or regulating, in any way, the functioning of the sugar industry. Starting in 1915, however, some limited regulations were applied to the then rapidly expanding sugar industry. Regulation of the sugar economy became more important from 1926 when world production exceeded consumption and international sugar prices fell. Restrictions were placed on the planting, harvesting and milling of sugar. These measures were not applied systematically, however, and they could not offset the effects of the worldwide depression. The crowning piece of legislation – and, consequently, the cornerstone of the Cuban political system until 1959 – was the Sugar Co-ordination Act of 1937 (Nelson 1951: 98: CERP 1965: 239-42, 325-7; Dominguez 1978: 84).

The Sugar Co-ordination Act and the supplementary regulations set forth in minute detail the rights and obligations of the various actors in the sugar sector. The act guaranteed to every *colono* registered as such in 1937 the right to sell 30,000 *arrobas* (345 tons) of sugar cane to a designated sugar mill. In return, the farmer agreed to limit production to the government's allowance. This "grinding factor" could be passed on to one's heirs but could not be renounced or sold. To make room for the small growers, the large sugar plantations and the sugar mills that owned cane fields were penalized. In addition, the act regulated minimum payments by the mill to the grower on the basis of the average sugar-cane yield (Nelson 1951: 100-3, 121; Dominguez 1978: 85).

The act established the "right of permanent occupancy". Every renter, sub-renter or sharecropper with a contract to engage in sugar cultivation in 1937 was guaranteed the right of permanent occupancy of the lands he worked so long as the grinding factor with the sugar mill was met (guaranteeing the mill a stable supply of cane) and rent was paid. If he complied he could not be evicted (Nelson 1972: 61; Dominguez 1978-85).

The "right of permanent occupancy" given to the *colonos* was extremely important. It gave the farmer practically all the advantages usually associated with ownership of land and at a rental which was nominal. This right implied a serious blow to the *latifundia* since it meant that most cane-land was left under the control of *colonos*. The measure was supposed to alleviate the problem posed by the fact that a very high proportion of the arable land was owned by a limited number of sugar companies, many of which were foreign (CERP 1965: 339, 343).

The Cuban Institute for Sugar Stabilization (Instituto Cubano de Estabilizacion del Azucar, ICEA) was in charge of enforcing sugar regulations. It was established in 1931 and was dominated by the sugar-mill owners. Besides enforcing sugar regulations, the Institute was charged with conducting the international relations of the sugar industry, severing them from official government agencies including the ministry of foreign affairs. Through that authority, it institutionalized access to political power for sugar-mill owners. The ICEA was the nerve centre in the system of sugar production and export regulations in Cuba. A part of government had been put into private hands, and thus private interests actually partly conducted government policy in this area. Private organizations came to control government agencies in charge of the country's domestic and international sugar policies (Dominguez 1978: 86; CERP 1965: 335).

Between 1933 and 1958, government did not take over any large segments of the economy, but it did increase its regulatory and distributive activity considerably. Sugar was regulated most extensively, from planting to international marketing. Because sugar was at the heart of the economy, this system ended up regulating much of Cuban economic life (Dominguez 1978: 90).

Changes until around 1980

Starting with the revolution in 1959, a socialist socio-economic system gradually developed in Cuba. As can be seen in Table 4.1, open unemployment was practically eliminated in the first decade of the revolution. Although unemployment increased during the first half of the 1970s, its magnitude did not reach the levels of the pre-revolutionary era or of the early 1960s. In the latter half of the 1970s, open unemployment stabilized at around 5 per cent and in the early 1980s it decreased again.

Table 4.2 presents some background figures on the size of the sugar cane harvest and cane yield per hectare.[4] The figures reflect the relative neglect of the sugar sector in the early 1960s as well as the enormous effort to

27

produce 10 million tons of sugar in 1970. To a large extent Cuba's development strategy during the latter half of the 1960s was dominated by this effort. In the 1970s the record shows a more balanced and gradual expansion of sugar production.

Table 4.2
Sugar Cane Production in Cuba, 1959-82

Year	1 *Total amount of cane produced per* zafra *(million tons)*	2 *Yield per hectare (tons)*
1959	48.0	45.0
1960	47.5	41.1
1961	54.3	43.1
1962	36.7	32.4
1963	31.1	28.9
1964	36.7	35.6
1965	50.4	47.8
1966	36.4	38.8
1967	50.5	46.9
1968	41.5	42.0
1969	41.7	44.2
1970	81.5	55.8
1971	52.2	41.7
1972	44.3	37.5
1973	48.2	45.0
1974	50.4	45.6
1975	52.4	44.4
1976	53.8	44.0
1977	60.3	53.1
1978	69.6	56.3
1979	77.3	58.9
1980	64.0	46.0
1981	66.6	55.1
1982	73.1	55.1

Sources: 1959-62, Moreno Fraginals (1978: 48); 1963-79, AEC (1979: table 7, p.68); 1980, AEC (1981: table 7, p.87); 1981-2, AEC (1982: table VIII. 12, p.213).

The first Agrarian Reform Law of May 1959 was the most important step taken in the early stage of the revolution.[5] According to the first law a maximum of 30 *caballerias* (about 1,000 acres or 403 hectares) was set for ownership by any one person or corporation. For rice, sugar and cattle, the maximum might be extended to 100 *caballerias* (1,341 hectares) provided that yields per hectare were at least 50 per cent greater than the national average. About 3,000 farms were expropriated under this law.

The law established the Institute for Agrarian Reform (INRA) to administer its provisions. INRA's authority was very broadly defined. The country was divided into 28 agrarian development zones, each to be governed by an appointee of INRA. INRA began without delay to exercise control over property confiscated from supporters of Batista. Large cattle ranches were taken over and managers appointed by INRA took charge. Co-operatives were organized to operate sugar cane plantations, the members consisting of the labourers previously employed. Since the managers were appointed by INRA, they never functioned like true co-operatives. Within a few years they were converted into state farms. In fact INRA took over all the functions of the Ministry of Agriculture and the ministry was dissolved in 1961. INRA also absorbed many agencies set up by the former government, including the Cuban Institute for Sugar Stabilization.

That portion of the agrarian reform which proscribed the *latifundio* naturally met with bitter objections from the mill owners, most of whom were large landlords themselves. The cane planters (*colonos*) did not fully accept the Agrarian Reform Law either. However, they favoured the expropriation of the sugar mill properties and supported that section of the law designed to enlarge the size of every Cuban farm to the so-called "basic minimum" of two *caballerias* (27 hectares).

The revolutionary government did design some of its policies to meet the cane planters' needs and interests. The mill owners were few in number and they lacked political authority and stature because they had long been identified with foreign interests. Thus their demands could safely be ignored. The *colonos*, on the other hand, were a sizeable group, and while INRA failed to meet some of their key demands, farmers in the 2- to 5-*caballerias* (27-67 hectares) category were allowed to purchase more land, and many small planters were brought up to the "basic minimum" of 2 *caballerias* (27 hectares). It is significant that there was no attempt to collectivize the planters forcibly, although the largest *colonos* did balk at the law. The Colonos Association of Cuba, whose anti-government agitation reached a climax at an extraordinary general assembly in August 1960, and which was dominated by the big planters, was dissolved in January 1961.

The rural proletariat provided the real basis for the consolidation of the regime's power. Cuba's agricultural workers, particularly the sugar workers, who outnumbered the *colonos* by about five to one, were the most favoured class of the revolution. Their main demand was for improved material conditions: increased employment, higher wages, schools, hospitals, etc. While meeting the demands of the rural proletariat, INRA was able to turn Cuba's large-scale seasonal unemployment into a political advantage for the new government. Most sugar workers eagerly joined the new Cane Co-operatives and Granjas del Pueblo (people's farms or state farms), which supplied off-season jobs cultivating expropriated lands, and which could therefore raise the annual incomes of the workers without significant increases in daily wages.

However, the expropriations started at a relatively slow pace. The real upsurge came in the summer and autumn of 1960 and the growing dispute with the USA was one of the major driving forces behind it. The definitive clash started not with sugar, however, but with oil. After a dispute over oil prices, the foreign-owned oil refineries were subject to "intervention" by the Cubans on 29 June 1960. President Eisenhower retaliated by suspending Cuba's remaining sugar quota imports for 1960. This led to a wave of nationalizations starting in August when most of United States investment in Cuba was seized, including all sugar mills and the oil refineries.

In October 1960, 287 larger companies, foreign as well as national, were expropriated. 105 of them were sugar mills. The US answer was a trade embargo – which is still in force – on everything except non-subsidized foodstuffs and medical supplies. By early 1961, 75 per cent of Cuban industry and 30 per cent of its land had been collectivized. This transfer of ownership liquidated the capitalist system, and it became clear that the revolution had entered into a socialist phase.

By the end of 1960, INRA controlled nearly four million hectares of sugar and grazing land and over two million hectares of rice and tobacco, and other properties. Almost one million hectares comprising administration cane land and the properties of a few large *colonos* were incorporated into the Cane Co-operatives, which were transformed into state farms in August 1962.

In addition to direct control over large amounts of land, INRA was also a monopoly supplier of working capital, technical aid and other resources to agriculture. Thereby INRA was in a position to wield considerable influence over the masses of *colonos* and other small farmers.

The private sector at this time consisted of farmers with less than 403 hectares. Most of the holdings were actually much smaller than that. These small farmers were mainly the former renters, share-croppers and squatters, who had been made owners by decree, as well as those who had owned their farms before the revolution.

The government and INRA attitude towards the middle farmers – cultivating between 5 and 30 *caballerias* (67-402 hectares) – was uncertain in the beginning, and no clear line developed until late in 1962. Some people pointed to the unfavourable consequences that could result from failing to integrate these farms into the planning of agriculture. In the autumn of 1962 plans were discussed to expropriate the entire middle sector.

The middle farmers cultivated nearly 25 per cent of Cuba's cane land, or roughly 22,000 *caballerias* (295,000 hectares). The new agricultural policy intoduced in 1963 implied a return to emphasizing sugar. The division of the cane fields between the private and public sector made the planning of the harvest and other kinds of co-ordination problematic. For example the rational utilization of the cane labour force grew more difficult.

A labour shortage developed during the last half of the 1961 sugar harvest and became successively more severe in 1962 and 1963. This was one of the reasons behind the Second Agrarian Reform Law of October 1963. Approximately 10,000 farms were affected by this law and they incorporated over 130,000 *caballerias* (1.7 million hectares) or somewhat less than 20 per cent of Cuba's farm land.

The Second Reform Law enlarged the state sector of agriculture to over 70 per cent of Cuba's total farm land. Nearly 155,000 farmers cultivating less than five *caballerias* (67 hectares) and all members of the National Association of Small Farmers (Asociacion Nacional de Agricultores Pequenos, ANAP) remained. Thus about 30 per cent of the land was still in the hands of small farmers.

In terms of actors in the sugar industry, the power of the sugar-mill owners was liquidated and the *colonos* became dependent on government institutions instead. Their associations were dissolved. The role of government had increased enormously in the process, so that various government agencies gradually became completely dominant as far as sugar and sugar technology policies were concerned.

The autonomy of the labour unions decreased. The government formulated policies in close contact with them. For example, detailed regulations for the cane co-operatives were hammered out in discussions between INRA and the National Federation of Sugar Workers. This was the basis for the formation of the General Administration of Cane Co-operatives on 3 March 1960 which provided an administrative basis for the collectivization of the sugar lands and guided the formation of many co-operatives.

It was mentioned above that INRA absorbed the Ministry of Agriculture in 1961. INRA operated the seven sugar mills that were taken over in 1959 through a department called Administracion General de Ingenios of INRA. In August and October 1960, when the rest of the sugar mills were confiscated, they were also taken care of by INRA. For a while, INRA also had a Department of Industrialization in charge of nationalized industries.

On 21 February 1961 the Ministry of Industries was established to direct and supervise Cuban industry and implement industrial policies. Thereafter INRA was in charge of cane cultivation, while the Ministry of Industries was in charge of sugar processing. The Ministry of Internal Trade took care of internal distribution of sugar and the Ministry of Foreign Trade handled exports. Co-ordination between these entities was, of course, difficult.

During the 1960s and 1970s frequent reorganizations of the state apparatus took place. New ministries were created and old ones were abolished or substantially modified. Nearly all of the new ministries were established as giant corporations, and under their wings were created huge Empresas Consolidadas (Consolidated Firms), which themselves controlled hundreds of production and service units. INRA and the Ministry of Industries were the largest and the most important of these combines.

The comprehensive Ministry of Industries was broken up in the mid-1960s. One of the new ministries created in that reorganization was the Ministry of the Sugar Industry. In 1976 a Ministry of Agriculture was re-established replacing INRA. In 1980 sugar cane agriculture was transferred to the Ministry of Sugar from the Ministry of Agriculture. Thereby both cane agriculture and sugar processing were administered by the same ministry, which can be expected to decrease problems of co-ordination.

CHOICE OF TECHNIQUE IN SUGAR CANE HARVESTING, 1958-83 – A DESCRIPTION

Having described briefly the structural stage upon which the choice of technique was made in Cuban sugar cane agriculture and identified the main actors, I will now describe the development and use of sugar harvest machinery in some detail. I will concentrate upon the tasks of cutting, cleaning and loading cane. Transport will be touched on only marginally. The presentation here will be descriptive, i.e. as free as possible from evaluation, interpretation and explanation. It will provide the empirical basis for the analysis in Part 3, where the Cuban and Jamaican experiences will be compared. Hence, the analysis of the data will not be presented until later, although many queries will undoubtedly arise in the minds of readers in the course of the description.

Pre-revolutionary Attempts to Mechanize Harvesting

The attempts to mechanize cane harvesting in Cuba have a history of more than 100 years.[6] The first patent application for a rudimentary machine "to cut cane and analogous products" was made in Havana in 1857 (Abreu 1973: 32). However, the breakthrough to mechanization of cane-cutting did not come until the 1970s.

During the first half of the 20th Century trials were made in almost all provinces in Cuba. However, almost all experiments originated from North American inventions and were carried out by US companies. Before 1930, sugar-mill owners, with administration cane and large cane farmers, showed a determined interest in looking for a solution to mechanical harvesting in Cuba. Different trials were carried out at various sugar mills, with the help of the owners, who saw future advantages in the development of harvest machines. During this period harvest workers had to be imported from other parts of the Caribbean, principally from Jamaica and Haiti, and the development of a harvest machine was seen as a solution to this problem. At the same time mechanization could increase profits by reducing harvest costs.

However, the situation changed radically with the depression of the 1930s. Unemployment became very high and the trials with new harvesters were terminated. The main reason was the low salaries of the agricultural workers and the abundance of manual labour. Under these conditions, mechanization experiments were not perceived to be economically attractive even for the large cane growers.

From this time on, the workers strongly opposed the introduction of mechanical harvest equipment. For example, during the trials of 1931 in the fields of the Baragua sugar mill, numerous breakdowns occurred, many of them caused by pales which the harvest workers placed in the cane furrows during the night in order to obstruct the experiments. This is not surprising, since more than half a million Cuban workers were unemployed (Suarez Gayol and Henderson 1966: 16).

In the late 1940s the trials started again at several sugar mills and cane farms. Also in this period the workers showed their hatred for the machines. For example, the North Americans who conducted the trials at the sugar mill Estrella in 1953 placed an armed guard to watch the harvester day and night after hearing threats that it would be destroyed. The resistance of the workers also took the form of burning a cane harvesting machine taken to Cuba for trials in Camagüey Province (Abreu 1973: 38; Mecanizacion 1977: 7).

Labour's fear of unemployment was justified. The sugar harvest lasted only for three or four months of the year, and seasonal unemployment rates were therefore high. Variations in unemployment rates occurred mainly from season to season within any given year, and they were relatively constant from year to year for each season, as we saw in Table 4.1.

However, in the period before 1959 no sugar harvester did provide a solution to the problem of mechanizing sugar cane harvesting in Cuba. There were several reasons for this. The sugar cane-producing countries were – and are – generally underdeveloped countries with an abundance of cheap manual labour. In most cases the machines could not compete with manual workers, because of the high cost of purchasing harvesters and the operation and maintenance of them as well. In addition, given that cane can be adapted to different kinds of soil and climate, local solutions are often difficult to implement in other areas. The opposition of the workers to the machines has already been mentioned.[7]

To my knowledge no attempts were made to mechanize cane-loading in pre-revolutionary Cuba. This is quite surprising since various loaders were offered on the world market and since mechanization of loading is relatively easy to achieve compared to cutting.

Early Efforts to Mechanize Harvesting in Cuba

Around 1960, the cutting and loading of cane was exclusively manual. The means of transportation were very antiquated. Ox carts, in combination with railroads, were the dominant means of transport and the transferring of the cane to the railroad wagons was accomplished by means of cranes often powered by animals. Unemployment was high, as shown in Table 4.1 (Abreu 1975: 38; Betancourt 1970: 36; Direccion Nacional 1976: 6).

After the revolution unemployment decreased gradually, but remained a problem for most of the 1960s. By 1970, however, it had dropped to 1.3 per cent. Thereafter it increased again and stabilized around 5 per cent during the second half of the 1970s. To some extent overt unemployment had been replaced by disguised unemployment – which was negative in terms of productivity, but preferable in terms of social status and security for those previously unemployed. In this way the negative social and psychological effects of unemployment were mitigated, but the negative impact of disguised unemployment (low productivity) for economic growth and efficiency remained. During the 1970s, the government made efforts to increase productivity and reduce disguised unemployment.

Indigenous Attempts to Mechanize Cutting
In cane harvesting, however, there was no disguised unemployment. On the contrary, already towards the end of the 1961 *zafra*, problems were experienced with the supply of cane to the factories because of a scarcity of harvest workers.[8] Because the cutting and loading of cane demanded the largest number of harvest workers in cane agriculture, the Ministry of Industry established The Commission for the Mechanization of the Cane Harvest (La Comision para la Mecanizacion de la Cosecha de la Cana) in 1961 (Abreu 1975: 38; Betancourt 1970: 36; Direccion Nacional 1976: 6; Mecanizacion 1977:7).

This was the first organizational expression of the interest in mechanizing sugar harvesting in revolutionary Cuba. Because of the shortage of cane-cutters – which became worse in 1962 and 1963 – the issue received priority, and quick results were hoped for. However, the task proved much more difficult than expected, and the result was a serious labour supply problem for the sugar harvest for many years – including the giant *zafra* in 1970, when an attempt was made to produce 10 million tons of sugar.

The number of professional cane-cutters declined radically during the 1960s, as shown in Table 4.3. This decline was supply-induced, i.e. there was a demand for a much larger number of cutters. A number of factors contributed to the decline. Many older workers retired, and younger men were extremely reluctant to take up cane-cutting as a lifetime occupation. They preferred less exhausting and more rewarding jobs. As a result of the comprehensive transformation of Cuban society associated with the revolutionary process, many new job opportunities were also created in non-sugar sectors, including other agricultural pursuits, the service sector and industry. This also meant occupational stability for many workers, which decreased the need for them to take a seasonal job like cane-cutting. Thousands of the country's youth, especially in the rural areas, were also incorporated in the armed forces as well as in the many schools which were established as part of the educational programme (Roca 1976: 46; Suarez Gayol and Henderson 1966: 16; Peralta *et al* 1980:59).

Table 4.3
Number of Professional Cane-cutters in Cuba, 1958-71

Year	Professional cane-cutters
1958	370,000
1963	210,000
1964	160,000
1967	143,368
1968	105,598
1969	88,300
1970	79,752
1971	72,986

Source: Roca (1976: 19).

This serious problem for the Cuban economy was paradoxically enough created by the revolution itself. The fear of unemployment and hunger no longer forced the rural workers to cut cane. The achievement of relative social and economic security had done away with "material incentives" of this kind. The solution to the problem of labour supply hoped for by the government was large-scale mechanization. But, as indicated, this was not a task that could be carried out easily and immediately. In the meantime the problem of shortage of harvest workers was "solved" by the seasonal mobilization of huge numbers of workers from other sectors of the economy. Most of them were certainly not very efficient as cane-cutters.[9]

The 1961 *zafra* constituted the beginning of the new government's attempts to mechanize the sugar harvest. Various Cuban engineers (Guerra, Ponce de Leon and Cruz) and technicians (Argibay and Bolanos) designed and constructed prototypes. These machines, of artisan production, began to be tested in the 1962 *zafra*. Betancourt mentions the cutters of type Argibay, Eca, Martin, Gerneth, Bolanos and Ecea. Abreu mentions a mechanical cane-cutter invented by José Argibay at the Guatemala sugar mill, and a continuous cane lifter and loader supervised by an engineer, José Guerras Romero, at the Venezuela sugar mill. In addition, the harvester INCA was imported from South Africa, and an International Harvester machine – Thornton Model F – which had been tested in 1948 and then abandoned, was put into operation. These early prototypes were designed to cut the cane at ground level, cut the tops off the plant and deposit the stalks in the furrow, but they could not separate the trash from the stalks (Abreu 1975: 38-9; Betancourt 1970: 36; Mecanizacion 1977: 7).

During the trials, elements of the INCA and the Thornton were combined into a third machine. This experimental machine was tested in the *zafra* of 1962 and a massive production was started for the 1963 *zafra*. As many as 680 units of this machine – known as the Ecea MC-1 – were produced for the 1963 harvest. It was on various occasions operated by the Minister of Industry, Che Guevara, during voluntary labour and he also personally proposed improvements to the machine (Abreu 1975: 39, 41; Betancourt 1970: 36; Peralta *et al* 1980: 59; Oviano 1973: 4; Mecanizacion 1977: 10; Suarez Gayol and Henderson 1966: 16). The government obviously considered harvest mechanization to be an important issue.

The MC-1 machines cut the cane at ground level, the tops were cut and the cane was then left on the ground. The cane was cut green (unburnt) and the machine had no mechanism to separate leaves, weeds and other trash from the cane. Therefore these machines needed the assistance of numerous workers following them to clean trash from the cane, pile it up and load it.[10]

In practice, the MC-1 machines did not produce satisfactory results. They did not increase productivity very much since they did not have a cleaning device. Although they cut a considerable quantity of cane, the machines frequently broke down and then the men assisting them were idle. Deficiencies in the organization of the maintenance and difficulties in the programming of the work were other problems. For these reasons the MC-1 was rejected and production was discontinued. Its intervention was of limited value in the 1963 *zafra* and it was not used thereafter (Abreu 1975: 39; Betancourt 1970: 36; Mecanizacion 1977: 10; Suarez Gayol and Henderson 1966: 16; Direccion Nacional 1976: 12).

During 1962 other models were, as mentioned above, designed and tried but none of these machines passed the tests and their development was not continued. The failure of these early indigenous attempts was partly due to the very limited experience of Cuban technicians in the field of cane harvester design and construction. Another important bottleneck to mechanization was the field conditions. Obstacles like trees and stones obstructed the machines, and the fields were often too small for the efficient operation of the harvesters.

In July 1963 a Soviet delegation of specialists visited Cuba to examine the conditions for cane harvesting in Cuba and study the machines then existing. The Cuban designers also continued working with new ideas, and in January 1964 the first prototypes which accomplished all necessary operations were tried. They cut the cane at ground level, eliminated the tops, cut the cane stalks into pieces, cleaned the cane and loaded it onto a means of transport. These were the machines designed by Ing. Ponce de Leon and a Cuban–Czech harvester largely developed by Ing. Bohumir Kotrech (Abreu 1975: 39-40).

The Breakthrough to Mechanical Loading in the 1960s
As in other cane-producing countries, successful mechanization on a massive scale was first accomplished in the lifting or loading of cane. The breakthrough to harvesting by means of combines came much later.

Before 1959, all the cane was loaded manually. This was an arduous and time-consuming task, representing about 40 per cent of the labour of the manual harvest workers (Mecanizacion 1977: 11). As a result of problems with the supply of harvest labour in the early 1960s, the design of machine prototypes to lift sugar cane started around 1962.

Once the massive production of the cutter MC-1 was terminated, the construction of lifting machines started in Cuba.[11] They were fitted to the Romanian tractor, Utos, and they heaped and lifted manually-cut cane. The prototypes were tested in the beginning of the 1963 *zafra* and already at the end of the same *zafra* there was a quantity of "criollas" lifters in service. About 440,000 tons were loaded with this equipment in the 1963 *zafra* (Betancourt 1970: 36-7; Direccion Nacional 1976: 11-12, Suarez Gayol and Henderson 1966: 16; Mecanizacion 1977: 10). Given that 31.1 million tons of cane were cut in 1963, this means that less than 1.5 per cent of the cane was loaded by the "criollas".[12]

However, in a convention with the Soviet Union concerning mechanization of cane-harvesting, a large order for cane loaders was included and the national production in Cuba was discontinued (Betancourt 1970: 36-7; Direccion Nacional 1976: 11-12). This cane loader – called PG 0.5 – was manufactured in the USSR and also designed with Soviet technical assistance (Suarez Gayol and Henderson 1966: 16).[13]

The Soviet mechanical loaders were introduced in 1964 and already in that *zafra* 20 per cent of the cane was mechanically loaded, as shown in Table 4.4. In the 1966 harvest there existed, according to one source, 3,500 machines manufactured in the USSR according to the new design as well as 200 machines of the original design, built in Cuba. Approximately 45 per cent of the cane was loaded with these 3,700 machines in the 1966 *zafra* (Suarez Gayol and Henderson 1966: 16). This means that about 16 million tons were mechanically loaded, since the total harvest was 36.4 million tons.

According to Table 4.5 the accumulated number of cane loaders imported from 1963 to 1969 was 9,143. However, the available or potential number in 1970 amounted to 7,332 loaders. In the 1970 *zafra*, from November 1969 until 31 March 1970, the average number of loaders in effective operation was 5,460 or about 75 per cent of the number potentially available (Betancourt 1970: 39). With these loaders almost 85 per cent of the manually cut cane was mechanically lifted in 1970 (see Table 4.4). Given the size of that *zafra*, close to 70 million tons of cane were lifted mechanically. In 1976 about 6,000 mechanical loaders were used to lift almost all the cane that was manually cut (Posada 1976: 21).

A comprehensive investigation of the amount of extraneous matter or impurities received at the sugar factories gave the results shown in Table 4.6. The difference between manual and mechanical loading over the period is about 1 per cent, which is an extraordinarily good result for mechanical loading. The table also shows a decreasing percentage during the first years. This was probably due to the increased skill of the operators. This was, in its turn, influenced by the results continuously published by the investigation, as well as by technical norms, based upon the investigation, which were implemented in the 1966 *zafra*. However, there are distinct disadvantages with mechanical loading. For example the cane lifted

Table 4.4
Mechanization of Cane-cutting and Loading in Cuba, 1963-81

	% of cane harvested by combine harvester	% of manually cut cane loaded mechanically
1963	—	1
1964	—	20
1965	1-2	26-32
1966	2-3	44-6
1967	2-3	53-7
1968	3	61-8
1969	2	65-74
1970	1	82-5
1971	3	87
1972	7	89-96
1973	11	93-4
1974	18	96
1975	25	96
1976	32	97
1977	36	97
1978	38	98
1979	42	98
1980	45	98
1981	50	98

Note: For many years, particularly in the 1960s, an interval rather than an exact figure is presented in the table. This is done because the various sources present different figures. In most such cases it has not been possible to determine which ones are correct. The reason is that the collection of statistics from the Cuban sugar sector was badly organized and had many deficiences, especially during the 1960s. As a result, many estimates have been made. The exact figures will never be known because of the lack of reliable primary data. Therefore I have chosen to be somewhat unspecific, rather than to present exact figures which may be false. (The degree of mechanization is measured in percentages of the weight of the cane.)

Sources: Betancourt (1970: 36-40); information received from the Cuban Ministry of the Sugar Industry (MINAZ); Oviano (1973: 4); Roca (1976: 54); Peralta *et al* (1980: 59); Sintesis (1982: 2).

mechanically contains four times more earth (0.38 per cent on the average for 1964-9) than the manually loaded cane (0.09 per cent) (Betancourt 1970: 41-2).

The Failure of Early Soviet Harvesters in the 1960s
Simultaneously with the trials of the harvesters designed by Leon and Kotrech, mentioned above, two combine harvesters constructed in the USSR were tested in January 1964. The KCT-1 was towed by a tractor while the KT-1 was self-propelled (Suarez Gayol and Henderson 1966: 18;

Table 4.5
Cuban Imports of Mechanical Cane-loaders from the USSR, 1964-70

Year	Number	Accumulated number
1964	3,500	3,500
1965	0	3,500
1966	1,635	5,135
1967	1,001	6,136
1968	1,507	7,643
1969	1,500	9,143
1970	1,355	10,498

Source: Betancourt (1970: 39); AEC (1975: 171); AEC (1982: 352-3).

Table 4.6
Percentage of Extraneous Matter with Manual and Mechanical Loading, 1964-69

% extraneous matter with:	1964	1965	1966	1967	1968	1969	average
Manual loading	2.63	3.03	2.71	3.25	2.90	3.29	2.97
Mechanical loading	6.16	4.24	3.09	3.47	3.64	4.38	4.16

Source: Betancourt (1970: 41). (In this source the average for mechanical loading was calculated to be 3.92 per cent, which is incorrect.)

Abreu 1975: 40-41). Both machines cut the stalks at ground level, topped them, eliminated leaves and other trash, cut the stalks into pieces 35 centimetres long and loaded them on the means of transport running alongside (Betancourt 1970: 42).[14]

Both the KCT-1 and KT-1 showed good results during the test period and it was decided to import them on a large scale. For the 1965 *zafra* (i.e. principally in 1964), 470 KCT-1 and 30 KT-1 machines arrived in Cuba and imports continued during the following years as shown in Table 4.7. In 1968, however, the importation was discontinued (Abreu 1975: 40-1).

Of the 500 harvesters which were imported for the 1965 *zafra*, 442 KCT-1 and 29 KT-1 – i.e. 471 units – went into operation. Accordingly the number of available units was 471, but the number in active service dwindled rapidly during the *zafra* as shown in Table 4.8 below. Only 10 per cent of the machines were in operation by the beginning of May 1965 (Betancourt 1970:44)!

In 1966 the number of available units was 728 (698 KCT-1 and 30 KT-1), but the maximum number of these which were in operation during any given week was only 521 machines. For the whole *zafra* the weekly average was 300 units per day, reaching 456 units per day at the culmination of the *zafra* in February and March (Betancourt 1970: 44).

Table 4.7
Number of Early Soviet Harvesters Imported to Cuba for the 1965-68 *Zafras*

	KCT-1	KT-1	Total	Accumulated total
1965	470	30	500	500
1966	250	—	250	750
1967	258	5	263	1,013
1968	6	—	6	1,019
Total	984	35	1,019	

Note: The exact timing of the imports is not clear. For example, many or most of the 470 KCT-1 machines which were imported for the 1965 *zafra* probably arrived in Cuba during 1964.

Source: Betancourt (1970: 43).

Table 4.8
Number of Early Soviet Harvesters in Operation during 1965

1965	Active	Inactive	% active
15 March	372	99	79
4 April	288	183	61
15 April	204	267	43
1 May	46	425	10

Source: Betancourt (1970: 44).

The performance of the early Soviet harvesters also declined between 1965 and 1966. In 1965 each machine cut 52 tons per working day and 34 tons per calendar day. For 1966 the corresponding figures were 38 tons and 26 tons, respectively (Betancourt 1970: 44).

From November 1969 until 31 March 1970 the number of available units was 498 harvesters, but the number in efficient operation was only 149. During the same part of the 1970 *zafra* the effective time in operation per day for each harvester was 2.8 hours. On the average 5.3 tons were harvested per hour by each machine. Thus, the productivity per day was about 15 tons (Betancourt 1970: 45).

Accordingly, six years after the start of the import of the Soviet harvesters only 149 out of 1,019 units – i.e. 15 per cent – were in operation. The productivity of these was very low and declined rapidly. It varied between 15 and 50 tons per day. This can be compared with the productivity of present-day harvesters which range between 115 and 140 tons per day, with a working day of 8 to 10 hours.

As regards the quality of cane, the amount of impurities was very high compared to manually cut cane. The average percentage of extraneous matter during 1964-9 for manual cutting combined with mechanical loading was about 4 per cent (Table 4.6). When the cane was cut with the Soviet harvesters the average was more than 13 per cent during 1965-9. Such an excessive quantity of impurities reduces the yield of sugar from the cane and overloads the transport system and factories. If all the harvesting had been carried out by these harvesters between 1965 and 1969, the total quantity of impurities brought to the factories would have been on average 6 million tons per *zafra* (Betancourt 1970: 46, 48).

The achievements of the early Soviet harvesters were very poor. They did not provide much of a solution to the problem of harvest mechanization. This is also indicated by the percentage of the harvest that was cut by harvesters during the 1960s, as shown in Table 4.4. The percentage harvested mechanically never exceeded 3 per cent and it was only about 1 per cent in the giant 1970 *zafra*.[15]

The KCT-1 and the KT-1 combine harvesters performed the technical task at hand, but they had important limitations. As we have seen, their productivity was very low. They could also only cut erect cane or cane with a maximum inclination of 30° (Direccion Nacional 1976: 12). Additionally they could not work in cane with a yield higher than 50-60 tons per hectare (60,000-70,000 *arrobas* per *caballeria*) (Abreu 1975: 40-1; Abreu 1981). In addition, both machines required fields with a maximum inclination of 5° and free from stones, trees, ditches and other obstacles. It was estimated that they could be used only in 30 per cent of the cane fields existing in Cuba in 1966 (Suarez Gayol and Henderson 1966: 28).

We have also seen that the operational reliability was very low. Breakdowns were common and many units became inoperative. Only a small fraction of the more than 1,000 machines that had entered Cuba were in operation in the last years of the 1960s. The import of the Soviet harvesters was stopped in 1968. In the giant *zafra* of 1970 most of the KCT-1 machines did not work. Of the KT-1 harvesters, 24 had been taken out of operation in late 1968 to be rebuilt into a Cuban model (Libertadora).[16] Thus only 11 remained, and only one or two of those worked. Only a handful of the Soviet harvesters imported during 1965-8 worked in the 1971 and 1972 *zafras*, and after 1972 none of them were in operation (Abreu 1981: Direccion Nacional 1976: 12).

Evidently, the effort to mechanize cane cutting in the 1960s was a failure. The Labour Minister, Jorge Risquet, stated in 1970:

> Our efforts in this complex task have been marked by insufficient systematiza-
> tion, and have been affected by the limitations of our mechanical industry and
> also by the low levels of organization, of knowledge, of qualifications of our
> agricultural workers and cadres who, with respect to machinery, sometimes
> and in some places, even manifested an anti-machine spirit . . . sometimes
> because they lacked trust that machines could in fact solve the problem and
> kept thinking that the only trustworthy method was the machete because it did
> not fail. Many times we found this attitude in the countryside, a deep mis-
> understanding regarding mechanization. And thus, for all these reasons, our

efforts to mechanize in time for the 1970 harvest failed and this forced the
country to employ 500,000 man-years.
(Quoted in Roca 1976: 56)

If large-scale mechanization could not solve the problem of lack of
professional cane-cutters, other means were necessary. The two methods
used were to let the army take over the cutting and to mobilize large
numbers of workers from other sectors for the sugar harvests. Without
dealing with these issues in detail, it can be noted that the military cut 20 per
cent of the giant sugar harvest in 1970. In the same year about 350,000
cane-cutters were used at peak times. All but 80,000 of them were
volunteers, civilian and military, transferred to cutting battalions from
various non-sugar sectors. The productivity of the voluntary workers was
very low which, in its turn, necessitated additional mobilization of
volunteers. As a result, production in many other sectors of the economy
suffered heavily. This high opportunity cost was one of the most important
negative consequences of the failure to solve the problem of mechanizing
harvesting (Oviano 1973: 4; Roca 1976: 35, 51, 58; Peralta *et al*
1980: 59).

Since a solution to the problem of harvest mechanization had not been
found, experimentation with different models designed by Cuban engineers
continued during the latter half of the 1960s. The Soviets also went on
experimenting with new variants and in 1965 and 1966, in addition to the
massive imports mentioned above, several other combine harvesters were
tested: CTK-1, KCC-1, KCC-1A, KTC-1, KTC-1A. In 1969 the self-
propelled machine KTS-1A was also tested (Abreu 1975: 42).

Dry Cleaning Stations
In Chapter 3 I discussed the problem of extraneous matter accompanying
the cane stalks into the factories. In order to reduce the quantity of
extraneous matter, cleaning can be carried out manually, automatically in
combine harvesters, in special cleaning plants or by burning the fields before
cutting. Various combinations of these methods are also used.

As indicated above, several different combinations of technique and
labour are available to accomplish the task of cleaning the cane before it is
processed in the sugar factories. These range from a combination of man and
machete to capital-intensive plants designed specifically for this purpose. The
choice of technique in cane-cleaning is, of course, a choice between the
various alternative techniques within this spectrum (compare Chapter 3).

In some countries – for example, Jamaica – water is used to clean the
cane of extraneous matter. These cleaning plants are normally located at
the factories. In Cuba, however, due to the shortage of water, pneumatic
and mechanical means are used to clean the cane in so-called dry cleaning
stations, or *centros de acopio*.[17] These plants were designed and developed
in Cuba in the mid-1960s by a team led by Ing. Roberto Henderson. They
are also manufactured domestically.

A *centro de acopio* is a stationary mechanical installation placed near the fields whose basic function is to clean the "dirty" cane from leaves, as well as to eliminate earth and other kinds of extraneous matter. A mechanical and pneumatic system cleans and chops the cane into pieces of about 40 centimetres – just as in combine harvesters – and deposits them in trucks or railroad wagons. Thus, it also provides a rapid means of reloading, i.e. it provides a substitute for the traditional crane, compared to which it has many advantages. It also serves as a central point of accumulation for the cane from the surrounding fields and as the point from which the cane is sent to the factory after having been cleaned.

The main idea with the cane conditioning centres was to release the manual cutters from having to clean the cane stalks of leaves and from having to cut the stalks into pieces. This saved time and effort for the *macheteros*. In trials it was reported that the productivity of the manual cutters thereby increased by between 80 and 150 per cent (Suarez Gayol and Henderson 1966: 18).

In May 1964 the initial prototype started to operate experimentally in the cane fields of the "Osvaldo Sanchez" factory in Havana province (Gonzalez 1972: 43; Suarez Gayol and Henderson 1966: 15; Salomon Llanes 1980: 38; Dpto . . . 1974: 63). In the 1965 harvest the trials were extended to four dry cleaning stations, with a new design for the three new ones. In the 1966 *zafra* 6 stations were in operation which cleaned 180,000 tons of cane. In 1967, 67 *centros de acopio* were functioning, two of which were double ones. These can manipulate 110-140 tons of cane per hour compared to the 60-70 tons of the single ones. Between 50-65 per cent of the extraneous matter is eliminated by the stations (Suarez Gayol and Henderson 1966: 15, 18; Gonzalez 1972: 44; Salomon Llanes 1980: 39).

As shown in Table 4.9, the importance of the dry cleaning stations increased rapidly after the initial phase of implementation. In particular, the number increased from 180 units in 1970 to 390 in 1971. The stations were, to a large extent, produced in the factory Cubana de Acero with 1,300 workers. From January 1970 to September 1971 – i.e. in 21 months – 320 units were fabricated in this factory (Gonzalez 1972: 44).

Towards the end of the 1970s the number in operation approached 500 units, so that in 1978 about 40 per cent of the total amount of cane harvested was processed in dry cleaning stations. Thus, these stations were of considerable importance in a quantitative sense, increasing the productivity of manual cane-cutters and thereby decreasing the number of *macheteros* needed in the *zafras*. In the 1960s the dry cleaning stations mainly received manually cut cane which was loaded mechanically. They were also, in the 1970s, used as a supplement to harvesting machines which failed to clean the cane properly.[18]

Table 4.9
Mechanical Cane Cleaning in Cuba, 1964-82

Year	Number of dry cleaning stations installed	Amount of cane treated by dry cleaning stations (million tonnes)	% of all cane harvested treated by dry cleaning stations	Sources
1964	1			(Gonzalez 1972:43; Suarez Gayol and Henderson 1966: 15; Salomon Llanes 1980: 38)
1965	4 (one of them was double)		0.2	(Gonzalez 1972: 44; Roca 1976: 54)
1966	6	0.18	0.5	(Suarez Gayol and Henderson 1966: 15; Roca: 1976: 54)
1967	67 (two of them were double)		6.8	(Gonzalez 1972: 44; Roca 1976: 54)
1968	150		13.0	(Betancourt 1976: 54; Roca 1976: 54)
1969	150 (166 acc. to Roca)		15.4	(Betancourt 1976: 54; Roca 1976: 54)
1970	180 (199 acc. to Roca)		25.0 (estimated)	(Salomon Llanes 1980: 38; Gonzalez 1972: 45; Roca 1976: 54)
1971	390			(Salomon Llanes 1980: 38; Gonzalez 1972: 45)
1973	440 (approx.)	16.49	32.9	(Oviano 1973: 4)
1974	445	17.39	33.8	(Salomon Llanes 1980: 40)
1975	450 (or more)	18.30	34.8	(Salomon Llanes 1980: 40)
1976	500 (approx.)	21.71	38.2	(Salomon Llanes 1980: 40; Posada 1976: 22)
1977		26.95	40.1	(Salomon Llanes 1980: 40; Mecanizacion 1977:11)
1978				(Salomon Llanes 1980: 40)
1979	481			(Salomon Llanes 1980: 38)
1980	511 (planned)			(Salomon Llanes 1980: 38)
1981				
1982	578			(Sintesis 1982: 2)

Note: For some years the figures on amount and percentage of cane treated by dry cleaning stations are inconsistent with the data on total amount of cane produced per *zafra* as presented in Table 4.2. However the deviations are marginal.

New Mechanization Efforts Starting around 1970

In the 1960s considerable efforts were made in Cuba to mechanize sugar cane harvesting. More than 80 per cent of the loading had been mechanized by 1970. About one fourth of the total amount of cane harvested was also cleaned by means of cane conditioning centres. These achievements increased the productivity of manual harvest workers. However, in the case of mechanical cutting, no breakthrough had been produced in spite of very substantial efforts. As a result, only 1 per cent of the 1970 harvest was cut by mechanical means.

When the failure to mechanize sugar cane-cutting in Cuba in the 1960s first became apparent, new attempts were made and new ideas were tried. In 1966 studies began in Cuba to try to find a machine that could cut all types of cane. At the beginning of 1967, it was announced by Fidel Castro that the work should be directed towards a machine that could cut all varieties and kinds of cane, however entangled and interwoven it may be, as well as fields with yields higher than 130 tons per hectare. This was an important modification of the dominant conceptions until then (Abreu 1975: 43-4).

It is important to stress that these new attempts did not start from scratch. The – sometimes costly – earlier efforts had created a very important pool of knowledge and experience. For example, thousands of workers had been educated to operate, maintain and repair harvesting machines. There had also been considerable "learning by trying" in harvester design and production. In addition the attempts to mechanize cutting had pointed to the crucial importance of preparing the cane fields in such a way that they were suited to the use of cane harvesters. However, no systematic burning of cane fields before harvesting had been tried, although this method had been used in other countries for many years in order to increase the productivity of manual cutters as well as to facilitate the operation of harvesting machines.

From approximately 1967, the continuing work can be divided into four different lines. Three "families" of harvesters were largely developed in Cuba: the Henderson, the Libertadora and the KTP-1. In addition, more than 400 Australian Massey-Ferguson harvesters were imported, starting in the 1971 harvest. The Henderson machine was a heavy and simple one which could cut and load, but not clean, the cane. It was developed in the late 1960s, but it was taken out of operation as early as 1972. The Libertadora was designed in the same period, also in Cuba. It was later improved and produced in West Germany and is still used in Cuba. The Massey-Ferguson was imported in large quantities from Australia during the first half of the 1970s. The KTP-1 was developed in the early 1970s by the joint efforts of Cuban and Soviet technicians. After trials, manufacturing was started in the Soviet Union, but there is now a large factory in operation in Cuba. It has a potential capacity of 600 units per year. In 1980 almost 2,000 KTP-1 machines were in operation in Cuba.

The four lines of development mentioned will each be discussed separately, but first, however, I will address the issue of burning the standing cane before harvest and the need to redesign and condition the cane fields in order to facilitate the operation of harvesting machines.

Burning and Reblocking of Cane Fields

In Chapter 3 and on pp.17-8 it was briefly mentioned that the quantity of extraneous matter in the cane can be reduced by burning the cane fields before harvesting. Through such burning the amount of trash is reduced but not completely eliminated. Still, it increases the productivity of manual cane-cutters and facilitates the operation of harvesting and loading machines as well as dry cleaning stations. Programmed burning of cane fields has been used, for example, in Australia, Hawaii, Mexico, Peru and South Africa for decades. In Jamaica it was introduced in 1961.[19]

In 1970-1 a group of Cuban specialists visited Australia, where they studied the cane harvest. One important difference, compared to Cuba, was that the cane fields were burnt in Australia before harvesting. Upon its return, the group proposed burning also in Cuba. Tests were made in the fields, and the political leadership made a decision to start burning in Cuba. Systematic burning was introduced on a large scale in the 1971 *zafra* (Vazquez 1972a: 18; Direccion Nacional 1976: 15; Mecanizacion 1977: 12). Once burning was introduced in Cuba, the practice spread very rapidly and in the 1972 *zafra* this method was used in approximately 70 per cent of the cane fields. The reason was that – at that time – burning was considered to be the only method to decrease rapidly the number of harvest workers needed to carry out the harvest. In the long run, however, the solution to this problem was expected to be combine harvesting (Vazquez 1972a: 19).[20]

As mentioned in Chapter 3, however, burning also has negative consequences and is a highly debated issue. Because of these negative factors, there was, in the second half of the 1970s, a shift back towards harvesting of green cane in Cuba (Pollitt 1981: 6). However, exact figures on the extent of burning for each year are not available.

One of the reasons behind the failure to mechanize cane-cutting in Cuba in the 1960s was the condition of the cane fields. Stones, trees and other obstacles obstructed the machines and caused stoppages and breakdowns. In addition the fields were often too small and irregular to allow an efficient use of combine harvesters.

Starting in 1970 investigations were begun to define the appropriate size of the cane fields to make possible more efficient mechanical harvesting as well as irrigation and drainage. The conclusion reached was that the optimal dimension of a cane field was approximately 500 × 160 metres. This unit was thereafter called a "typical field". Twelve of these constitute together a *bloque* which is about km^2 in size (Direccion Nacional 1976: 6; Mecanizacion 1977: 7-8). From 1972 all fields were designed according to this scheme when they were replanted. Stones, trees and other obstacles were also removed in this process of reblocking the fields. By 1975 about

40 per cent of the Cuban cane fields were designed in this way (Vazquez 1975: 25-6).

The Henderson Harvesters

The Henderson harvester was developed by a group led by Ing. Roberto Henderson principally to cut cane with high yields. It was attached to a Soviet crawler tractor (T-100 M) of 108 horsepower. The front part of this bulldozer was taken out and replaced with a sugar cane-cutting mechanism. The cutting at the bottom was done by round segmented knives. The machine also had a lateral knife to cut fallen cane at the side of the furrow and knives which cut the cane into pieces of about 35 centimetres (Abreu 1976: 6; Betancourt 1970: 48).

The cane pieces were carried to the discharge conveyor and directly to the cart. In other words, the machine collected all the cane plant without having the means to clean it. Green and dry leaves, tops, weeds, etc. accompanied the cane into the carts. The idea was that it should work in co-ordination with dry cleaning stations (*centros de acopio*) which were being installed in large numbers at the same time as the Henderson harvesters were being tried. Because of its strength, and since it was attached to a crawler tractor, this harvester was not very demanding in terms of land conditions, although, of course, the best results were obtained on prepared land, flat and free from obstacles (Abreu 1976: 6; Betancourt 1970: 49).

The Henderson machine was heavy and simple and designed in such a way that it would be easy to construct in Cuba, by adapting a heavy tractor. It could cut cane of any yield, erect or lying down. On the average it cut 35 tons per hour and it could cut as much as 70 tons of burnt cane with a yield of 215 tons per hectare (Betancourt 1970: 49).[21]

The Henderson machine was developed in early 1968; experimental tests were conducted in 1969. The importance of solving the serious problem of cane-cutting in the vast *zafra* of 1970 made it necessary to introduce the machine on a large scale. A total of 148 units of Henderson Model 1(1-CFH) were therefore produced in "Fabric Aguilar" in Santa Clara for the 1970 harvest (Abreu 1976: 6; Betancourt 1970: 48-9).

These 148 units were sent to the province of Camagüey which was the region with the lowest population density and therefore most in need of the harvester (Abreu 1976: 6). As a matter of fact, most of the mechanically cut cane in 1970 (1 per cent) was cut by the Henderson harvesters in Camagüey province (Abreu 1981). This means that the early Soviet harvesters actually cut almost no cane in the huge *zafra* of 1970, contrary to what some other authors argue.

The Henderson Model 1 machines were used in the 1970 and 1971 *zafras*, but the results were not very satisfactory and this made it necessary to improve the working parts of the machine. Model 1 was taken out of operation and in 1971 100 new units of an improved version were produced. They are known as Model 3(3-CFH) and attached to the 150 horsepower Italian FIAT BD-14. These units were used in the Province of

Las Villas in the 1972 *zafra*. In this line of harvesters other experimental models, called Hector Molina and Mini-Henderson, were also designed (Abreu 1976: 6).

The fact that the Henderson harvesters did not clean the cane meant that about 30 per cent of the material collected by them was extraneous matter. This led to overloading of the means of transport. In addition, the dry cleaning stations could not clean efficiently the vegetal mass collected by the Henderson machines. The amount of extraneous matter was simply too much.[22] This, in turn, created serious problems for the sugar factories. The operational reliability of the Henderson harvesters was also low (Abreu 1976: 6).

In spite of their high cutting capacity per hour in operation, then, the Henderson harvesters had important disadvantages when compared with the other harvesters – to be dealt with below – which existed in Cuba in the early 1970s. In the middle of 1972, it was therefore decided to terminate the development of all the Henderson models (Direccion Nacional 1976: 13).

The Libertadora Harvesters
More or less the same group of Cuban technicians were working on cane harvester design from 1962-3 on. The design and development of different models could, therefore, build upon each other and overlap. It is thus sometimes difficult to judge exactly when the development of a certain model started, but sometime around 1965 the development of the Libertadora was begun. In 1967 an experimental model was created by the "cane group" at Instituto para el Desarrollo de la Maquinaria (ICDM) in its prototype workshop "Rufino Suarez Albo" in Guanabacoa just outside Havana. A chassis of the Czech tractor PKUS-45 and an additional Robur engine were used (Abreu 1976: 4-5).

This was the first machine of Cuban design which could cut inclined and entangled cane and which managed the technical process of cutting, cleaning and loading to a sufficiently high standard. It was provided with a cutter for the tops with mechanical drive, lateral knife, two round knives to cut the bottoms of the stalk, a knife which cut the cane stalks in pieces of about 30 centimetres, a conveyor mat, pneumatic cleaning by means of a ventilator or fan and final delivery to a trailer or truck by means of a conveyor belt. Trials were made in fields with a yield up to 130 tons per hectare with lying cane (Abreu 1976: 4-5; Betancourt 1970: 49). During tests in Oriente on 7 April 1968 this machine was named Libertadora by Fidel Castro, implying that this harvester would liberate man from the arduous task of hand-cutting (Abreu 1976: 4-5).[23]

This model was modified step by step, and for the 1969 *zafra* 24 machines were manufactured in Planta Mecania, Santa Clara. This model was called Libertadora 800. These 24 machines were built on the chassis of the self-propelled Soviet harvester KT-1 which was taken out of operation at the end of 1968. A 97 horsepower motor was used, and the power for the propulsion of the harvester was in this version supplied by an hydraulic system. These machines did not yet have a high rate of operational reliability, which resulted in a low utilization of the working day. However, the productivity of these harvesters was still twice as high as the productivity obtained by the Soviet harvester KCT-1 (Abreu 1976: 4-5; Betancourt 1970: 49).

Development and testing continued in order to produce more productive machines. In 1970 the Libertadora 1400 and 1600 appeared, both bigger than the 800 model. The 1400 model, in particular, showed very positive results when it was tested in the field during 1970 (Abreu 1976: 5-6).

In 1970 negotiations concerning collaboration were carried out with the Claas Maschinenfabrik in the Federal Republic of Germany. A collaboration agreement was signed, the drawings of Libertadora 1400 were taken to Germany by a group of Cuban technicians, and some modifications were made by the Germans on the machine. Thereby the Claas-Libertadora was born. The fabrication of this machine started in Germany and the patent rights were handed over to the Germans in exchange for a low price for a certain quantity of the machines (Diaz Hernandez and Alvarez Portal 1981: 49; Andérez 1981; Abreu 1981).

The production of the Libertadora in Germany was contracted in 1970 and the first two prototypes were already in Cuba by the 1971 *zafra*. In the following years this model was to be implemented on a large scale in Cuba as can be seen in Table 4.10. During the 1972-4 period 169 units were delivered to Cuba (Stephenson and Loeser 1982). Table 4.1, based upon information originating from Cuba, shows that the maximum number of Libertadoras in operation was 167. 157 of them were still in operation in 1980.[24]

The Massey-Ferguson Harvesters

The Massey-Ferguson 201 (MF 201) is a combine harvester, also called a chopper harvester. The machine is hydrostatically driven and powered by a 140 h.p. Perkins V-8 diesel engine. After burning, the standing cane is topped at the desired height by the hydraulically adjustable topper, gathered and somewhat straightened by the gathering walls which incorporate the spiral crop lifters. The cane is then cut near to, at, or just below soil level by the twin base-cutter. The cut cane is drawn into the machine base first by a big roller and conveyed to the chopper by a series of rollers. At this stage loose soil drops out (van Groenigen 1970: 57; Lee and van Groenigen 1973: 184).

The chopper consists of two sets of contra-rotating ("kissing") blades which chop the cane in pieces of approximately 30 centimetres and throw them into the first elevator. An air blast blows out trash when the cane drops from the first to the second elevator. An extractor fan on top of the second elevator sucks out trash when the cane drops into the cart (van Groenigen 1970: 57; Lee and van Groenigen 1973: 184). The development

Table 4.10
Number of Various Kinds of Cane Harvesters Operating in Cuba,
1971-82

	Henderson 1 and 3	Libertadora 1400		MF 201 (102 and 205)		KTP-1		Total
		no.	%	no.	%	no.	%	
1971	148	2[a]		20		2[a]		172
1972	100	19		115		2[a]		236
1973	—	123	29.6	249	60.0	43	10.4	415
1974	—	163	22.3	387	53.0	180	24.7	730
1975	—	167	16.6	418	41.5	422	41.9	1,007
1976	—	162	12.6	439	34.2	683	53.2	1,284
1977	—	166	10.5	432	27.4	979	62.1	1,577
1978	—	166	8.3	435	21.7	1,405	70.0	2,006
1979	—	157	6.8	407	17.7	1,734	75.5	2,298
1980	—	157	6.5	365	15.1	1,901	78.4	2,423
1981	—	n.a.		n.a.		n.a.		2,712[b]
1982	—	n.a.		n.a.		n.a.		3,000[c]

[a] Experimental machines
[b] Estimated in the following way $\dfrac{2,423 + 3,000}{2} = 2,711.5$
[c] Approximately

Note: In 1971 and 1972 also a very limited number of KCT-1 and KT-1 machines operated, as indicated on p.41.

Sources: 1971-80, information received from the Cuban Ministry of the Sugar Industry (MINAZ); 1982, Sintesis (1982: 2).

of the MF 201 was completed in 1969 when serial production started in Australia. It was the successor to the MF 515 which will be discussed on p.126 below. In contrast to its predecessor it was self-propelled and also improved in many other respects. The MF 201 and the Libertadora 1400 constituted – independently of each other – a technical breakthrough in sugar cane harvesting. They were the first combine harvesters which could successfully, and with high productivity, cut almost any kind of cane. There was, however, one important difference. The MF 201 was designed for burnt cane and the cleaning system was not efficient enough for green cane harvesting (Hackett 1984: 1). The Cuban/Claas joint venture was more efficient in green cane (Hackett 1984: 1). Although they were designed simultaneously, and probably independently of each other, large-scale production of the Libertadora 1400 started somewhat later (1971) than in the case of the MF 201 (1969). However, the modern chopper harvester concept was more successfully introduced by the Cuban/Claas venture as the Libertadora could be used in green cane. In spite of this, the Massey-Ferguson eventually achieved larger shipments of harvesters to Cuba, as shown in Table 4.10.[25]

A collaboration agreement was established between Cuba and Massey-

Ferguson (Australia) Limited and the first MF 201 harvesters arrived in Cuba in December 1970: 20 machines were available in the 1971 *zafra*. As shown in Tables 4.10 and 4.11, the MF 201 was introduced, on a large scale, in Cuba during the following years.[26]

Table 4.11
Massey-Ferguson Sales of Cane Harvesters to Cuba by Model, 1969-76

Model	1969-70	1970-1	1971-2	1972-3	1973-4	1974-5	1975-6	Total
MF 201	20	100	90	130	90	—	—	430
MF 102	—	—	—	1	—	—	20	21
All models	20	100	90	131	90	—	20	451

Source: Hackett (1982).

As we can see from Table 4.12, it was principally the MF 201 harvester that produced the breakthrough as regards mechanization of cane-cutting in Cuba. Of the mechanically cut cane in 1972, 4 out of 7 per cent was harvested by the MF 201. About half or more of the mechanical cutting during the first four years (1972-5) of successful mechanization was done by this machine. However, the Libertadora contributed to the breakthrough: 27 per cent of the mechanically cut cane in 1973 was harvested by this machine. From the mid-1970s, the relative importance of the Massey-Ferguson and Libertadora machines declined, and in 1980 only 20 per cent and 9 per cent respectively of the mechanical cutting was carried out by these harvesters.

Table 4.12
Percentage of Cane Mechanically Cut by Various Harvesters in Cuba, 1971-80

	Libertadora 1400	Massey-Ferguson	KTP-1	Others	Total
1971	—	1	—	2	3
1972	1	4	—	2	7
1973	3	7	1	—	11
1974	4	10	4	—	18
1975	4	12	9	—	25
1976	5	13	14	—	32
1977	4	13	19	—	36
1978	4	10	24	—	38
1979	4	10	28	—	42
1980	4	9	32	—	45

Note: The machines included in "others" were mainly Henderson Models 1 and 3, since only a handful of the early Soviet harvesters worked in the 1971 and 1972 *zafras* (see pp.41 and 47).

Source: Information received from the Cuban Ministry of Sugar Industry (MINAZ).

The KTP-1 Harvesters

In 1969 La Direccion Nacional de Mecanizacion (DINAME) constructed a new prototype called CCAT-910 with the aim of cutting green cane in fields with high yields. After some trials this harvester was sent to the Soviet Union within the framework of a collaboration agreement. There, two identical prototypes were produced on the basis of the CCAT-910, but also using the experience acquired by the Soviet specialists during the tests, mentioned earlier, in Cuba in the mid-1960s.

The two prototypes were taken back to Cuba and in the 1971 *zafra* the development of this new Cuban–Soviet machine – the KTP 1 – started at the testing station in Artemisa. Its principal initial characteristics were a double feeding conveyor in the front part, two side knives for separation, a knife to cut the cane into pieces, pneumatic cleaning by means of two diametrical ventilators, a discharge conveyor and a 105 h.p. diesel engine (Abreu 1976: 8).

After the tests the two machines were taken back to the USSR, but the following year the same two machines returned to Cuba again. They were now improved. The feeding conveyors were replaced by drum feeders and endless collectors and the engine was now 150 horsepower. The front parts of the two units were also different.

The tests in 1972 were considered successful, and in the 1973 *zafra* the large-scale introduction of the KTP-1 started. Some 50 units were imported from the Soviet Union, and the imports increased rapidly to a yearly rate of about 200-300 units by the mid-1970s. The mass-produced version was self-propelled and could efficiently cut the cane at ground level, chop it into pieces, clean it and deposit it on the truck or tractor cart following the combine. Thus, the KTP-1 harvesters are similar in principle to the MF 201.[27]

The number of KTP-1 harvesters in operation during various years is shown in Table 4.10. The number increased rapidly from 1973 onwards and in 1976 more than half of the machines in operation were KTP-1 harvesters. In 1980 this figure was almost 80 per cent. Table 4.12 shows that more than half of the mechanical cutting was done by these Cuban–Soviet machines in 1977 and in 1980 this figure was 71 per cent. By the late 1970s, the KTP-1 was the dominant combine harvester in operation in Cuba. As mentioned earlier, the KTP-1 was first manufactured in the Soviet Union. In 1977, however, a factory was inaugurated in Cuba to produce these machines. This is now the biggest cane harvester factory in the world, with a capacity of 600 units per year.[28]

Notes

1. The organization previously in existence was the Asociación de Hacendados de Cuba.

2. Other *colonos* associations existed earlier, but membership in them was not compulsory. Until 1934 the Asociación Nacional de Colonos was the organization representing the cane planters.

3. The importation of contract labourers was forbidden by the 1940 constitution.

4. The sugar content of cane is about 10 per cent.

5. The information regarding agrarian reforms presented below is taken from CERP (1965), Brundenius (1984), Dominguez (1978), MacEwan (1981), Nelson (1972) and O'Connor (1968).

6. The history to follow in this section builds mainly on Abreu (1973).

7. Several additional factors which complicate the mechanical cutting of cane were mentioned in Chapter 3.

8. This shortage of harvest labour co-existed with a general unemployment rate of more than 10 per cent in 1961, as shown in Table 4.1.

9. These mobilized workers are not included in Table 4.3.

10. The loading could in principle have been done mechanically, but mechanical loaders were not introduced in Cuba until the very end of the 1963 *zafra*; see p.37.

11. The number of machines mentioned varies between 400 and 500 units, depending on the source.

12. Since the number of units in operation is not known, this says little about the performance of the machines.

13. The Soviet machine is a grab-loader. It is suspended on the tractor (Byelarus) MTZ-5LC or MTZ-5MC and grabs a bundle of cane to place it on a truck or cart. It lifts 500 kilos to a height of 3.2 metres, and the work cycle is 1 minute and 38 seconds. Its potential capacity is 14 tons per hour, but the official norm was set at around 10 tons per hour. At tests in Ciego de Avila, the average achieved was 11.2 tons per hour (Betancourt 1970: 37-9).

14. The KCT-1 worked attached to the Byelarus MTZ-5MC tractor or similar ones. The working parts of the harvester were powered by the tractor engine by means of a driving shaft.

15 Most of this percentage was not cut by the Soviet machines, as will be seen on p.47.

16. See p.48.

17. In Spanish, "centros de recepcion y beneficio en seco de la cana", or, for short, "centros de acopio".

18. This was, as we shall see, tried in particular with the Henderson harvester. It should also be mentioned that the leaves separated in the dry cleaning stations can be used as a supplementary cattle fodder.

19. See p.69.

20. In Chapter 7, p.116, I will discuss some implications of the fact that the decision to start burning came very late in Cuba.

21. However, the Henderson harvesters primarily cut green cane.

22. In other words, the capability of the dry cleaning stations had been overestimated.

23. The names of the prototypes before 1968 were CCE-1 and CCE-2, CCE being short for *C*ombinada para *C*ana *E*nredada, meaning combine for entangled cane.

24. On the whole the German and Cuban data seem to be consistent in this case. However, according to information received from MINAZ in 1982, Claas

produced 172 units for Cuba of the Libertadora 1400; two (experimental) units arrived in Cuba for the 1971 *zafra*, 20 units for the 1972 *zafra*, 100 units for the 1973 *zafra*, and 50 units for the 1974 *zafra*. Claas also manufactured a prototype "Hector Molina" in the Henderson family, which was tried and rejected in the 1972 *zafra*. In addition, Claas produced two more prototypes in the Libertadora family (Libertadora 1200-A and 1200-B) for the 1974 and 1975 *zafras* respectively. Hence, according to MINAZ, Claas manufactured in total 175 machines for Cuba.

25. It should also be mentioned that the Toft and Don companies in Australia produced efficient combine harvesters almost at the same time.

26. Table 4.11 shows the number of machines sold to Cuba and is based on information received from the supplier, while Table 4.10 shows the number of machines operating in various *zafras* and is based on information from Cuba. Given that the tables are based on differently defined years, and that a certain number of machines normally become inoperational, the two tables seem to be consistent with each other. However, it must be noted that Table 4.11 shows when the machines were manufactured and delivered from Australia; they started to be used in Cuba considerably later. For example, the first 20 units were sent from Australia in 1970 and started to be used in Artemisa during the 1971 *zafra*.

27. Just like the MF 201, the KTP-1 is equipped with a conical cane separator on either side of the throat, a base-cutter with blades mounted on a disc, feed-rollers pulling whole cane into chopping knives, a detrashing mechanism and a two-stage elevator with extractor fans for removing trash and tops and loading the cane into carts. However, the KTP-1 is not equipped with a topping mechanism. Elevators have the usual 180° traverse in a lateral direction and can load carts either alongside or behind the machine when breaking fields.

28. This will be discussed further in Chapter 7, pp.133-4.

5. Jamaica: 1958-83

STRUCTURE AND ACTORS IN THE SUGAR SECTOR

Capitalist Jamaica was a British colony until 1962 and is still largely economically and technologically dependent in the early 1980s. Much of the role previously played by Britain has now been taken over by the USA. Imperialist penetration and domination is still a major obstacle to development, and Jamaica is – in contrast to Cuba – a typical case of a developing country which has not developed. With regard to technical change in sugar cane harvesting, Jamaica has been less dynamic than Cuba during recent decades. For these reasons, I will devote less space to the description of the case of Jamaica than to the Cuban case.

Jamaica has a parliamentary political system of British model, dominated by two parties. In the first ten years after independence, the conservative Jamaican Labour Party (JLP) was in power. In the 1972 election, the reformist social democratic People's National Party (PNP) took over. The PNP election victory was repeated in December 1976, but in 1980 the JLP returned to power.

As indicated by Table 5.1, chronic unemployment has been a severe problem in Jamaica for decades. The unemployment data is, however, sparse and quite unreliable before the 1970s. The decline in unemployment between 1943 and 1960 was not due to the capacity of the economy to absorb labour at a rapid rate, but because high rates of emigration depressed the growth of the labour force to less than the rate of growth of unemployment. It seems reasonable to assume that without wide-scale emigration, the unemployment rate in 1960 would not have been much, if at all, below the 1943 rate (Jefferson 1972: 30).

In the late 1970s, unemployment increased rapidly, and in 1979 it was close to 28 per cent. According to the World Bank, it was about 30 per cent at the end of 1977 (World Bank 1978b: 11). Finally, it must be added that the figures presented do not take into account the severe problems of underemployment and disguised unemployment.

The present-day sugar sector can trace its roots to 1938, when a large and extremely modern sugar factory was built at Frome, by the newly-formed West Indies Sugar Company (WISCO), controlled by Tate & Lyle

Table 5.1
Unemployment in Jamaica. Selected Years, 1943-80 (per cent of
Labour Force)

1943	25.1	1974	21.2
1953	17.5	1975	20.5
1957	17.1	1976	22.4
1960	13.5	1977	24.2
1967	20.2	1978	24.5
1972	23.2	1979	27.8
1973	22.5	1980	27.3

Sources: 1943-67, Jefferson (1972: 28, 32); 1972-3, World Bank (1978b:
5); 1974-8, National Planning Agency (1978: table 15.1); 1979-80,
National Planning Agency (1980: table 14.1).

in London. Sugar production increased from 178,000 tons in 1946 to an all-
time record of 506,000 tons in 1965, when the sector directly employed
over 60,000 people, and over 30,000 cane farmers delivered cane to 18
factories. Since 1965-6, however, the acreage devoted to cane cultivation,
cane yields and total cane production have steadily declined (Mordecai
1967: 78; World Bank 1978a: 6; see also Table 5.2).

Main Actors in the Jamaican Sugar Sector in the late 1950s

> At the time of the Mordecai Report (1967) the structure of the industry was
> relatively simple, there being three groups of interested parties: estate owners,
> independent cane farmers and sugar workers.
> (World Bank 1978a: 7)

Although the Government did not play a dominant role in the sector at that
time, it none the less did have a role. Government and government agencies
must be added to the three actors mentioned by the World Bank.

The structure of the sugar sector had not changed very much during the
decade before 1967. Therefore the information presented in the Mordecai
report in that year can be used to describe the picture in the late 1950s,
although, in actuality, it refers mainly to the early 1960s.

Estate Owners

The estate owners were the dominant actors in the Jamaican sugar sector
around 1960. The estates were defined by the fact that each of them owned
a sugar factory. Together they also owned and worked approximately half
of the cane acreage in Jamaica. In 1959 there were 20 sugar factories in
Jamaica and by the mid-1960s the number had decreased to 18 factories

Table 5.2
Sugar Cane Production in Jamaica, 1955-82

	(1) Total amount of cane produced per year (million tons)	(2) Yield per acre (tons)		(1) Total amount of cane produced per year (million tons)	(2) Yield per acre (tons)
1955	3.6	34.8	1969	4.0	28.1
1956	3.2	32.9	1970	4.2	27.2
1957	3.4	33.8	1971	4.0	26.2
1958	3.2	30.6	1972	4.1	26.9
1959	3.8	33.1	1973	3.6	25.1
1960	4.3	34.6	1974	3.8	26.8
1961	4.4	33.0	1975	3.5	27.0
1962	4.1	30.7	1976	3.6	25.6
1963	4.5	33.4	1977	3.2	24.8
1964	4.6	30.6	1978	3.5	27.6
1965	4.7	32.0	1979	2.9	26.2
1966	4.9	32.1	1980	2.7	24.0
1967	4.4	29.3	1981	2.4	23.4
1968	4.4	28.7	1982	2.5	24.2

Note: The yield per acre is not available for cane produced by cane farmers until 1964. Therefore the yields concern only estates until 1963. Thereafter the average yield is for both cane farmers and estates. 1 acre = 0.4047 hectares.

Sources: Minster (1976: 1.1); Page (1981: table 3); National Planning Agency (1980: table 6.7); Shaw (1982: 6).

owned by 17 companies (Goldenberg 1960: 1; Mordecai 1967: 15; Page 1981: 2). The Sugar Manufacturers' Association (SMA) – formed in 1929 – represented all the sugar and spirit manufacturers in the island. The association also marketed all export sugar, molasses and distilled spirits, and it also owned and conducted a Sugar Research Division near Mandeville, mainly on behalf of its member estates.

A large part of Jamaican sugar production was controlled from abroad. For example, the three largest estates – Frome, Monymusk and Bernard Lodge – were externally controlled. Frome and Monymusk were owned by Tate & Lyle of the UK and Bernard Lodge by United Fruit of the USA. Together these three estates in 1966 and 1970 produced about 45 per cent of all sugar in Jamaica (Minster 1976: 33). Part of the cane was produced by the estates themselves, but they also processed cane bought from cane farmers. Coupled with the fact that the estate-factories exercised an explicit leadership function in relation to other actors in the sector, this external influence can be expected to have considerably affected the policies of the Jamaican sugar sector.

Cane Farmers

The independent cane farmers' share of total cane production increased from 30 per cent in the late 1940s to 50 per cent in the late 1960s and the 1970s. In 1958 there were about 20,000 cane farmers, but in the mid-1960s some 30,000 cane farmers owned and operated about half of the cane acreage (Mordecai 1967: 79, 140, 166). The formation of the All-Island Jamaican Cane Farmers' Association (AIJCFA) in 1941 grew out of general discontent by the cane farmers with the price they were paid by the estates for their cane. Since it was created, the AIJCFA has functioned as an interest organization of the cane farmers in many areas.

However, the members of AIJCFA were a quite heterogeneous group. In 1964 420 cane farmers supplied 60 per cent of all farmers' cane, and 2,300 farmers supplied 76 per cent. The rest were medium and small-sized farms, the former delivering an average of 60 tons each and the latter 12 tons each. The contribution of the large number of very small farmers was therefore rather small in volume. At the same time, a few farmers operated on a larger scale than the smaller estates (Mordecai 1967: 16). Thus a large number of cane farmers grew only a few acres of cane, but at the other end of the scale were farmers who grew as much as 1,500 acres. The latter were virtually small estates but they were not classified as such because they did not have their own sugar factories (World Bank 1978a: 7).

Sugar Workers

Average field employment of non-staff workers on sugar estates during the harvesting season fell from 35,700 to 22,300 between 1955 and 1965 (Mordecai 1967: 204). In 1967 23,000 workers were employed in the fields and factories of the sugar estates and 9,000 by the cane farmers. Two trade unions, the Bustamente Industrial Trade Union (BITU) and the National Workers' Union (NWU) represented various categories of workers in the sugar sector. The two unions together claimed a total membership of 131,000 (1964), some 30,000 of whom were sugar workers (Mordecai 1967: 19). An important fact is that each of the two principal unions are closely associated to one of the two big political parties: the BITU to the JLP and the NWU to the PNP.

Negotiations between the unions and the Sugar Manufacturers' Association were conducted annually and were usually protracted. The relationship between the unions and the Sugar Manufacturers was considered "unhealthy" by the Mordecai report (Mordecai 1967: 19).

Government

The most important government agency intervening in the sugar sector was the Sugar Control Board which was established in 1929. The first International Sugar Agreement was completed in 1937, and was intended to stabilize prices in the free world market by instituting export quotas for those producing countries which were parties to the pact. Related to this agreement the board was given the powers to distribute equitably any restriction in Jamaican production among the sugar manufacturers themselves and among the estates and cane farmers. However, the Sugar Control Board played a largely passive role until it was dissolved in 1970 when it was replaced by the Sugar Industry Authority (Mordecai 1967: 11, 193).

CHANGES UNTIL AROUND 1980

The sugar sector of Jamaica has now been in a crisis for more than 15 years. Cane yields have declined – as shown in Table 5.2 – and the quality of the cane has deteriorated. Many factories were run down by the late 1970s due to the failure over many years to maintain and repair old machinery and equipment. Conflicts between labour and estate management and between the estates and cane farmers have contributed to the decline of the sector. As a result, Jamaica has developed into an inefficient and high-cost producer of sugar. The government, has, however, decided to rehabilitate and revitalize the sugar sector. The implementation of a rehabilitation programme – partly financed by the World Bank – started during the latter half of the 1970s. This programme did not concern cane agriculture very much; it was instead concentrated upon the industrial part of the sector.

The most important changes in the structure of the sector during the 1970s were the relatively rapid decline of the influence of the estates, increasing government participation and control, and the emergence of cane co-operatives. The government control has been exercised by the formation of the Sugar Industry Authority (SIA), the purchase of estate-owned cane lands, and more recently by the acquisition of five of the remaining twelve sugar factories.

The government has channelled most of its recent efforts to rehabilitate the sugar sector through the Sugar Industry Authority (SIA), a statutory body established in 1970. The authority, while nominally accountable to the Minister of Agriculture, operates autonomously and is a strong centralizing power which brings together representatives of the manufacturers, cane farmers and trade unions (World Bank 1978a: 35; Minster 1976: 12).

SIA directs the marketing of sugar, provides loans to cane farmers and sugar factories, proposes prices for cane and raw sugar to the government and co-ordinates relations between the actors in the sugar sector. SIA also administers the Sugar Industry Research Institute (SIRI) which has replaced the research department of the SMA. SIRI is responsible for research, extension and training related to both cane-farming and sugar-processing (World Bank 1978a: 35).

Growers of sugar cane have been traditionally classified into two categories – estates and farmers. In 1974 a third element was introduced in the form of co-operatives. Cane was, during the latter half of the 1970s, produced by eight sugar estates, 23 primary sugar cane co-operatives and about 15,000 independent cane farmers.

Estates have traditionally developed in conjunction with the factories to which they supply all their cane. They generally have good land and historically a high level of management capability coupled with fairly substantial capital resources. As a result, cane yields have been, on the average, 3 tons per acre higher than those of farmers. However, in recent years high overheads and manning levels have restricted profits and reduced viability. As the estate system is also regarded as the epitome of colonialism, gradual phasing out of this kind of unit is taking place.

Government ownership of significant sections of the sugar sector began in 1970-1, when it bought the three largest estates on the island, namely, Frome, Monymusk and Bernard Lodge. At that time the government bought only the land and not the three factories attached to the land, the original idea being to subdivide the land into medium-sized parcels and sell it off freehold to independent cane farmers. To manage its new assets while this was being done, the government established the Frome Monymusk Land Co. (FMLC) (World Bank 1978a: 7, Minster 1976: 3B2).

However, in the election of 1972, the reformist social democratic People's National Party took over from the conservative Jamaican Labour Party. Thereby policies also changed in relation to the cane lands. The PNP had long been committed to the co-operative idea and the PNP chairman, Michael Manley, was determined to find a way whereby the workers could share in the ownership. Therefore the new government was averse to the concept of selling off the land freehold and instead favoured co-operative or leasehold titles (Higgins 1980: 11). FMLC did not, however, have the facilities to operate the acquired land (about 57,000 acres), and, since the government wished to avoid disruption of cane supplies to the three factories, the bulk of the newly-acquired lands were leased back to their original owners. Three sections, one per estate, were however retained by FMLC, and on these were established three pilot cane-growing co-operatives in 1974 (World Bank 178a: 7).

Later on, the process accelerated under strong popular pressure from the workers and in 1975-7 all the former estate lands – apart from three farms at Frome – were subdivided into 23 co-operatives (World Bank 1978a: 7-8; Minster 1976: 382). The 23 cane-growing co-operatives were the basic units. Called primary co-operatives, they operated farms averaging about 2,000 acres which corresponded to the old sections of the former estates. Estate co-operatives at each of the three areas provided administrative and technical services, including transport, to the primary co-ops. All co-ops were represented by United Sugar Workers' Co-operation Council (USWCC) in negotiations with the government and its agencies (World Bank 1978a: 40).

When the estates were originally bought they were overmanned, partly because the previous owners could not afford the severance pay to which workers were entitled if they lost their jobs and partly because of strong union pressures. When the estates were co-operativized, each farm section became a co-operative and the workers who had worked on that unit became members of the co-operative. Hence the co-operatives inherited an acute overmanning situation, with too many people relative to the output of a co-operative if union wage rates were to be maintained (World Bank 1978a: 40). The co-ops also suffered from a weak financial position from the beginning (Higgins 1980: 13).

After the change of government in 1980 – when the JLP, under the leadership of Edward Seaga, won the election – the policy in relation to the co-operatives also changed. In November 1981 the JLP government declared the 23 sugar worker co-operatives bankrupt and transferred their assets back to government control. The govenment characterized the co-operatives as incompetent and inefficient, and accused them of mismanagement (Seaga Government 1981: 1-2). Although it was true that most of the co-ops were bankrupt, it can be argued that they were not given a fair chance. They would have needed a much longer time to succeed as well as adequate financial resources and training of their members.

Cane farmers are the third category of producers and contributed between 17 per cent and 43 per cent of factory throughput in 1975 as far as the three largest factories were concerned. Island-wide, just over 16,000 farmers made cane deliveries in 1974. In 1975 deliveries were received from 14,600 farmers. Thus the number of farms had decreased by half from the mid-1960s. The farms ranged in size from several thousand acres to just a few acres. While there were a large number of farmers involved in the industry it is important to note that 176 farmers produced 67 per cent of all farmers' cane in 1974 (Minster 1976: 39).

Although the choice of sugar-processing techniques will not be dealt with in this study, it is appropriate to describe very briefly the structural changes in this sector. When buying the sugar cane land, the government had no intention of buying sugar factories. But circumstances and policies changed. The factory owners were not averse to selling, and after a series of lengthy and complicated manoeuvres, by 1977, the government had become sole holder of the equity of the Frome, Monymusk and Bernard Lodge factories. By doing so it in effect became the owner of 65 per cent of the sugar-processing capacity of the country (World Bank 1978a: 8). These factories are owned by the National Sugar Company Ltd, which was formed in October 1975. It is a holding company and its shares are owned by government agencies. National Sugar also operates two ports.

As can be seen in Table 5.3, the sugar sector provides a considerable amount of employment.

The characteristics, role and position of the unions have not changed dramatically since the early 1960s. However, representatives of the unions have become members of SIA and other agencies in the sugar sector. This has strengthened the already strong position of the unions. The close relation between each union and one of the political parties remains.

61

Table 5.3
Peak Direct Employment in the Jamaican Sugar Sector during Harvesting,
Selected Years, 1967-74

	1967	*1972*	*1973*	*1974*
Sugar Estates	23,000	21,000	18,598	18,850
Cane Farmers	9,000	13,900	12,300	12,500
Self-employed	28,000	17,812	17,042	16,029
Total	*60,000*	*52,712*	*47,940*	*47,379*

Note: Indirect employment not included (e.g. contractors)

Source: The Table is taken from Minster (1976: 1.1).

As we saw on p.56, the industry structure was relatively simple around
1960. Estates, cane farmers and labour were organized in national
organizations: the estate owners' association (SMA), the cane farmers'
association (AIJCFA) and the two labour unions (BITU and NWU).
Government involvement was limited.

By the end of the 1970s the 18 sugar factories had been reduced to 12.
Eight of these had, in the early 1980s, been taken over by a public Jamaican
corporation (National Sugar Co.) (Page 1981: 2). The influence of the
private estates had decreased considerably, as can be illustrated by the fate
of their organization (SMA), which no longer exists. The rise and fall of the
cane co-operatives implies that the state now also controls a dominant part
of the sugar land. Thus government influence has increased not only by
regulation through SIA, but also through extensive direct ownership.[1] The
process can perhaps be characterized as a combination of indigenization
and nationalization. It occurred largely during the PNP period, i.e. before
Seaga came to power in 1980. Since the change of government, attempts
have been made to reprivatize the sugar sector.

CHOICE OF TECHNIQUE IN SUGAR CANE
HARVESTING, 1958-83 – A DESCRIPTION

The previous section provides the context in which choices of technique are
made in Jamaican sugar agriculture. The actors identified and described are
the social entities that can influence choice of technique. They do so within
the constraints imposed by general socio-economic and political structural
conditions also briefly outlined.

The Situation in the late 1950s

Traditionally, cutting and loading of sugar cane have been manual tasks in
all countries. Jamaica in the 1950s was no exception. Stalks were cut by a

machete or cane-knife, the leafy top severed, and the dry trash removed from the millable cane. Bundles of cane stalks were later manually loaded onto vehicles for transport to the factory. In Jamaica no cane fields were burnt before 1961, except experimentally as discussed on p.64 (Shillingford 1974: 86).

While some small farmers harvest their own cane, most crops are reaped and loaded by wage-labourers, so that the total seasonal labour demand in the crop period is very substantial, as we saw on pp.58 and 62. Under the most favourable conditions a good cutter could cut and load up to five tons of cane in an eight-hour day, but in Jamaica the output of a cane-cutter seldom exceeds three tons in green cane (Mordecai 1967: 88). In Jamaica it is customary to carry out the harvesting as two distinct operations – cutting and loading – and the work is carried out by two groups of workers (Mordecai 1967: 89).

As mentioned before, the Jamaican sugar sector has now been in a crisis for a long time. Several government commissions have been appointed to investigate the problems of the sugar industry and to propose remedies. One of them was the Mordecai Commission in the mid-1960s. The work of this commission was presented in a detailed report (Mordecai 1967). For information about sugar in Jamaica in the 1950s and 1960s the Mordecai report is extremely valuable. The commission also dealt with the problems and possibilities of mechanization and made very specific recommendations in these matters. For these reasons I will quote at some length from the Mordecai report. The quotes also tell the reader a little about the views and prejudices of the commission. This is important since the Mordecai report will be referred to frequently later in this chapter.[2]

> Development [of the sugar industry] in the modern era, dating from about 1938 was still founded on the premise of an abundance of rural labour and low wage rates; expansion depended on the employment of more and more manual workers for pre-harvesting work, and then for cutting and loading the grown crop for delivery to the factory. But this reliance upon manual labour was soon naturally confronted by problems. The workers became organized into trade union groups, demanding better working conditions and a more generous share of the fruits of their labour. Wage levels steadily increased until the weekly pay of a field worker plus intermittent bonus payments is now many times that of 1938.
> (Mordecai 1967: 115)

> But the trouble is that meantime the market value of the product has not kept pace with the increased wage and material costs. The industry has therefore been confronted by the choice between bringing costs under control by developing methods of increasing the productivity of its manpower and a gradual but certain extinction. The former course has, in some cases many years ago, been taken by Jamaica's competitors in the world market for sugar. Jamaica meantime has made marginal progress in pre-harvesting and loading operations.
> (Mordecai 1967: 115)

The crucial problem facing the sugar industry is that of high costs. Labour and its supervision represents approximately 60% of total production costs: in comparison with other sugar producing regions the Jamaican industry is highly labour intensive.
(Mordecai 1967: 204)

The sugar industry must solve the twin problem of competition from lower cost producers in external markets, and that of a shrinking supply of labour, particularly cane cutters and loaders, whose productivity is comparatively low. Both estates and cane farmers see their best hope of lowering costs in more use of mechanical methods of harvesting cane and bulk loading sugar at ports. Other countries whose costs of production are allegedly lower than that in Jamaica, have resorted successfully to such modern methods, under similar pressures and the same doubtful prospects of greatly improved sugar prices.
(Mordecai 1967: 204)

The Advent of Mechanical Loading in the 1960s

Large-scale Introduction of Mechanical Loading at Monymusk Estate
In 1957 the first mechanical loader was introduced in Jamaica at the Monymusk sugar estate owned by WISCO, a Tate & Lyle company (British). It was a Thomson "Hurrycane" loader mounted on an Allis Chalmers tractor which means that it was a grab-type loader fitted to a crawler tractor. This loader was operated for several years, but only experimentally (Blanchard 1959: 51).

In the trials the cane was first burnt, then manually cut and laid in heap rows, four rows per windrow. The loader then travelled down the windrow, lifting the cane into tractor carts which were drawn along beside the loader by a second crawler tractor. Five men followed the loader as it passed down the heap row and picked up cane that was dropped or missed by the loader and threw it into the next windrow to be loaded on the way back. The capacity of this loader was approximately 400 tons of cane in a 16-hour day (Blanchard 1959: 51).

In the 1961 crop – starting in December 1960 – the first large-scale commercial conversion to mechanical loading was made in Jamaica at the Monymusk estate. Eight mechanical loaders were introduced. They were Broussard push-pile loaders mounted on D4 tractors (Blanchard 1964: 78). Simultaneously harvesting was made more efficient by introducing pre-harvest burning of cane, which increased the daily output of the cutters (Mordecai 1967: 120).

The estate owners' reason for introducing mechanical loading was a desire to increase the productivity of field labour and to cope with absenteeism and a large turnover of workers, which were severe problems for the estates. To counter these problems, the Monymusk estate had been forced to employ numbers far in excess of standard requirements. In theory a force of 1,130 cane-cutters would have been required to reap the 1960 crop, while in practice the turnover was 4,096. In the previous year the turnover was 4,333 cutters (Mordecai 1967: 120).

In September 1960, the West Indies Sugar Company began paying compensation to over 800 workers at its Monymusk estate whose services would no longer be required as a result of the plans to mechanize cane loading. At the same time notice was served that about 400 fewer cane-cutters and a number of dray contractors and their employees would also not be required for the 1961 crop. This had the effect of reducing the crop employment by a fifth (Central Planning Unit 1961: 26).

The cabinet decided to have a limited study done of those people who were displaced by mechanization to find out what happened to them and, in particular, to investigate the rate at which they were absorbed into other jobs and pursuits. The survey was conducted during November 1960. Some of the main findings of the study were:

- The number of persons affected by mechanization exceeded previous estimates. At least 1,600 persons were directly affected and if one applies the dependency ratio of the survey (1 breadwinner to 3.6 dependants) the total number affected exceeded 7,000.

- A large proportion of these persons had been "attached" to the estate for a long time and depended to a large extent on earnings from the crop for their living; some 60 per cent had been living in the Monymusk area for over ten years.

- At the time of the survey, much of the severance pay had been spent, although not many had alternative employment. Only 23 per cent of all persons surveyed were "at work" during the reference week. For persons under 30 years of age only 14 per cent were "at work". The majority were self-employed, as there seem to have been few jobs available at the time.

- The majority reported that they were living off the severance pay and even those "at work" suggested that they had to draw on savings and the severance pay to supplement earnings.

- Nearly 30 per cent of those receiving severance pay between September and October had left the area by November. Nearly a third of those that could not be found were known to have emigrated to the UK.

- On the basis of the intentions stated it would seem that about 26 per cent of those interviewed contemplated emigrating to the UK in addition to those who had already done so. 26 per cent planned to farm on their own account. Some contemplated using the severance pay to help in purchasing land, fishing gear or trucks. About 14 per cent planned to pursue other self-employed work beside farming such as "higglering", petty trading and trucking. Only 11 per cent of those interviewed planned to get a job and 18 per cent had plans which they could not disclose.

- Investigators reported tension in the area and a general restlessness on the part of the workers, although there were no incidents during the survey (Central Planning Unit 1961: 34-5).

According to the Mordecai report, the impact on employment on the Monymusk estate was severe. From a weekly average of 7,038 field workers employed in 1959, the number plummeted successively to 5,579; 3,658; 2,785, 2,939 and rose to 3,128 in 1964. In 1965 the average for the crop rose to 3,246. The average number of field workers out of season fell similarly: from 3,798 in 1959 to 1,866 in 1965. Aggregate earnings of field workers rose from £825,371 (excluding bonus) in 1959, to £1,131,145 in 1964. Fewer people were earning more money. Severance of £150,000 was paid, but it took several seasons for the employment pattern of the "surplus" labour force in the surrounding area to settle down again or migrate (Mordecai 1967: 120).

Table 5.4
Harvesting Costs at Monymusk (Mechanical Loading) and
Frome (Manual Loading) Estates, 1961-66 (pounds per ton)

	Monymusk	*Frome*	*Note*
1961	1.61	1.56	—
1962	1.87	1.53	—
1963	1.45	1.60	Wage inc. average 8⅓%
1964	1.50	1.60	—
1965	1.66	1.86	Minimum wage increase (Douglas), average 8⅓%
1966	1.53	1.84	—

Source: Mordecai (1967: 121).

The swing in Monymusk harvesting costs following the adoption of mechanized loading in 1961 indicates that, after a necessary period for operational adjustments, substantial savings could be expected. In Table 5.4, harvesting costs at Monymusk are compared with its sister estate, Frome, where hand loading was the practice. From 1962 onward (the "teething" year) the Monymusk harvesting costs showed a relative downward trend (Mordecai 1967: 121). Accordingly, mechanical loading probably reduces harvesting costs.

Mechanical Loading and Employment
Many estates reported a shortage of both manual cutters and loaders in the mid-1960s. In spite of the very high levels of unemployment in the towns, 13 out of 18 estates reported shortages of cane-cutters during 1965. Nine estates reported a shortage of manual cane loaders in the same year. For 1966 the corresponding figures were 12 and 9 and for 1967, 10 and 7 respectively. The shortage of manual cutters and loaders amounted to

1,500-2,000 men in both years (Annual Report 1967: 101). Thus there was a shortage of manual labour for agricultural work in a country where the actual open unemployment was very high. Large general unemployment co-existed with a critical manpower shortage in sugar harvesting. This can probably be explained by the heavy and non-stimulating character of manual harvesting in combination with low status and pay.

The Mordecai Commission reported in 1967 that:

> The estates have had increasing difficulty during recent years in maintaining their field workers at full strength. Some complain of a shortage of cutters, others have trouble obtaining loaders. In order to alleviate the situation, most estates have introduced some measure of mechanical loading.
> (Mordecai 1967: 127)

In the middle of the same decade, mechanical loading also attracted the attention of the larger cane farmers (Mordecai 1967: 89). The Cane Farmers' Association stated that by 1967, the degree of mechanization on about 15 cane farms which had resorted to mechanical loading was just sufficient to offset the decline in the available labour force. But the Mordecai Commission was unable to form any opinion on the amount of redundancy of workers on commercial cane farmers' lands, since no data was available (Mordecai 1967: 204).

The number of mechanical cane loaders rose gradually and so did the proportion of the crop that was mechanically loaded. In the 1960 crop – starting in December 1959 – almost none of the cane was mechanically loaded, whereas approximately 30 per cent of the 1967 crop was loaded mechanically (Mordecai 1967: 116). In 1969-71 the percentages were 66, 76 and 91 respectively, i.e. in the early 1970s the cane was loaded mechanically everywhere except on small farms, mostly in hilly areas (Shillingford 1974: 41; van Groenigen 1972: 96).

The dominant harvesting system can from the 1970s, thus be said to have the following characteristics. The cane is burnt prior to harvesting, cut by hand, loaded by mechanical loaders and transported to factories by tractors and trailers and trucks. Some cane is transferred to railway wagons to be transported to the factories.

Each field is divided into sections of four rows by the length of the field. Each such section is considered to be a task and allocated to a pair of cutters, who cut the cane and lay it in a windrow or pile it into heaps across the two centre rows. Mechanical loaders pick up the cane and deposit it into trucks or tractor-drawn trailers which proceed directly to the factories. In a few areas there are reloading stations.

Mechanical loaders are of two types, the slewing self-propelled grab and the push-piler. The former picks up cane from pre-piled heaps and because it can rotate through 360° can load from three heap rows in one pass. Damage to fields from the passage of equipment is therefore kept to a minimum. The machine is, however, relatively expensive, requires modifications for successful operations in Jamaica, suffers from appreciable down-time due to mechanical failures in Jamaica and has a relatively low output rate (Sugar Industry Research Institute 1975: 5). The push-piler is either self-propelled or mounted on a mobile power unit. The loader has a piler which pushes the windrow of canes, forming piles which are picked up by the grab and deposited in trucks or trailers moving alongside the loader. The boom has a 90° rotation and such a reach that only one heap row can be loaded at a time. The machine is relatively simple in design and easy to maintain, but it picks up more extraneous matter than the grab loader. Its loading speed is high, although the present industry daily average is less than 150 tons per day. Even at this rate each loader loads about 20,000 tons of cane per crop over 150 crop days. It is estimated that there are 160 loaders in operation in the industry (Sugar Industry Research Institute 1975: 6). In 1983 the number of mechanical loaders in Jamaica was roughly 190-200 units. In the latter half of the 1970s the number of push-pile loaders increased and the number of grab loaders decreased (Burgess 1983).

As we have seen, the potential of mechanical loading for displacing field workers was very great. However, Jamaican sugar cane production increased between 1962 and 1966 (see Table 5.2).[3] Thereby the potentially drastic impact of the mechanical loaders on employment throughout the industry was to some extent mitigated by the expanding demand for manual cutters. Where manual loaders were displaced by machines, they could be absorbed in cutting gangs which were short of labour.

The first introduction of the loader led, however, to mass redundancies of workers and significant social problems. This was due to the very rapid changeover to mechanical loading on the Monymusk estate. It also resulted in a large severance pay bill (£150,000). Because of this, other estates introduced mechanical loaders more gradually as labour shortages occurred. Mechanical loaders have also allowed management to cope with the shortage of cutters by enabling it to shift manual loaders to cane cutting. In spite of this, however, some redundancy has occurred in the continuing process of loading mechanization (Shillingford 1974: 73).

Mechanical Loading, Extraneous Matter and Cane Cleaning
Over the past 20 years, cane harvesting and loading practices in Jamaica have changed drastically. Whereas cane was once cut green, de-trashed and bundled by hand to be passed into field trailers and secured by sling chains, the practice now is to burn the cane fields, arrange the cut cane in rows on the ground and load the cane mechanically. Mechanical loading – particularly push-pile loading – normally leads to an increase in the amount of extraneous matter, like soil, stones, trash, etc., in the cane delivered to the factories. This may damage the equipment and reduce the crushing rate as well as the amount of sugar extracted in the factories. Such a deterioration in the quality of the cane occurred with the introduction of mechanical loading at Monymusk in 1961. A similar experience was reported by the New Yarmouth sugar factory, following the wider-scale

adoption of mechanized loaders by farmers supplying that factory. The remedy employed in both cases was to install a cane-washing plant (Mordecai 1967: 107-8).

At Monymusk rudimentary cane-washing with water was introduced in 1962, i.e. one year after the massive implementation of mechanical cane loaders. A full-scale washing system along the lines of the Hawaiian plants, but reduced in complexity, was installed for the 1963 harvest (Blanchard 1964: 78). Such cane-washing facilities are expensive to operate, utilize precious water and leach juice from the cane.

CANE-CUTTING IN THE 1970S

A ripe sugar cane field consists of the sugar stems or stalks, their leafy tops and a mass of dead leaves free or adhering to the stems. These cane leaves, both dead and green, have to be eliminated in the harvest operation. To effect this, controlled burning of cane fields has been introduced in recent years. Up to 1961, practically all cane was cut green in Jamaica, but by 1969, nearly 70 per cent was burnt before harvest (Shillingford 1974: 86). Pre-harvest burning had become the general practice in Jamaica from the early 1970s, principally in order to increase the output of the manual reapers. It is said to double the productivity of a manual cane-cutter (Shillingford 1974: 80). Burning also facilitates the work of loading machines and combine harvesters.[4]

Experiments with Cane Harvesters in the early 1970s
We saw earlier (pp.66-7) that the majority of the sugar estates reported shortages of manual cane-cutters and loaders in the mid-1960s. The estate owners and their Sugar Manufacturers' Association (SMA) argued before the Mordecai Commission, which investigated the Jamaican sugar industry in 1966, that conversion to mechanical cutting was necessary and inevitable. The SMA proposed that the industry be permitted to import one or more harvesters for experimental purposes. This was also recommended by the Mordecai Commission.

After these recommendations, and a representation to the government by the sugar manufacturers, the Jamaican Labour Party government in 1967 agreed to the importation of up to five mechanical harvesters for use in trials to be carried out under the auspices of the Sugar Research Department of the Sugar Manufacturers' Association (Lee and van Groenigen 1973: 183). The experiments with mechanical harvesters had two elements: first, a short-term programme for the introduction of whole-stalk harvesters, which replace only the manual cane-cutter, and do not affect the system of loading and transportation. Heavy, recumbent and brittle cane could not be cut by these machines. Second, a long-term programme for the introduction of combine harvesters. The combine harvester was expected to be the final solution, as it was considered capable of handling a large range of yields without including a high percentage of extraneous matter in the cane sent to the factory (SMA 1970: 35).

Three machines were imported: a soldier-type whole-stalk cutting machine called Cameco "Cost-Cutter" and two chopper-type combine harvesters, a Massey-Ferguson machine, model MF 201 and a Wyper Brothers machine, Don Mizzi 740. During the 1970 crop the SMA tested two mechanical harvesters, the Cameco "Cost-Cutter" and the MF 201 (van Groenigen 1970: 57). The Cameco machine is a Louisiana-type, also called soldier-type or whole-stalk harvester. It is designed for the relatively light, erect crops in Louisiana. Green cane is gathered by the gathering chains and brought upright for topping by the adjustable topper. After topping, the cane is held erect by conveying chains as the machine passes over the cane until the base-cutter cuts the stalks at ground level. The cane is then carried by the machine and deposited in the heap row by sticker chains. A maximum of six rows can be piled across two banks in the heap row. The cane is then burnt in the pile to get rid of the trash. The subsequent loading of the cane can be done by hand or by a mechanical (push-pile) loader. The harvester is powered by a Cat D 330 diesel engine. It is a tall, somewhat unstable, three-wheeled machine. The maximum recommended operating side slope is 8 per cent (SMA 1970: 44; Lee and van Groenigen 1973: 183).

The Cameco was imported in 1970 from Louisiana to meet the short-term aim of the programme, as the machine replaces only the manual cutter in the existing harvesting system. In 1970 operations were planned for the Bernard Lodge estate, owned by the United Fruit Company, "but the labour situation at this estate was such that management decided to postpone the mechanical harvesting operations and finally called them off" (SMA 1970: 44). Instead, the machine operated at the Worthy Park and Trelawny estates. In 1971 and 1972 it was also tried at four other estates.

The MF 201 combine harvester was described on p.49. This machine was introduced to the export market in 1970, after one year of commercial operation in Australia. The machine tried in Jamaica was actually one of the first two MF 201 units in operation outside of Australia (Briscoe 1970: 24). In Jamaica the machine was used at the Frome estate in 1970 and at Monymusk in 1970-2. Both these estates were owned by WISCO at the time.

The operation of the MF 201 was promising during the 1970 crop. This led to the introduction of another Australian combine harvester, the Don Mizzi 740, which is substantially different from the MF 201. The Don Mizzi is not considered an all-purpose machine, but is useful under certain conditions. The main reason for this is the side mounting of the machine on a tractor, which is normally a disadvantage, but has advantages on steep land. However, the basic principles of the two machines are very similar. This machine was used at Monymusk in 1971 and at Worthy Park and on the Jamaican Sugar estates in 1972 (SMA 1970: 47; SMA 1971: 55).

The trials with combine harvesters in the early 1970s did not result in commercial introduction for reasons which will be discussed on pp.91-6. As a consequence, in 1983 all cane was still being cut manually by means of machetes in Jamaica.

Notes

1. However, the character of the Jamaican state is, of course, very different from the Cuban.

2. When using the term "sugar industry", the Mordecai Commission means both cane agriculture and sugar processing.

3. This expansion was partly a result of the US embargo on Cuban sugar, which increased the demand for Jamaican sugar.

4. As mentioned in Chapter 3, however, burning also has negative consequences and is a highly debated issue.

Part 3: Analysis and Comparison

6. Determinants of the Choice of Technique

On the basis of the theoretical framework outlined in Chapter 2 and the descriptive material in Chapters 4 and 5, an analysis and explicit comparison of the two cases will be presented in Part 3 of this study. In doing this, theoretical considerations will be fused with the empirical material presented.

In the introduction to this study, "socio-economic aspects" of choice of technique were defined to include determinants as well as consequences of the choices. In Chapter 6 the determinants of the choice of technique will be addressed, and in Chapter 7 I will discuss certain consequences. I will also evaluate and compare the processes of mechanization in the two cases.

It is not always possible to distinguish completely between determinants and consequences of the choice of technique. For example, the employment situation on a particular occasion is often an important determinant of the choice of technique, but the choices made may also have employment consequences. In other words, the employment situation is both cause and effect.[1]

I begin with some conceptual and theoretical specifications which will be used in analysing and comparing the determinants of the choice of technique in Cuba and Jamaica.

SOME CONCEPTUAL AND THEORETICAL SPECIFICATIONS

Descriptive and Analytical Comparative Studies

One objective of this study is to try to compare socio-economic aspects of technical change in sugar cane harvesting in Cuba and Jamaica. But there are different types of comparative studies in the social sciences. Here I will limit myself to two general types which have quite different objectives: descriptive and analytical comparisons.[2]

If the objective of a comparative study is purely descriptive, data are needed for the variables to be compared, e.g. rate of literacy, total cement production, GNP per capita or choice of technique for the countries or regions compared. The data are then simply presented in a comparative manner, i.e. the descriptions are compared. This is the most common kind of comparative study.

Descriptive comparisons are valuable as indicators of relative performance in different countries, or over time. However, they do not provide scientific explanations; that is, they say nothing about causes and consequences. The methodological problems associated with descriptive comparative studies concern the availability (existence and access), reliability and comparability of empirical data. These problems may be considerable. This is particularly true for developing countries, where the statistical system is less developed, and in cases where access to information is limited.

Analytical comparative studies deal with comparisons between determinants of similar or parallel processes in two or more cases. Methodologically they are much more complicated than descriptive comparisons, since scientific explanations are necessary preconditions for them. And explanations are associated with numerous problems, particularly in the social sciences. For example, practically all social processes are multi-causally determined and one cause cannot be isolated in an experimental fashion – as is often the case in the natural sciences – in order to measure or estimate its influence.[3]

Social Carriers of Techniques

The analytical framework presented in Chapter 2 consisted of an integration of a structural and an actor-oriented approach. Here, this framework will be made somewhat more specific.

Concepts and theories are necessary tools if a social process is to be explained. If the objective is to carry out an analytical comparison, i.e. to compare the explanations in various cases, the theoretical framework should have certain specific characteristics. For explanations to be comparable they should be expressed in a common conceptual framework or language, since the problems of communication, and thereby comparison, can be quite serious between different frameworks. This means, however, that an appropriate theoretical framework tends to be quite abstract, particularly if societies with different structural characteristics are to be compared. An exclusively structural approach is insufficient since it can only explain change – including technical change – in a sweeping way and since the "distance" between structural theory and reality is often quite great.

One way to reduce these problems is to supplement the structural approach with an actor-oriented one, as was proposed in Chapter 2. Such a combination of structural and actor-oriented perspectives will be employed below to identify the determinants of the choice of cane harvesting techniques. However the concept of "actor" is a rather general and abstract one. In order to decrease the level of generality and connect the theoretical framework explicitly to techniques, we need an actor concept that is related specifically to the choice of technique; a social concept that is technique-centred.

"Social carriers of techniques" is such a concept. A social carrier of a technique is a social entity which chooses and implements a technique; it "carries" it into the society. It is defined in the following way. For a certain technique to be chosen and implemented in a specific context or situation, the technique must, of course, actually *exist* somewhere in the world, i.e. it must be "on the shelf". But some additional conditions[4] must also be fulfilled:

1. A social entity that has a subjective *interest* in choosing and implementing the technique must exist.[5]
2. This entity must be *organized* to be able to make a decision and also be able to organize the use of the technique properly.
3. It must have the necessary social, economic and political *power* to materialize its interest, i.e. to be able to implement the technique chosen.
4. The social entity must have *information* about the existence of the technique and functionally similar ones.
5. It must have *access* to the technique in question.[6]
6. Finally, it must have, or be able to acquire, the necessary *knowledge* about how to handle, i.e. operate, maintain and repair, the technique.

If all the six conditions listed above are fulfilled, the social entity is a *social carrier of a technique*. The carrier may be, for example, a private company, an agricultural co-operative or a government agency. Every technique must have a social carrier in order to be chosen and implemented. If the six conditions are simultaneously fulfilled, the technique will actually be introduced and used. In other words, the six conditions are not only necessary but, taken together, they are also sufficient for implementation to take place.[7]

"Social carriers of techniques" are specific kinds of actors. The intention is that this actor concept – and the six conditions defining it – shall function as a conceptual bridge, or intermediary link, between the structure of society and technical change, to make it easier to study the interaction between techniques and society in a detailed manner.

The concept "social carriers of techniques" was formulated as a tool to deal with choices among existing technical alternatives. As mentioned in Chapter 3, however, the choice among existing techniques can, in sugar cane harvesting, sometimes not be separated from the process of developing new ones and adapting existing ones to local conditions. Therefore the concept cannot be employed uncritically in this study. It has to be supplemented with an analysis of research and development efforts in the field of sugar cane harvesting techniques. After the presentation of the concept "social carriers of techniques" and with a glance at the empirical data collected and presented in Chapters 4 and 5, it is now possible to specify the general framework presented in Chapter 2.

The structural characteristics of a society are important in an analysis of determinants of choice of technique. For example, structural changes may lead to the emergence of new actors and the disappearance of others. Thereby the character of the socio-economic system influences the array of actors that exist in a society as well as in its sugar sector. The distribution of power among the actors is also affected by the character of the socio-economic system. In addition, the actors are highly influenced by the employment situation, i.e. another structural phenomenon. For example, the employment situation certainly affects the interests of some actors in relation to various choices of technique.

Accordingly, the power and interest of various actors are directly associated with structural phenomena. As a corollary, structural conditions influence which actors are transformed into social carriers of various techniques, i.e. for which actors the conditions defining a social carrier of a technique are fulfilled. This means that the concept of social carriers of techniques is intrinsically "structure-based" in the sense that it is defined, in part, from a structural point of view.[8]

Therefore, structural conditions, actors and social carriers of techniques are not independent of each other, but constitute together a pattern or hierarchy of partly related factors, which influence the choice of techniques. The discussion below will be carried out within the framework of this pattern. However, it is certainly beyond the ambitions of this study to try to lay bare this hierarchy in detail and as a whole. Therefore I will concentrate the discussion of determinants on one level in the hierarchy of factors explaining the choice of technique. To make this discussion as specific as possible, it will be pursued mainly in terms of the six conditions defining a social carrier of techniques, i.e. it will be concentrated at a low level in the hierarchy.[9]

The objective of developing the concept of social carriers of techniques was to enable a more specific analysis of the relations between techniques and social conditions. The six conditions are more helpful in a specific empirical analysis than the composite concept as such. Therefore, in the analysis below, the concept as such will be used less than its elements. What will concern us is to investigate in some detail *who*, has the *interest, organization, power, information, access* and *knowledge* to choose and implement a certain technique as well as the *constraints* to which these actors are subject when choosing.[10]

Both the social carriers of techniques and the structural constraints must be analysed in a study of the determinants of choice of technique. In this context it must not be forgotten that some of the six conditions are intrinsically related to structural phenomena. In other words, structural factors will be implicitly reflected in the discussion below of the six conditions. At various points, explicit references to structural phenomena will also be made.

DETERMINANTS OF THE CHOICE OF TECHNIQUE IN CUBA

We will begin the analysis by specifying when the various conditions defining a social carrier are fulfilled for which actors in Cuba and Jamaica respectively. In other words, the six conditions are confronted with reality.

The Pre-revolutionary Period

The situation in terms of structure, actors and choice of technique in Cuba in the late 1950s and around 1980 is summarized in Figure 6.1. For reasons of convenience and since the classification of actors is here somewhat altered, the description in Chapter 4 is first briefly summarized.

Figure 6.1
Structure, Actors and Choice of Technique in the Cuban Cane Harvest in the late 1950s and around 1980

Late 1950s	*Around 1980*
1. Capitalism	*2. Socialism*
12-15% unemployment	*About 5% unemployment*
Plantations	State farms
Small cane farms	Small cane farms
Sugar workers and unions	Sugar workers and unions
The state and its agencies	The state and its agencies
Manual cutting and loading	Cutting mechanized to 50%. Loading almost completely mechanized

Until 1959, Cuba was an underdeveloped capitalist country heavily dependent upon the USA economically, technologically and politically. The overall annual rate of unemployment was in the order of 12 to 15 per cent, but during the non-harvest season this figure increased to more than 20 per cent. The most important actors in sugar cane agriculture were plantations, small cane farms, sugar workers and unions and the state and its agencies.

In 1958 there were 161 sugar mills in Cuba. Many of these produced sugar cane in large quantities themselves and were, therefore, also large sugar cane plantations. They were organized in the Sugar Mill Owners' Association which had a very strong influence over the sugar industry during the pre-revolutionary period. The mill owners were the most influential sugar plantation owners in Cuba. A large number of them were foreign.

The cane farmers or *colonos* were another important group in cane production. They produced approximately 90 per cent of all the cane in the 1950s. All of them were organized in the Cane Farmers' Association of Cuba. The number of cane farmers was around 60,000 in the 1950s.

The heterogeneity among the *colonos* was extreme. For example, in 1952, 61 per cent of the cane farms produced only 8.6 per cent of the total amount of cane and 1.2 per cent (730 in number) of the *colonias* produced 29 per cent of all cane. Accordingly, the larger cane farms must also be considered plantations, since they were carrying out large-scale private capitalist agriculture employing many wage workers. The other *colonos* are included in the category "small cane farms".

Several hundred thousand field workers were employed by the plantation owners during the harvest season. Most of them were organized in the Sugar Workers' Federation which was the most important labour union in the 1950s. Government intervention in the sugar industry was quite extensive during the 1950s and the most important state agency was the Cuban Institute for Sugar Stabilization.

No mechanized cane-cutting or loading was carried out in the 1950s, although experiments with various harvesting machines had been carried out for decades.

In pre-revolutionary Cuba, plantations owners showed an *interest* in looking for ways to make cane-cutting more efficient through mechanization. This interest is indicated by their efforts in carrying out trials at many plantations. These actors were obviously also *organized* to be able to make decisions about, and to carry out experiments with, cane harvesting machinery.

The small cane farmers were not in a position to introduce or experiment with harvesting machines. The size of their productions units, of course, explains their lack of interest in mechanization.

The interest of the workers and unions as regards mechanization was completely contrary to that of the plantation owners. This was demonstrated by the threats and attempts of workers to destroy the machines tested by means of sabotage. The main rationale for these actions was, of course, the high unemployment rate prevailing in Cuba, i.e. a structural feature of the system influenced the interest of the workers and unions in this respect. They tried to defend those jobs that existed, even if manual cane-cutting was heavy, seasonal and badly-paid work. Unemployment was considered worse.

Thus, labour in capitalist Cuba opposed mechanization, fearing it would result in increased unemployment. The policy of unions in other spheres of sugar production was similar. In the loading and shipping of sugar a protracted battle over mechanization took place between unions and sugar capitalists. Labour long resisted bulk loading of sugar because bulk shipment would have greatly decreased the demand for dockworkers for the handling of sugar bags. In an agreement in 1955 it was stated that sugar must be moved in bags from the sugar mills to the ship's hatch, where the bags could be opened and emptied. In this way the sugar enterprises could save labour outside Cuba, but not inside the country (Chacon Reyes 1966: US Department of Commerce 1956: 24).

The state had no explicit policy in the field of cane harvest mechanization. State agencies were not, for example, involved in the experiments with harvest machinery. The government was indifferent to the choice between machetes and harvesters, which meant neither active support nor restrictions on the attempts of the plantation owners to introduce mechanical harvesting equipment; the matter was left to market forces and class struggle.

As regards cane loading, there are, to my knowledge, surprisingly enough, no indications that plantation owners – or any other actor – had an interest in mechanization. If no one had a subjective interest in introducing mechanical loaders, it is not very useful to discuss whether the rest of the six conditions were fulfilled in the case of loading.

Before the revolution, no cane harvesters suited to Cuban conditions existed in the world.[11] Hence, the main problem for plantation owners in their mechanization efforts was that they did not have *access* to an efficient harvesting machine. Therefore most of the efforts of the plantation owners was spent gathering *information* about various technical alternatives, on trying to adapt existing machines to Cuban conditions, and on building up a pool of *knowledge* about how to use, maintain and repair harvesting equipment. But not much was achieved. Except for the use of trucks and tractors – and the railroads – to transport cane to the mills, no mechanization of the harvest work had taken place on a commercial scale before 1959.

What, then, about the *power* condition? It is, of course, hypothetical – and perhaps futile – to speculate about whether the plantation owners would have had enough socio-economic and political power to introduce mechanical harvesters on a large scale if they had had access to harvesters that could have been used efficiently in Cuba. It can be said, however, that the most important opposition to mechanized cane-cutting was that of the agricultural workers who feared losing their jobs with little prospect of finding suitable alternative employment. Organizationally, the influence of the sugar workers' union always worked against the use of agricultural machinery which would reduce the amount of manpower required. The resistance of the workers even took the anarchic form of direct sabotage against the trials with mechanical harvesters, as we saw in p.33. But given that Cuba was a capitalist country, the sugar capitalists had a general structural advantage in terms of power in relation to the workers and unions in a possible struggle over the introduction of harvest machinery. This structurally determined advantage in terms of balance of power means that the plantation owners could probably have mechanized if they had found it profitable to do so. An indication in this direction is that they obviously did have enough power to carry out experiments.

The only possibility for workers and unions to prevent mechanization in the short run would have been a massive mobilization and an intensive struggle. In the long run they would probably have needed the support of the state. In other words, the position taken by the state in such a struggle would have been decisive.

In summary, the main reason for the complete lack of mechanization of cane-cutting in the 1950s was that the Cuban plantation owners did not have access to a cane-cutting machine which was suitable to Cuban conditions.

MECHANIZATION IN REVOLUTIONARY CUBA

Starting with the revolution in 1959, a socialist socio-economic system gradually developed in Cuba. Although Cuba was still a developing country in the late 1970s, open unemployment gradually decreased from 13.6 per cent in 1959 to 1.3 per cent in 1970. During the first half of the 1970s it increased somewhat and stabilized around 5 per cent during the later half of the decade. In the 1970s, close collaboration with the Soviet Union had been developed and Cuba became a member of Comecon.

The agrarian reforms of 1959 and 1963 led to the disappearance of the plantations in sugar cane agriculture (see Figure 6.1). Their land-holdings were taken over by the state farms – established in the process – or were distributed to small private cane farmers.[12]

Almost 155,000 private farmers (not only cane farmers), cultivating less than 67 hectares each, remained. However, the small cane farmers were quite dependent upon government institutions for credit, technical assistance and other resources. They were also gradually integrated in the planning system for agriculture. For example, holdings of small cane farmers were integrated in the co-ordinated planning of the sugar cane harvest. A current policy is also to stimulate private farmers to fuse their lands and form co-operatives.

The number of professional cane-cutters had decreased to less than 100,000 in the early 1970s. The character of the unions had changed. They were no longer independent interest organizations in wage bargaining, but were organizations dealing with social welfare questions and with campaigns to increase productivity.

The changes in Cuban sugar cane agriculture have meant a strong centralization and an enormous increase in the role of the state. At present, various government agencies are completely dominant in regard to sugar and sugar technology policies.

In Figure 6.1 "state farms" and "the state and its agencies" are listed as different actors. State farms are micro production units and state agencies are mainly administrative institutions. However, the state farms are certainly not independent of state agencies but subordinate to them, and their freedom of action is therefore highly limited.

The state is a comprehensive, heterogeneous and composite kind of social entity which has the function of superior responsibility for the coherence and management of the society. This is true for the state in capitalist societies, but even more pronounced in socialist ones, where the power of the state over the economy is even more extensive. At the same time, the state – both in capitalist and socialist countries – intervenes directly in the sugar industries and influences the choice of technique in cane agriculture. For example, it may prohibit or support the introduction and use of certain harvesting techniques.

The state in revolutionary Cuba is of course fundamentally different from the Cuban state in the 1950s or the Jamaican state with regard to the class base as well as its objectives and the means available for their achievement. This is linked to the structural environment in which the state is situated, i.e. to the different character of the socio-economic systems. The Cuban Revolution implied fundamental changes in the structure of ownership and in the character of the socio-economic system, and in Figure 6.1 we can see that it was also accompanied by an important change in the array of actors in sugar cane agriculture. The private plantations disappeared and were transformed into state farms. As we have seen, the character of the actors, the relations between structure and actors and among actors themselves also changed significantly. As a result of the structural changes and of a conscious government policy, almost all cane-loading and half of the cane-cutting was mechanized in Cuba by 1980. The process leading to these results will now be discussed.

The general rate of unemployment – i.e. one of the components in our concept of structure – was reduced after the Cuban Revolution, although considerable unemployment remained for some time (see Table 4.1). In sugar cane agriculture, however, a sectorial shortage of harvest workers had already emerged in 1961, and this caused problems with the supply of cane at the sugar factories. This shortage was aggravated during the 1960s when the number of professional cane-cutters dwindled from almost 400,000 in 1958 to approximately 80,000 in 1970. Thanks to the expansion of other sectors of the economy, and to the social security system, the fear of unemployment and hunger no longer forced the rural workers to cut cane. This serious problem of labour shortage *for* the Cuban Revolution was paradoxically enough created *by* the revolutionary process itself.

The government hoped that rapid mechanization would solve the problem of the shortage of harvest labour. As a part of the efforts to accomplish this, the Commission for the Mechanization of the Cane Harvest was formed in 1961.

First, it can be noted that this initiative came very soon after the revolution. Secondly, it implied that the state now took an active part in the attempts to mechanize harvesting and pushed this issue very strongly. From the early 1960s mechanization became a conscious policy of the government, and the state took almost complete charge of the process through a large number of agencies.

This, in turn, reflects several things. First, the state as an actor was influenced by the labour shortage in cane harvesting. This implied that the state and its agencies had a strong *interest* in pursuing mechanization for the simple reason of economic survival. In public statements it is often said that the reason for the efforts was twofold: solving the problem of labour shortage and abolishing the very heavy and boring tasks of cutting and loading sugar cane manually. This is a reflection of the socialist–humanistic values of the revolutionary leadership and this is certainly related to the new character that the state apparatus assumed after the social transformation (Pino Santos 1980). Hence, the strong efforts to mechanize cane harvesting were motivated by humanitarian as well as by economic reasons – and the two reasons coincided.

Secondly, another structurally conditioned change in regard to the state apparatus is that it had much more *power* after the consolidation of the Revolution than before. Apart from the traditional political functions of the state apparatus, in socialist Cuba the state also assumed a completely dominant economic role because of the nationalizations and the formulation and implementation of centralized economic plans.

In the specific case of cane production, the state had become responsible for a major part of production through the agrarian reforms. This meant the abolition of private plantations and the establishment of state farms. In terms of actors – as noted earlier – it is therefore somewhat problematic to distinguish between "the state and its agencies" and "state farms", since they are organizationally linked, and, in the last instance, both controlled by the political leadership. On the other hand this reinforces the powerful position of the state in the field of choice of technique in sugar cane harvesting. Through INRA the state also exercised a considerable influence over the cane co-operatives. Thus the state had a strong interest in mechanization and the power to pursue such a policy.[13]

The small cane farms were not nationalized in the agrarian reforms, which means that a considerable portion of Cuban agriculture is still in private hands. As a result of the reforms, many of the smallest farms grew in size. However, most of them did not grow enough to be able to introduce expensive, capital-intensive and complex mechanical harvesting machinery. But since the maximum size of the private holdings after the second agrarian reform was as large as 67 hectares, at least some mechanical harvest equipment could have been introduced. There was also the possibility of several private cane farmers owning mechanical units in common. However, the state – represented by INRA – was a monopoly supplier of technical and other resources to agriculture. Therefore, even if some small private cane farmers had an interest in implementing mechanical harvesting equipment, they were highly dependent on the state in this respect. The small cane farmers did not have enough power to mechanize harvesting by themselves, nor did they have access to machines unless the government decided to provide them. Given the shortage of harvest workers, the state gave priority to its own state farms in regard to mechanization.

Due to the labour shortage and because of the influence of the state over the cane co-operatives, their leadership had an interest in cane harvest mechanization. However, this interest never materialized because of the short period of existence of the co-operatives.

As a result of the structural transition from capitalism to socialism, the character of the labour unions changed. The unions more or less lost their role of independent workers' interest organizations and became more concerned with social questions, with problems of the organization of work and how to increase productivity. The exodus of professional cane-cutters from the sugar harvest clearly showed the preference of the workers for mechanization, and this was reflected in the labour union policies in this field.

To sum up: given the fundamental structural changes of the Cuban socio-economic system, the decreasing general rate of unemployment associated with this transformation, and the severe shortage of labour in cane harvesting, *all* actors in the Cuban sugar industry had a common interest in the mechanization of cane harvesting from the early 1960s on.

A considerable portion of the Cuban population was mobilized for harvest work throughout the 1960s, and particularly in the 1970 *zafra*. Most of them certainly did not appreciate this arduous manual work, although many of them recognized the necessity for it. Therefore, the interest in harvest mechanization was shared by almost all social classes, groups and organizations, and there was a broad consensus in Cuba that the sugar harvest should be mechanized as rapidly as possible.[14]

The state was certainly equipped with sufficient social, economic and political power to pursue a strategy of mechanization. The obstacles to mechanization in revolutionary Cuba were of other kinds, which will now be discussed.

In the case of cane-loading, there were – in the first years of the 1960s – problems with the availability of *information* about different mechanical loaders being used in other countries. Cuba did not have access to an efficient mechanical loader during the early part of the 1960s, although such machines existed in other countries.[15]

An indigenous attempt to design and manufacture a mechanical loader was made in 1962-3, but production of this model had already been discontinued in 1963 when a large order for grab-type cane-loaders was placed in the Soviet Union. The Soviet loaders were introduced in 1964, and in the same year lifted 20 per cent of the cane. Thereby, Cuba acquired *access* to an efficient cane-loader produced in the Soviet Union: ten years later, practically all manually-cut cane was mechanically loaded.

As late as in the 1970 *zafra*, 25 per cent of the 5,460 potentially available machines were not in operation. This indicates that problems regarding *knowledge* about now to operate, maintain and repair the machines persisted through the whole of the 1960s. In the beginning there were also *organizational* problems, but these were gradually solved, as indicated by the rapid increase in the degree of mechanical loading during the 1960s.

In summary, all the six conditions necessary and sufficient for a massive implementation of mechanical cane-loaders were – from the mid-1960s – fulfilled in the case of the dominant actor in the Cuban sugar cane agriculture. The state (agencies) responsible for the introduction of mechanical cane-loaders had become a social carrier of this technique. The record shows a breakthrough in mechanization of cane-loading in the latter half of the 1960s (see Table 4.4).

In the case of cane-cutting many types of machines were designed, tried and either produced in, or imported into, Cuba from the early 1960s onwards. As many as 680 units of the indigenously designed MC-1 were manufactured in Cuba for the 1963 *zafra*, but this simple model did not work satisfactorily and was taken out of operation in the same year. Co-operation with the USSR was initiated, and between 1965 and 1968 about 1,000 units of the KCT-1 and the KT-1 models were manufactured for Cuba in the Soviet Union. However, the productivity was low and the majority of the units became inoperative very quickly.

The almost complete failure of all machines tested in the 1960s is indicated by the fact that the percentage of cane harvested mechanically never exceeded 3 per cent in the 1960s and that only 1 per cent of the great 1970 *zafra* was harvested mechanically (see Table 4.4).

During the 1960s it was not lack of interest or power on the part of the government that inhibited mechanization of cane-cutting. Instead the main problem was that the KCT-1 and KT-1 machines – as well as the indigenous MC-1 – simply did not constitute a reliable solution to the task of cutting sugar cane mechanically. In other words, Cuba did not have *access* to a satisfactory machine. This is shown by the data presented on p.39. Only 10 per cent of the 471 Soviet harvesters were in operation at the end of their first *zafra* (1965), and the number in operation decreased rapidly. Their productivity was also quite low and became even lower as the years went by. In addition the high percentage of extraneous matter showed that they did not clean the cane properly. Finally, they could not be used in cane which did not grow straight or in fields with a high yield per hectare.

All these problems can be explained mainly by the technical deficiences of the machines, but they were also reinforced by lack of *knowledge* about how to operate, maintain and repair such complicated equipment satisfactorily. The task of *organizing* the use of such a large number of machines was not an easy task to solve either.

The question is whether there was also a problem of *information* about the various cane-cutting machines in other countries. Were there, in other words, machines in other countries which could have been used successfully in Cuba? I will argue below (p.125-7) that the Massey-Ferguson 515 harvester would probably have suited Cuban conditions. However it was never imported to Cuba and the Cubans may have been insufficiently informed about its characteristics.

The labour shortage problem in the sugar harvest was still serious in the early 1970s. As a consequence, efforts to mechanize continued, partly along new lines, but also on the basis of previous unsuccessful attempts. To make the cleaning of sugar cane more efficient, dry cleaning stations were introduced during the latter half of the 1960s. As we saw, these plants were successfully implemented quite rapidly during the late 1960s and early 1970s. The Henderson harvesters were designed to work in combination with the dry cleaning stations, but this machine was not successful. Instead the Massey-Fergusson 201, the Claas-Libertadora and the KTP-1 combine harvesters were introduced on a large scale in the early 1970s. They were all successful to various degrees, and as a result 50 per cent of the cane harvest was cut by means of combine harvesters in 1981.

The breakthrough in mechanical harvesting in the 1970s could perhaps be regarded as more surprising than the failure of the 1960s. This is particularly evident if one compares Cuba with other developing countries which were in a similar situation in the 1950s. In regard to cane-cutting, Cuba is currently among the most mechanized countries in the Third World. In the case of mechanical loading, Cuba gained access to a Soviet machine in the mid-1960s and the breakthrough came very soon thereafter. But in the mechanization of cutting, more than a decade was needed before a solution was found. In the 1960s there were no major social obstacles to mechanical cutting, i.e. the conditions of *interest* and *power* were certainly fulfilled by the state and its agencies. The main problems were instead of a technological character, i.e. they concerned *information, access* and *knowledge*. In addition the problem of *organization* was not completely solved.

In the 1960s the Cubans did not have access to any mechanical harvesters that suited Cuban conditions. Both the changing of conditions and the adaptation and development of machines were tried to solve this problem. Fields were levelled and reblocked, stones and trees were removed from the fields, etc. Simultaneously, sizeable efforts were devoted to adapting existing cane-cutting machines and developing new models.[16]

Finally, the problems of information, access, knowledge and organization were solved and the state (and its agencies and farms) became a social carrier of combine harvesters. The Massey-Ferguson 201, the Libertadora 1400 and the KTP-1 combine harvesters provided the technical basis for the growth of mechanization in the 1970s.

DETERMINANTS OF THE CHOICE OF TECHNIQUE IN JAMAICA

Figure 6.2 summarizes the situation in terms of structure, actors and choice of technique in Jamaica in the late 1950s and around 1980. For the purposes of comparison, the corresponding information regarding Cuba in Figure 6.1 is repeated here.

The most important actors in Jamaican cane agriculture in the late 1950s were similar to those in Cuba. "Plantations" included those 18 sugar cane producing estates which were attached to the same number of sugar factories and the limited number of large cane farms run independently of sugar factories. Some of these farms operated on a larger scale than the smaller estates, but they were not classified as such because they did not have their own sugar factories. Both estate owners and large farmers employed a considerable number of field workers. Thus, the plantations represented large-scale private capitalist agriculture.

The estate owners were the dominant actors in the Jamaican sugar industry around 1960. They were organized in the Sugar Manufacturers' Association (SMA) which was the strongest institution in the Jamaican sugar industry. Some of the largest estates were controlled from abroad.

Figure 6.2
Structures, Actors and Actual Choice of Technique in the Cuban and Jamaican Cane Harvests in the late 1950s and around 1980

Country	Late 1950s *1. Capitalism* *12-15% unemployment*	Around 1980 *2. Socialism* *About 5% unemployment*
Cuba	Plantations Small cane farms Sugar workers and unions The state and its agencies	State farms Small cane farms Sugar workers and unions The state and its agencies
	Manual cutting and loading	Cutting mechanized by 50% Loading almost completely mechanized
	3. Capitalism *About 15% unemployment*	*4. Capitalism* *About 27% unemployment*
Jamaica	Plantations Small cane farms Sugar workers and unions The state and its agencies	Plantations Small cane farms Cane co-operatives Sugar workers and unions The state and its agencies
	Manual cutting and loading	Cutting completely manual. Loading almost completely mechanized.

Just as in Cuba, the independent cane farmers, who were organized in the Cane Farmers' Association (CFA), were quite a heterogeneous group. Thus the vast majority of the approximately 30,000 independent cane farms – which are designated "small cane farms" in the figure – grew only a few acres of cane, mainly by means of their own labour. Accordingly these small-scale peasants who owned their farms and tools were simply commodity producers.

The average number of non-staff field workers employed on sugar estates during the harvesting season was approximately 35,700 in 1955. In 1967 23,000 workers were employed in the fields and factories of the sugar estates and 9,000 by the larger cane farmers. Most of the workers were organized in the Bustamente Industrial Trade Union (BITU) and the National Workers' Union (NWU) respectively.

Although the state did not play a dominant role in the 1950s, it imposed some regulations upon the sugar sector, most importantly through the Sugar Control Board. The state and its agencies must therefore be mentioned as a fourth actor.

In the late 1950s all cutting and loading of sugar cane was carried out manually in Jamaica. No mechanical equipment to accomplish these tasks existed in the country, except for one cane loader used for experimental purposes.

By 1980 Jamaica was no longer a colony, but still a capitalist developing country heavily dependent upon the outside world both economically and technologically. Now this dependency was more on the USA than on the UK. The rate of unemployment had risen to more than 25 per cent. In terms of the array of actors in sugar cane agriculture, some changes had occurred. In the early 1970s foreign capital was, to a large extent, withdrawn from cane production in Jamaica, and the category of plantations had been reduced to 12 sugar estates and a limited number of large cane farms. The SMA had been dissolved, reflecting the decline in the influence of the estates which no longer exercised a clear leadership position in the industry. In the mid-1970s about 15,000 independent cane farmers remained, i.e. the number had decreased by half. The majority of the independent cane farms were small, as in 1960.

A new type of cane production unit had emerged through the transformation of the three largest foreign controlled estates into 23 primary cane co-operatives; these produced almost one third of all cane in Jamaica. These represented a new kind of actor in Jamaican cane agriculture. The workers participated themselves in the management of their production units. Thus, self-management had replaced private capitalist cane agriculture on a considerable portion of Jamaican cane acreage. However, in 1981 the co-operatives were dissolved.

State participation and control had increased considerably, for example through the formation of the Sugar Industry Authority (SIA) and extensive direct ownership. The character of the government had changed from conservative (JLP) in the 1960s to reformist socialist (PNP) in 1972 and back to conservative (JLP) again in 1980. Sugar estates and cane farms in the mid-1970s employed about 30,000 workers and the position of the unions had been strengthened since the 1960s.

Although trials with combine harvesters were carried out in the early 1970s, this did not result in their commercial introduction, and all cane-cutting was still carried out by means of machetes in the early 1980s. In the case of cane-loading, however, almost complete mechanization had been achieved during the early 1970s.

In the 1950s and 1960s the plantation owners expressed a strong *interest* in the mechanization of cane-loading and cutting because of shortages of harvest workers at many plantations and for reasons of productivity and profit. For example, a mechanical cane-loader could replace at least ten manual loaders and the productivity gains were large. As in Cuba the small cane farmers had no possibilities of mechanizing on their own and therefore no interest in mechanization.

The co-existence of shortages of harvest labour and a very high (20 to 30 per cent) general rate of unemployment – discussed on p.67 – can at least partly be explained by the extremely heavy character, low pay and low status of manual harvesting. The workers and unions were reluctant to accept mechanical loaders and harvesters because of the fear of increased unemployment. Thus the attitude of the workers was, on the whole, negative (Central Planning Unit 1961: 26).

In the 1950s the government prohibited the use both of mechanical loaders and of combine harvesters on the grounds that they would displace labour and aggravate an already critical unemployment problem (Shillingford 1974: 70). If the capitalist state in Jamaica is understood as an actor guaranteeing the coherence of the society but also balancing various social interests in the society, it was – in this period – thus acting in the interests of the workers.

In the case of cane-loading, however, trials – but not commercial introduction – with mechanical loaders were allowed by the government and carried out at the Monymusk sugar estate in the late 1950s. *Information* about and *access* to mechanical loaders were no problems for WISCO – the British owner of the Monymusk plantation – since such machines were widely used in other countries and could readily be bought on the world market. During the experiments WISCO also accumulated *knowledge* about how to operate and maintain the machines and how to *organize* the use of them properly. These abilities are not very difficult ones to appropriate since the loading machines are not very complicated and since they could quite easily be fitted into the traditional harvesting system.

Accordingly, we have a situation in which five of the six conditions defining a social carrier of mechanical cane-loaders were fulfilled by plantations. Although the structure of the socio-economic system and the sugar industry was such that the plantation owners were the dominant actor in sugar agriculture, they did not have enough *power* to introduce mechanical cane loaders on a large scale because of the government prohibition, combined with – and perhaps also motivated by – the resistance of the workers and unions. This resistance was, in turn, motivated by the structural phenomenon of high unemployment.

When the state in 1960 changed its position, and decided to allow imports of mechanical cane-loaders for commercial use, the power balance between the plantation owners and the workers shifted in favour of the former. The plantation owners became social carriers of mechanical cane-loaders. A large-scale introduction now took place at Monymusk. As we saw on pp.65-6, this led to large redundancies and severe social problems for the workers who were made superfluous. However, the mechanical loaders decreased harvesting costs and thus spread to other plantations, both estates and large cane farms. In 1971 about 90 per cent of the crop was mechanically loaded.

In the case of cane-cutting the story was quite different. As mentioned earlier, there was a shortage of manual cane-cutters reported by a majority of the sugar estate in the mid-1960s. This led the estate owners and their Sugar Manufacturers' Association (SMA) to argue, in their evidence to the Mordecai Commission in 1966, that conversion to mechanical harvesting was necessary and inevitable. Their arguments were summarized in the Mordecai report; in short, they were: that there was a shortage of manual field labour at many estates and large cane farms; that about a quarter of the costs of a ton of cane were costs for manual harvesting; that in Jamaica a much greater number of man hours were necessary for harvesting than in competing countries; that the pressure for higher wages could only be countered by increased harvest mechanization, and that mechanization was inevitable if the standard of living for sugar workers was to be improved (Mordecai 1967: 118-9). The SMA found it impossible to estimate in any reliable way the savings in costs which would accrue from the use of mechanical harvesters on all estates (Mordecai 1967: 119). In retrospect it seems that they – at the time – overvalued the advantages in the short run and disregarded many of the problems associated with the introduction of combine harvesters.

However, it can be concluded that the estate owners and their SMA had a very strong subjective *interest* in mechanization of cutting in the mid-1960s. The interest of the large cane farmers was similar to that of the estates. However, the smaller cane farmers did not have the same interest in – nor possibilities for – the mechanization of cutting.

When mechanical loaders were introduced at the Monymusk estate, the reduction in the number of workers was severe during quite a short period of time. On this basis it is understandable that the unions were opposed to increased field mechanization. However, the wages at Monymusk also increased considerably.[17] There seemed to be a choice for the unions between saving all jobs and keeping some of them at higher wages. If all workers who lost their jobs because of mechanization could have been secured other jobs, this would not have been a dilemma, but because of the structural characteristics of the Jamaican economy this was not possible. As long as unemployment continues to be one of the major problems of Jamaica, the unions will probably also continue to be opposed to increased mechanization.

Thus the labour unions organizationally tried to resist the mechanization of cane-cutting. The sugar workers also constituted a threat to mechanization in a more anarchic manner. This is indicated by the following quotations:

> The planned programme to cut cane at Bernard Lodge and Caymanas Estates
> was postponed and finally cancelled as enough suitable cane was not avail-

able at Caymanas, and it was thought that the operations of the machine might increase labour unrest in the area.
(SMA 1972: 37)

Insurance. During this introductory period a full comprehensive policy with riot and fire risk is considered important and this makes the cost of this insurance high.
(SMA 1972: 39)

Operations [with the Cameco machine] were planned at Bernard Lodge, but the labour situation at this estate was such that management decided to postpone the mechanical harvesting operations and finally called them off.
(SMA 1970: 44)

Travelling of the machine could be reduced by parking the harvester in the field or at a nearby farm, but this seems to be risky.
(van Groenigen 1970: 58)

The interest of the workers and unions in preventing mechanization was also a considerable obstacle to mechanization due to the strong power position of the unions. The close relation between unionized labour and the two major political parties is also an important basis for the power position of the unions, each of the two principal unions being associated to one of the two parties.

The unions seem to care only about the quantitative employment consequences of the choice of technique. This is understandable in a country characterized by high unemployment. However the content and character of the jobs as well as the wages paid are very different in, for example, manual and mechanical harvesting. The character of the jobs, as well as the technical training of harvest workers, would be revolutionized through mechanization.

In line with the arguments of the SMA, the Mordecai Commission made the following recommendations to the government: that the sugar industry, under regulation, be permitted to explore and pursue a policy of the gradual extension of the use of mechanical harvesters; and that initially, in order that tests and evaluations of performance which are essential to regulating a gradual conversion to mechanical methods could begin, a limited number of mechanical harvesters (not more than five of selected types) should be introduced (Mordecai 1967: 226). Until the late 1960s, the government had prohibited the import of mechanical harvesters. The JLP government's negative attitude to sugar cane harvest mechanization "was said to be due to a concern for . . . particularly the employment effect" (Shillingford 1974: 210).

As in the case of loading, the government changes its position from support of the interest of workers into support of the cane capitalists' demand for experiments, after pressure from the latter. Two Australian and one US produced harvester were imported and comprehensive trials were carried out by the SMA in the early 1970s. This constituted an important change in government policy.

As we saw on p.70, the estates owned by Tate & Lyle and United Fruit were among the first to experiment with mechanical cane harvesters. As with mechanical loaders, the foreign-controlled companies were the first to introduce mechanical cane-cutters.

The trials with mechanical cane harvesters were described on p.70. Approximately 75 per cent of estate-managed and about 60 per cent of privately-farmed cane lands in Jamaica are adaptable for mechanical harvesting. The average cost of adaptation, including the investment for land forming and reblocking to improve irrigation and drainage efficiencies, is estimated at £32 per acre (Lee and van Groenigen 1973: 184).

Average cane yields in Jamaica are 25-35 tons per acre, but yields of 40-55 tons per acre are common in plant cane and first ratoons. Where yields are high the cane has a heavy, leafy top and a high degree of recumbency occurs, especially after burning. Some brittleness causing stalks to break before being cut by the base-cutters has been experienced. This has led to cane losses, especially with the whole-stalk machine (Lee and van Groenigen 1973: 184).

Satisfactory performance of the Cameco "Cost-Cutter" can be expected in erect cane with a yield under 35-40 tons per acre. In addition, flat lands or gently rolling land without deep twigs or quarter drains are required (van Groenigen 1970: 63). Because of the severe limitations concerning cane yield and recumbency the machine is only suitable for a small proportion of the cane acreage in Jamaica (SMA 1970: 47). In other words, the Cameco did not handle fields with average Jamaican yields satisfactorily (Lee and van Groenigen 1973: 185). This means that the short-term programme – which would not require large investments in the system of loading and transportation – was not viable.

Both the MF 201 and the Don Mizzi 740 have proven to be capable of handling the variety of crop and field conditions present in Jamaica (Lee and van Groenigen 1973: 186). The Don Mizzi machine seemed capable of handling most of the cane grown in Jamaica (SMA 1971: 64). The mass-produced Massey Ferguson machine has shown an ability to work under Jamaican conditions without basic modifications. It can quite satisfactorily handle the vast majority of the cane grown in Jamaica. The main limitations are the conditions of the fields (SMA 1970: 43; van Groenigen 1970: 60).

In an evaluation of three years of mechanical cane harvesting trials in Jamaica the following conclusions were drawn (Lee and van Groenigen 1973: 189, 190, 201, 202):

1. Whole-stalk mechanical harvesting, a method which would fit better into the present harvesting system and organization than combine harvesting, cannot be considered until a suitable machine becomes available.

2. Combine harvesters are able to harvest cane grown under Jamaican conditions.
3. In order to lay a sound basis for the acceptance of the combine harvesting machinery available on the world market, field and crop conditions will have to be improved. Without these preparations, harvesting costs will be exorbitant.
4. Combine harvesting will require high investments in auxiliary equipment and factory yards. It demands personnel for the operation and maintenance of machines and with organizational skills. These qualifications are scarce at the present and without overcoming this problem, successful harvesting does not seem economical.
5. The 1973 cost for manual cutting and mechanical loading was approximately 1.20 Jamaican dollars per ton.[18] The actual cost incurred by the MF 201 during the 1972 operations was 2.08 dollars per ton. This cost was reached when operating under less than ideal conditions. The maximum capacity of the machine was not utilized, which also led to higher cost. The time perspective used in the calculation was five years. The cost estimated for improved Jamaican conditions was 1.45 dollars per ton and the Australian machine manufacturer's (Massey-Ferguson) estimate for a fully developed system was 0.82 dollars (SMA 1972: 43).

> Costs of mechanical combine harvesting even under improved Jamaican conditions are presently considerably higher than the cost of hand cutting plus mechanical loading. Rising labour costs and/or unavailability of labour for hand cutting will eventually make mechanical harvesting inevitable.
> (Lee and van Groenigen 1973: 189)

> It is hoped that eventually mechanical harvesting will reduce the steep rise in harvesting costs which is presently being experienced.
> (Lee and van Groenigen 1973: 190).

Accordingly, the experiments showed that the combine harvesting machines worked well in a technical sense and would be able to harvest most of the cane grown in Jamaica. However, the cost per ton during the experiments, i.e. in the short run, was considerably higher for combine harvesting than for hand-cutting combined with mechanical loading at prevailing wages. The experiments were terminated in 1974.

Since combine harvesters were shown to be unprofitable at the level of the firm (plantation) – at least in the short run – the plantation owners lost interest in the mechanization of cutting. Another reason for this was the fact that there was no longer any shortage of manual cane-cutters during the first half of the 1970s. This increasing supply of harvest labour was related to a considerable increase in cane-cutters' wages in 1973-4 (Lee 1983). Thereby one of the plantation owners' strongest arguments for mechanization had disappeared.[19]

For these reasons, no actor with an interest in the mechanization of cane-cutting remained. After the trials in the early 1970s there was no actor in Jamaica which could be transformed into a social carrier of combine harvesters since the condition of interest was not fulfilled for any social entity.

It could be mentioned that the trials had indicated that the conditions of *organization, information, access* and *knowledge* were fulfilled in the case of plantation owners. The condition of *power* would probably have been fulfilled if the government had supported a demand from plantation owners to introduce combine harvesters commercially. However a discussion like this is hypothetical since no one had an interest in the mechanization of cutting. This condition was not fulfilled even for the plantation owners.

Although the lack of interest is a sufficient explanation for the fact that there is still no mechanical cutting in Jamaica, there are several factors that may possibly have contributed to this situation. Below I list several such factors without trying to evaluate their relative importance.

● From 1966 to 1976 the amount of cane harvested decreased from 4.8 million tons to 3.6 million tons, which in turn led to decreased demand for manual cutters.

● In the 1970s Jamaica experienced a continuously deepening economic crisis and the general unemployment rate increased.

● Another aspect of the economic crisis is the lack of foreign exchange which made the importation of expensive harvest machinery difficult. The relative price of such machinery has also increased.

● In the light of the increased general unemployment rate and the disappearance of the harvest labour shortage, the opposition of the workers and unions to mechanization has increased and their arguments against it have been strengthened.

● As we saw on pp.59-62 the Jamaican sugar sector went through radical structural changes in the 1970s. New actors emerged or existing ones became more important and powerful. Others disappeared or lost influence: (a) The dominant influence of the private estates of the 1960s has diminished drastically. Not only has the interest of the private units in mechanizing decreased, but so has their power to do so. For example foreign sugar companies, which were the main proponents of mechanization in the 1960s, are no longer in Jamaica, and the SMA does not exist as an organization. (b) Instead, large parts of the sugar-processing industry have been nationalized and much of the cane was farmed by co-operatives between 1975 and 1981. These were overstaffed and their interests differed fundamentally from those of private estates and cane farmers. For example, for the co-operatives the objective of securing employment for their members was in the short run more important than increased productivity. Thereby their interest in mechanized cutting was minimal in the late 1970s.

Because of their financial difficulties, their opportunity to gain access to harvesting machines would also have been limited. In the 1960s, government involvement and control over the sugar industry was very limited. As a result of the structural changes in the industry during the last decade, this has changed and the sugar processing industry has gradually been developing into a government controlled one. The major part of the sugar factories has now been taken over by a government-operated company. Thus the direct influence of government in the sugar industry has increased radically.

Government policy also changed when the social democratic PNP took over from the conservative JLP in 1972. The objective of decreasing unemployment was a very important one for the PNP government.[20] Mechanization of cane-cutting was in conflict with this objective. The close links between the PNP party and one of the unions (NWU) may also have made the government even more reluctant to support the mechanization of cutting. As a result of this and as a reaction to the growing economic problems (unemployment, scarcity of foreign exchange, etc.), "the introduction of mechanical harvesting would be totally unacceptable to government in this period of high unemployment throughout the island" (World Bank 1978a: 20). In an interview in 1979, a PNP government official even argued for a *decrease* in the level of mechanization (in cane-loading) in order to create more jobs (Fletcher 1979).

COMPARISON OF CHOICE OF TECHNIQUE IN CUBA AND JAMAICA

As stated in the introduction, one of the ideas behind the design of this study was to make possible a comparison between choice of technique in two developing countries with different socio-economic systems. Sugar cane harvesting in Cuba and Jamaica was chosen as the object of the comparison. The two countries are situated in the same part of the world and both have a colonial and neocolonial history. The sugar industry has for a long time been the single most important economic sector in both countries. It is a major employer of labour and a quite significant foreign exchange earner in both countries. However, sugar is more important for Cuba than it is for Jamaica.

The time period studied stretches from the late 1950s to the early 1980s. In respect to the degree of mechanization, Cuba and Jamaica were at about the same level in the late 1950s. At present Cuba is more mechanized, but both countries are quite advanced in mechanization compared to other developing countries.[21].

As mentioned on pp.75-6, a descriptive contrast is simply a matter of presenting the data on choice of technique in a comparable manner, which was done in Figure 6.2. The descriptive comparison shows that in both

Cuba and Jamaica the degree of mechanization of loading increased from zero to practically 100 per cent between the late 1950s and around 1980. In the case of cutting, no mechanization took place in Jamaica during the time period in question. In Cuba, however, the degree of mechanical cutting increased from zero in the late 1950s to 50 per cent in 1981.

Obviously such a descriptive comparison is quite superficial and says nothing about differences or similarities in regard to causes or determinants of the processes of mechanization in the two countries. It is left to the reader to speculate over which factors influenced the processes descriptively compared.[22]

Summary of Determinants

On pp.79-96 I discussed empirically, and in some detail, the determinants of the actual choices of cane harvesting techniques in Cuba and Jamaica with the help of the theoretical considerations presented earlier. I will now try to make some analytical comparisons, i.e. I will try to compare determinants of the choices of cane harvesting techniques in Cuba and Jamaica. The results attained in the empirical analysis of determinants are first summarized in Figures 6.3 and 6.4. In interpreting these figures it is appropriate to study them in relation to Figure 6.2.

Figure 6.3
Interest in Harvest Mechanization by Actors in Jamaica and Cuba

	Jamaica				*Cuba*		
	Loading		*Cutting*		*Loading*	*Cutting*	*Cutting and loading*
	1958	*From 1960*	*Late 60s*	*Mid-70s*	*1958*	*1958*	*from 1961*
Plantations	yes	yes	yes	no	no	yes	—
State farms	—	—	—	—	—	—	yes
Small cane farms	no	no	no	no	no	no	yes[b]
Workers and unions	no	no	no	no	no	no	yes
State and its agencies	no[a]	yes	no[a]	no	no	i	yes
Co-operatives	—	—	—	no	—	—	yes[c]

yes = the actor has an interest; no = the actor has no interest
— = not relevant; i = the actor is indifferent
[a] However, the state gave permission for trials.
[b] The larger ones had an interest in harvest mechanization.
[c] The co-operatives were transformed into state farms in 1962.

Some temporal analytic comparsions within countries have already been implicitly made on pp.79-96. This also includes inter-system comparisons in the case of Cuba, but as far as cross-country analytical comparisons are concerned, practically nothing has been said so far.

Since the number of theoretically possible comparisons between determinants is quite considerable, the discussion below has to be restricted to some of them. I will deal with cane-loading quite briefly, and concentrate more on comparisons between the determinants of the choice of technique for cane-cutting, since these are more interesting with regard to comparisons between socio-economic systems.[23]

Figure 6.4
Conditions Defining a Social Carrier of Techniques Fulfilled or not Fulfilled in the Cases of Plantation Owners in Capitalist Cuba and Jamaica and State Agencies in Socialist Cuba

	Jamaica				Cuba				
					Plantation owners	State agencies			
	Plantation owners		Cutting		Cutting	Loading		Cutting	
	Loading		Late 60s	Mid-70s	Before 1959	Before 1964	After 1964	1960s	1970s
	1958	From 1960							
Interest	yes	yes	yes	no	yes	yes	yes	yes	yes
Organization	yes	yes	yes	yes	yes	?	yes	?	yes
Power	yes[a]	yes	yes[a]	?	yes	yes	yes	yes	yes
Information	yes	yes	yes	yes	no	?	yes	?	yes
Access	yes	yes	yes	yes	no	no	yes	no	yes
Knowledge	yes	yes	yes	yes	no	?	yes	?	yes

yes = condition fulfilled; no = condition not fulfilled
? = it has not been possible to judge empirically whether the condition was fulfilled or not
[a] For trials only.

Cane-loading

In the case of cane-loading, the Jamaican plantation owners had an interest in mechanization in the late 1950s. In Cuba no actor had an interest before the revolution, but thereafter the state – and its agencies and farms – rapidly developed an interest in mechanization of loading (see Figure 6.3).

In Jamaica all the conditions defining a social carrier were fulfilled for plantation owners in the very early 1960s. In Cuba they were satisfied for state agencies from 1964 (see Figure 6.4). Thereafter processes of mechanization took place in both countries. One difference was that the social carriers of mechanical cane-loaders were not the same in the two countries. This is a reflection of the different socio-economic structures in the two countries, of the different sets of actors as well as of the differing relations between them, for example, in terms of relative power.

Another important difference between the processes of loading mechanization in the two countries is their relation to the structural phenomenon of unemployment. In Jamaica mechanization of loading led to extensive redundancies and large social problems for those workers laid off. In Cuba the process of the mechanization of loading took place simultaneously with a gradually decreasing general rate of unemployment. The latter was a consequence of the expansion of other sectors in the economy, an expansion connected with the construction of socialism. For example between 1958-9 and 1970 employment increased by 50 per cent in industrial activities, by 90 per cent in construction, by 100 per cent in transportation and communication and by 23 per cent in services (elaboration on Brundenius 1983: table 2). Therefore the mechanization of loading did not result in increased unemployment in Cuba.

Another observation is that the interest in mechanization in Cuba was practically unanimous. In Jamaica the small cane farmers had no direct interest in mechanization; the unions in particular opposed it. In Jamaica it was accordingly a conflict issue. This reflects the employment consequences discussed above, but also the fact that the character, role and position of the unions were different in capitalist Jamaica and socialist Cuba. This issue will be addressed further in the discussion of the mechanization of cane cutting below.

In spite of the fact that mechanization of loading started in 1961 in Jamaica and in 1964 in Cuba, Cuba had reached a higher degree of mechanization (85 per cent) than Jamaica (75 per cent) by 1970. Hence, the process was considerably faster in Cuba. This may be partly explained by the fact that all actors had the same interest in Cuba, while in Jamaica there was a certain resistance on the part of workers and unions. Another reason was that the Cuban social carrier (the state) had many more resources at its disposal than the Jamaican one (the plantation owners).

Cane-cutting

In the case of cane-cutting, the picture was more complex. Before the Cuban revolution, the plantation owners had an interest in introducing combine harvesters, and many experiments were carried out. They were not successful, however, since the plantation owners did not have access to an efficient machine which suited Cuban conditions. After the revolution, all the actors in sugar cane agriculture had an interest in the mechanization of cane-cutting. The state – and its agencies and farms – was then the completely dominant actor because of the structural changes, the changes in the set of actors and the changes in terms of power between them. The main obstacle to mechanization was the same as during the pre-revolutionary period – the state did not have access to a suitable harvester during the whole of the 1960s. This is indicated by the "no" concerning access to cutting machines in the 1960s in Figure 4.4, and a "no" in this figure indicates that there is an obstacle which constitutes a direct constraint for the process of mechanization. In a policy of pursuing mechanization it thereby constitutes a point of intervention.[24]

The state agencies in Cuba certainly devoted a lot of resources to trying to develop or buy a suitable machine in the 1960s. In the early 1970s, the problem of access – as well as others – was solved, and all of the six conditions were fulfilled. The degree of mechanization increased rapidly during the 1970s.

In Jamaica in the mid-1960s the plantation owners pressed for the mechanization of cutting, but they were the only actor that had an interest in introducing cane harvesters. After demands from the plantation owners, however, the government allowed the import of harvesters for experiments around 1970. Thereby all conditions necessary for the introduction of combine harvesters seemed to be fulfilled for plantation owners (see Figure 6.4). However, the power condition was satisfied "for trials only" which indicates that a social carrier of mechanical cane-cutters "almost" existed.[25]

When the experiments had been carried out, the results made the plantation owners change their minds, i.e. they lost their subjective interest in the mechanization of cutting, because in the meantime, the shortage of manual cane-cutters had disappeared. Combine harvesters were also shown to be unprofitable for plantation owners in the short run as compared to hand-cutting combined with mechanical loading. In the mid-1970s there was thus a situation where none of the actors in sugar cane agriculture had an interest in the mechanization of cutting. No social carrier of mechanical cutters has come into existence in Jamaica since then, and all cane-cutting is still carried out manually.

In addition to the fact that the percentage unemployed was much higher in Jamaica than in Cuba, there was another crucial difference between the two countries in regard to the employment situation. In Cuba the workers left the cane fields first and thereafter the harvest was mechanized. In Jamaica it was the other way around. At Monymusk the manual loaders were forced out of the fields by the machines. In the case of the trials with mechanical cutters, the temporary labour shortage disappeared during the experiments, which meant that one of the main reasons for mechanization was gone.

In summary, *all* actors in Cuba and *none* of the actors in Jamaica had an interest in the mechanization of cutting in the mid-1970s. Thus there was harmony of interest among actors in both countries, but it was a consensus about opposing things. This striking difference must be attributed to the differences in the socio-economic system and the employment situation in the two countries, i.e. to structural conditions.

In Cuba the situation is currently quite stable. All actors have an interest in increased mechanization (Figure 6.3) and all the conditions necessary for its achievement are fulfilled (Figure 6.4) In Jamaica there are, in the early 1980s, indications of a renewed interest in mechanization of cutting. Before discussing this, I will, however, add a few comments related to the evaluation of the trials carried out during the first half of the 1970s (see pp.93-6).

In that evaluation, it was concluded that combine harvesters were unprofitable for the Jamaican plantation owners. However, the evaluation dealt only with private profitability in the *short* run. The time perspective employed in the evaluation was only five years. This is too short for several reasons. First, the initial investments in, for example, training personnel, reblocking of cane fields, adaptation of transport systems and factory yards are very large. These costs should be distributed over a longer time period. Second, the lifetime of a combine harvester may very well be more than five years, particularly if its maximum capacity is not utilized.[26] Third, the performance of an agricultural machine of the complexity of a combine harvester is always very low in a poorly prepared trial situation. Fourth, we know that in Cuba a decade was needed before the breakthrough in mechanical cutting was achieved.

Although it is certainly not an easy task to carry out an analysis with a longer time perspective, this should have been tried. If the costs and benefits had been estimated in a *longer* time perspective – e.g. 10 or 15 years – it is likely that the outcome would have been more favourable to a large-scale introduction of combine harvesters. The fact that the private estates in Jamaica would perhaps not have been willing to accept losses for such a long period is another matter. This fact is related to the character of the actors and their objectives. These objectives are, in turn, imposed upon the estates by the laws of motion of the socio-economic system. In Cuba the social carrier was another actor subject to different objectives imposed by another system. Losses could therefore be accepted over a longer period.

On p.94 it was also noted that the increase in the cane-cutters' wages in the first half of the 1970s contributed to the disappearance of the previous shortage of manual cane-cutters. In addition to attracting more manual workers, however, such a wage increase simultaneously makes mechanical harvesting more interesting for plantation owners, since it means a rise in manual harvesting costs. This is probably one of the reasons why a renewed interest in mechanization of cutting in Jamaica emerged in the late 1970s. There is again talk about trials with cane harvesters. For example, a KTP-1 harvester was "almost" brought in from Cuba in 1979. There has also been interest in testing a cane harvester from Barbados. Finally, the SIRI was in 1982-3 discussing with the Claas company the possibility of shipping a Claas machine to Jamaica (Shaw 1983a; Burgess 1983). Some of the cane plantations – for example, New Yarmouth, Innswood and Rowington – became interested in introducing mechanical harvesters around 1980. They have prepared themselves by reblocking their fields so that they are ready to receive mechanical harvesters (Shaw 1983a; Burgess 1983).

The Seaga government which came to power in 1980 is less sensitive to union demands than the Manley government and would not object to the importation of small numbers of harvesters for experiments. Whether the government would agree to large-scale mechanization is dependent upon whether new trials would show that the costs of sugar cane production can really be considerably decreased in this way (Burgess 1983).

Although the Manley government (1972-80) was certainly not an active supporter of mechanization of cane-cutting, it obviously accepted the idea of bringing a KTP-1 harvester from Cuba in 1979. This machine was a gift from the Cubans, reflecting the good relations between the two governments at that time. All arrangements were made for the trials with the Cuban harvester. Everything and everybody was ready: the harvester, the supporting systems, interpreters and other personnel, etc. The harvester was already on the wharf to be shipped to Jamaica, and it had been decided at which plantations it was to be tested. Then the unions took an interest. Although it is not documented, they threatened to interfere. One of the plantations where the machine was supposed to be tested then decided to pull out of the trials because they feared sabotage. By the time three of the main plantations had pulled out, it made no sense to bring the harvester into Jamaica. Therefore the Jamaicans requested that the whole affair be postponed (Shaw 1983b).

Hence, it was the resistance to mechanization from the workers and unions which made the estate owners pull out of the trials with the Cuban machine. The situation was peculiar. A socialist government wanted to assist Jamaica by supplying a combine harvester. The Jamaican government and the plantation owners were positive and interested. However, the workers in the capitalist country would not accept trials with a machine which the workers in the socialist country had nothing against. As we have seen, the Cuban workers, as well as all other actors there, were eager to mechanize cane-cutting as soon as possible. In other words, the socialist government acted in the interests of plantation owners and against the interests of the sugar cane workers in Jamaica – at least against their short-term subjective interests – and the workers in the capitalist country managed to stop the trials with the machine. The plantation owners had an interest but not power enough to introduce the machine.[27]

As mentioned earlier, there is currently renewed interest in several countries in going back to green cane harvesting. This is also the case in Jamaica. The Cane Farmers' Association started a campaign for a return to green cane harvesting around 1980. Therefore the chairman of the association visited Barbados twice in 1981 to observe the "Carib Cane Cutter" which is used in Barbados to cut green cane (AIJCFA 1981: 17). The Carib Cane Cutter was developed in a collaboration between a British farm machinery manufacturer (E.W. McConnel) and the Barbadian sugar producers. The objective was to solve the problems caused by the shortage of cane-cutters in Barbados during the 1960s. The machine is really only a reaping aid which is attached to a standard tractor. It gathers the cane in the row, cuts the cane at ground level and windrows it along the row that is being cut. Workers follow and the cane is topped and detrashed with machetes. The cane is piled and later loaded by standard mechanical loaders. The Carib Cane Cutter gives a reduction in labour requirement of about half compared with hand-cutting. The Barbados machine could perhaps be labelled an intermediate technology in relation to manual cutting with machetes and combine harvesting. However, it has also been characterized as a rudimentary machine which is not particularly efficient. I was also informed that the Barbadians will soon go over to the Massey Ferguson 205 combine harvester (Shaw 1983a; Burgess 1983).

As late as in its 1982 Annual Report the Cane Farmers' Association argued that the Jamaican sugar industry should experiment with the Barbados machine to see if it were suitable for Jamaican conditions (AIJCFA 1982: 13). Such tests have also been considered, but it was necessary to cancel them "for more or less the same reasons as in the case of the Cuban machine" (Shaw 1983b).

The discussions in 1982-3 concerning the introduction of a Claas harvester in Jamaica should also be seen in the context of the increasing interest in returning to green cane harvesting, since the Claas machine is one of the best in green cane harvesting. To my knowledge the discussions with the Claas company have not yet resulted in the importation of a harvester.

Although there is at present no significant shortage of manual cane-cutters in Jamaica, the average age of the cutters is increasing, since relatively few young men are joining the cutting gangs (Sugar Industry Research Institute 1975: 7). Therefore it is a common view in Jamaica that a shortage of harvest labour will, sooner or later, develop again. This would force the Jamaican cane producers to try to mechanize cutting.

The best policy for the cane producers and their organizations is therefore to prepare themselves for mechanization in order to be ready for it when a need develops. All experience – including the Cuban example – shows that it is impossible to be too prepared when it comes to the introduction of new techniques. In order to be prepared for mechanization in 1990 the preparations must start now. The cane producers should therefore continue to clean and reblock their cane fields. Perhaps even more important, however, is the provision of adequate training of harvester operators and repair and maintenance crews. Equally important is the adaptation of harvesting equipment to suit Jamaican conditions as well as the adaptation of the transport system for combine harvesters. However, training and adaptation require the presence of at least a few mechanical harvesters in Jamaica. This is, as we have seen, strongly opposed by the labour unions which also have shown themselves powerful enough to prevent the import of cane harvesters for testing, training and adaptation.[28]

Notes

1. Accordingly, consequences will also partly be touched on in Chapter 6 and the discussion in Chapter 7 will to some extent be based on the analysis of determinants.

2. This distinction is inspired by Erik Baark (1981). It is important to note, however, that the two kinds of comparisons mentioned are ideal types, and most comparative analyses carried out include elements of both.

3. It could also be mentioned that *all* explanations of events or processes in the social sciences are actually – at least implicitly – comparisons with counterfactual situations, i.e. situations where the phenomenon explained has not occurred. In this sense, analyses which include attempts to explain things are always comparative analyses. Accordingly, analytical comparisons require explanations of the cases to be compared, i.e. comparisons between factual and counterfactual situations. Thereafter, the explanations arrived at in the various cases can be compared.

4. These conditions are elaborated upon in Edquist and Edqvist (1979: 31-2), where the concept was theoretically developed in a rationalistic manner, and defined. Some minor changes have since been made in relation to the presentation there.

5. The concept of "interest" is problematic. Sometimes a distinction is made between objective and subjective interest, the difference reflecting the possibility that an actor may or may not be conscious of its "true" interest; it is not conceived as an adequate goal. In our definition, however, only subjectively perceived interests matter – however "false" they may be – since only perceived interests can be a basis for decisions and actions. (Thereby we avoid the problem of who has the possibility of determining an actor's objective interest as well as a complex discussion of relations between objective and subjective interests). Subjective interests are revealed by actions or statements of actors. It seems sensible, however, to allow for the possibility that perceived interests may change as a result of changes of consciousness. The (perceived) consequences – in terms of employment, work conditions, division of labour, productivity, profitability, etc. –of the implementation of a technique influence whether an actor has an interest in the choice of it or not (Edquist and Edqvist 1979: 31).

6. If the condition of information is fulfilled for an existing technique, this does not mean that the technique is available for the social entity. The latter must also be able to gain access to the technique in a physical sense, e.g. by purchasing it. Therefore, it is useful to treat information and access as separate conditions, although they are partly overlapping.

7. This is analytically true, and not an empirical hypothesis. The empirical work instead concerns determining when the various conditions are fulfilled for which actors in which structural contexts. This will be investigated in the following sections. In this study I concentrate on choice among, and implementation of, existing techniques. It would, however, be possible to extend the analysis and discuss also "social carriers of inventions" or "social carriers of innovations" in a similar way. This would, however, require modifications of the concept of social carriers of techniques.

8. That the actor concept is structure-based avoids the voluntaristic fallacy mentioned in Chapter 2. It also means that the approach employed in this study is less actor-oriented than it may seem at first glance.

9. Therefore, my attempt is rather an interpretation in terms of the six conditions than a complete causal explanation.

10. These six conditions will be italicised in the text as they are addressed.

11. Later (see pp.125-7, Chapter 7) it will be argued that the Massey-Ferguson 515 combine harvester would probably have suited Cuban conditions. It was developed in Australia in 1956, but serial production did not start until 1960.

12. At first, cane co-operatives were established, but they never really functioned as independent co-operatives and were soon formally transformed into state farms.

13. However, the 1960s was a decade of failures in regard to mechanized cutting, but success in mechanized loading. This difference cannot be explained solely by considering the aspects of interest and power: other factors, to which we will turn later, must also be considered.

14. In economic terms, a precondition for investment in mechanization was lower consumption. The interest in mechanization shared by all social groups meant that people implicitly accepted this in order to escape manual cane-cutting. Although most Cubans were also fed up with the low consumption levels prevailing around 1970, mechanization and increased consumption could not both be achieved at the same time.

15. The US embargo against Cuba contributed to these problems.

16. We have seen that many mistakes were made during this period, but such costs are common in a process of building up a technical capability in any country.

17. The wage of a machine operator is several times higher than that of a manual cutter or loader.

18. In September 1969, the Jamaican dollar (J$) replaced the Jamaican pound (J£) as the official currency. The Jamaican pound was divided into shillings and pence, after the imperial British system. The Jamaican dollar is divided into 100 cents.

19. However, the wage increase also meant higher manual harvesting costs – which should have been an incentive for mechanization. This aspect will be discussed later in the chapter.

20. However, it was certainly not successful in this respect, as can be seen in Table 5.1.

21. See Chapter 3.

22. In another context I have tried such a speculation built exclusively upon the empirical information provided in the descriptive comparison above (Edquist 1982b). It led to trivial and even absurd results in terms of explanations. It simultaneously indicated, however, that empirical data as such are by no means sufficient to explain processes of technical change. It shows that theoretical work is also a necessary element in an attempt to create some order out of chaos. Accordingly, Edquist (1982b) may be of interest in a methodological sense. Its main conclusion was thus that a much more detailed and specific analysis is required if the results are to be scientifically interesting and/or useful for policy-making purposes.

23. The discussion will also be focused on the three most important (plantation owners, the state and the unions) of the six possible actors. Among the six conditions defining a social carrier of techniques, the three most important are interest, power and access. (However, all six conditions must of course be fulfilled in order for implementation to take place.)

24. Hence, an analysis of this kind may have direct policy implications. For example, an actor with an interest in introducing a certain technique and with ambitions to become its social carrier must, in its strategy or policy to achieve this,

concentrate upon those conditions among the six defining a social carrier which are not fulfilled. These are different for various actors, but also for similar or corresponding actors situated in different structural environments (see Figure 6.4). In a strategy, the missing conditions must be identified by the policy-maker and the means to overcome these obstacles must be sought.

25. It also indicates that another actor (the state) had a veto power.

26. Table 4.10 indicates, for example, that the Libertadora harvesters used in Cuba lasted for more than five years.

27. In different terms, the workers and unions had a veto power by virtue of their sabotage threats.

28. The policies of workers and unions will be discussed in Chapter 7, pp.153-7.

7. Consequences of the Choice of Technique

INTRODUCTION

In the previous chapter, the determinants of the choice of technique in the two cases were first addressed separately and then compared. In this chapter, the discussion of conquences of the choice of technique as well as some other aspects related to the two cases and the comparison between them will be integrated, i.e. various "themes" will be addressed in regard to both countries in the separate sections.

The two main consequences which will be discussed are generation of technological capability (pp.121-46) and employment effects (pp.146-57). In addressing these it becomes necessary and natural to deal also with other aspects of mechanization as a background. Therefore mechanization as such will first be discussed on pp.108-20. There the performance of various combine harvesters will be dealt with in some detail since it is a necessary basis for the later analysis of capability generation and employment.

In this chapter the data presented in Chapters 4 and 5 will be examined; trends, tendencies and correlations will be looked for and teased out of the data. In other words, the analysis in most of the chapter will be "close to" the empirical material. It will not have abstract theory as a point of departure. This is a reflection of the fact that the theoretical framework – presented in Chapter 2 and on pp.76-8 – was developed primarily for the study of determinants of the choice of technique. It is less relevant for the study of consequences of technical change.

In some sections below we will "take off" from the safe empirical ground and present more speculative discussions of various issues related to the consequences of the different choices of technique in the two countries. Various reasons for indigenous production of capital goods will be discussed against the background of the experience in Cuba and Jamaica. Costs and benefits of mechanization will be touched on as well as the issue of technical dependence. Finally the different interests and strategies of workers and unions in capitalist Jamaica and socialist Cuba will be discussed and related to Luddite machine destruction and the concept of "appropriate technology". The main emphasis in this chapter will be on consequences of the choices of techniques in cane-cutting, and cane loading will be dealt with only marginally. As we have seen, there has been much more mechanization of cane-cutting in Cuba than in Jamaica. As a natural consequence the discussion in this chapter will deal more with Cuba than with Jamaica.

MECHANIZATION OF CANE-CUTTING – A BACKGROUND

In discussing the mechanization of cane-cutting in Cuba it may be useful to compare planned goals with actual performance. In the case of Jamaica the state has not intervened actively in the choice of technique and therefore there are no government mechanization plans that can be compared to the actual record. Below, the explicit objectives with regard to mechanization of cane-cutting in Cuba are compared to the actual achievements during various periods.

(a) "To obtain the sugar output planned for 1970, Cuba needs to mechanize at least 30 per cent of cane cutting" said Minister Carlos Rafael Rodríguez at a 1966 FAO conference (quoted in Roca 1976: 51). The almost complete failure of the early Soviet harvesters in the latter half of the 1960s meant that only about 1 per cent of the cutting was mechanized in 1970 (see Table 4.4).

(b) A mechanization plan for cane-cutting was formulated for the 1973-6 period. The goal was to reach degrees of mechanization of 11, 19, 26 and 34 per cent respectively in these four years (Direccion Nacional 1976: 14; Mecanization 1977: 12). The actual record shows the following percentages: 11, 18, 25 and 32 (see Table 4.4). Thus, the plan was almost completely met.

(c) For the 1976-80 five-year period a new mechanization plan was formulated, according to which the degree of mechanization should be 60 per cent in 1980 (Thesis 1978: 123; Direccion Nacional 1976: 15; Gonzalez Eguiluz and Garcia Nunez 1977: 11). The percentage achieved was 45, hence the plan was not fulfilled (see Table 4.4).

(d) The goal for 1985 is to mechanize 50 per cent of sugar cane-cutting, 10 per cent less than the 1980 goal and only 5 per cent more than actual mechanization in that year (2nd Congress 1981: 246, 42). The 1985 goal was easily achieved already in 1981, but the harvest in that year was smaller than in 1979, affected by a pest. The amount of cane harvested mechanically was only marginally larger than in 1979 (see Table 7.1).

In summary, the goals were too optimistic in the 1960s, were realistic and achieved in the 1973-6 period, and were again too optimistic in the second half of the 1970s. The modest goals for the first half of the 1980s will most probably be achieved.

However, a mere comparison between planned targets and actual achievements is not a thorough method of evaluating a process of technological change in a socio-economic sense. For one thing, the feasibility and rationality of the targets as such should also be discussed and questioned. The unfulfilment of a plan target does not, as such, mean an economic failure. A better evaluation procedure would be to compare socio-economic costs and benefits of the process in the long run. Because of the paucity of data, such an analysis cannot be pursued in a detailed and exact manner, but a very general discussion of this matter is presented on pp.140-4.

Performance of Sugar Cane Combine Harvesters

Average Performance over Time

Table 7.1 repeats some figures related to sugar cane harvesting which were presented in Chapter 4. Some additional information as well as some calculations based upon the data are also presented.

The performance of the Cuban efforts to mechanize sugar cane-cutting is normally measured in terms of percentages of the cane harvested by combine harvesters each year (column 2 in Table 7.1). However, it could be more appropriate to use the total amount of cane harvested mechanically (column 3) as a measure of performance, as well as a planning goal. Since the total amount of cane harvested (column 1) increased from 1972 to 1979, this absolute measure would also give a better record.

Column 4 shows the number of cane harvesters operating each year and in column 5 the yield per harvester per *zafra* in Cuba is calculated. It shows that the yield was fairly stable during 1972-9. Thereafter it decreased somewhat. In column 6, the total length of the various harvest campaigns in calendar days are presented. If the yield per harvester per *zafra* (column 5) is divided by the number of days in each *zafra* (column 6) we arrive at a measure of the yield per harvester per harvest day (column 7). In column 8 Brian Pollitt's data on yield per combine harvester per day is presented (see footnote to Table 7.1). The figures in column 7 and 8 of Table 7.1 are graphically shown in Figure 7.1.

Pollitt has not explained how the "yields per combine" in column 8 are calculated. However, the pattern coincides largely with that of the yields per combine harvester per harvest day presented in column 7 and calculated on the basis of information presented in Table 7.1.[1] Therefore, we will, in the following, regard the general pattern illustrated by column 7 as a good approximation of the real yield per combine harvester per harvest day. It increased from 1971 to 1975 and decreased from 1975 to 1978. During 1978-80, it was fairly stable and thereafter it increased again.[2]

Relative Performance of Various Harvester Models

In Table 7.2 the amount of cane harvested per machine per *zafra* is calculated for each of the combine harvester models used in Cuba during the 1971-80 period. If we limit ourselves to the three models currently in use, we can see that the average amount of cane harvested per machine per *zafra* was 15,988 tons for the Libertadora, 16,798 tons for the Massey-

Table 7.1
Average Performance of Sugar Cane Combine Harvesters in Cuba, 1970-82

Zafra	(1) Total amount of cane harvested (million tons)	(2) Percentage of cane harvested by combine harvesters (%)	(3) Amount of cane harvested mechanically $\frac{1 \times 2}{1000}$ (thousand tons)	(4) Number of cane harvesters operating	(5) Yield per harvester per zafra 3/4 (tons)	(6) Length of zafra (days)	(7) Yield per harvester per harvest day 5/6 (tons)	(8) Yield per combine per day (tons)
1970	81.5	1	815	n.a.	n.a.	217	n.a.	n.a.
71	52.2	3	1,566	172	9,105	166	54.8	n.a.
72	44.3	7	3,101	236	13,140	153	85.9	56.3
73	48.2	11	5,302	415	12,776	135	94.6	88.5
74	50.4	18	9,072	730	12,427	128	97.1	108.1
75	52.4	25	13,100	1,007	13,008	123	105.7	113.8
76	53.8	32	17,216	1,284	13,408	130	103.1	106.9
77	60.3	36	21,708	1,577	13,765	141	97.6	95.4
78	69.6	38	26,448	2,006	13,184	168	78.5	83.9
79	77.3	42	32,466	2,298	14,128	182	77.6	82.8
80	64.0	45	28,800	2,423	11,886	149	79.8	n.a.
81	66.6	50	33,300	2,712[a]	12,278	136	90.3	n.a.
82	73.1	n.a.	n.a.	3,000	n.a.	n.a.	n.a.	n.a.

Sources: (1) table 4.2; (2) table 4.4; (4) table 4.10; (6) AEC (1981: 109) AEC (1979: 88); AEC (1977: 86); Junta Central (1970: 136); (8) Pollitt (1981: table 6b).

a estimated (see Table 4.10).

b Pollitt's source is: "Memorias", Ministerio de la Agricultura, Havana, 1980. In Pollitt's table the data is said to measure "yield per combine" only. The only sensible interpretation is that "yield per combine per day" is actually meant. However, we do not know if the figures apply to yield per combine for each calendar day of the *zafra*, for each day when harvesting was actually carried out or some average for each day of actual operation of the harvesters. In addition Pollitt mentions that "the data for combine-yields were inevitably somewhat rough and ready" (Pollitt 1981: 5).

Figure 7.1
Yield per Combine Harvester per Harvest Day in Cuba, 1971-81

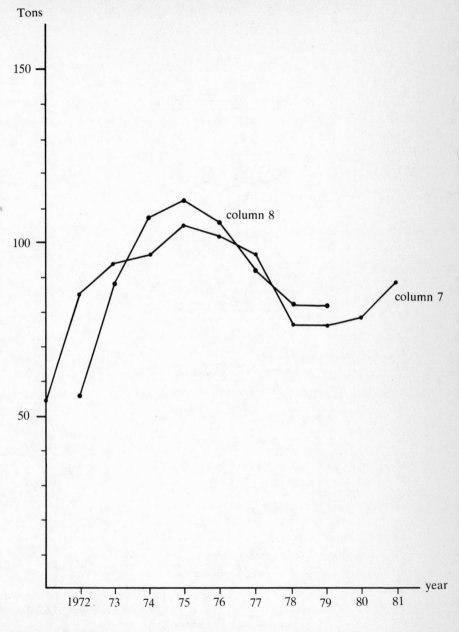

Source: Columns (7) and (8) in Table 7.1.

Table 7.2a
Relative Performance of Various Harvesters in Cuba, 1971-80

Year	Total amount of cane harvested per zafra (million tons)	Libertadora				Massey-Ferguson			
		%	Amount (thousand tons)	Number of machines	Amount per machine per zafra (tons)	%	Amount (thousand tons)	Number of machines	Amount per machine per zafra (tons)
1971	52.2	–	–	2[a]	–	1	522	20	26,100
72	44.3	1	443	19	23,315	4	1,772	115	15,409
73	48.2	3	1,446	123	11,756	7	3,374	249	13,550
74	50.4	4	2,016	163	12,368	10	5,040	387	13,023
75	52.4	4	2,096	167	12,551	12	6,288	418	15,043
76	53.8	5	2,690	162	16,604	13	6,994	439	15,932
77	60.3	4	2,412	166	14,530	13	7,839	432	18,146
78	69.6	4	2,784	166	16,771	10	6,960	435	16,000
79	77.3	4	3,092	157	19,694	10	7,730	407	18,993
80	64.0	4	2,560	157	16,306	9	5,760	365	15,781
Average					*15,988*				*16,798*

[a] Experimental machines.

Sources: Table 4.2, Table 4.10, Table 4.12.

Table 7.2b

	KTP-1				Others[b]			
Year	*Amount (thousand tons)*	*%*	*Number of machines*	*Amount per machine per zafra (tons)*	*%*	*Amount (thousand tons)*	*Number of machines*	*Amount per machine per zafra (tons)*
1971	–	–	2[a]	–	2	1,044	148	7,054
72	–	–	2[a]	–	2	886	100	8,860
73	482	1	43	11,209				
74	2,016	4	180	11,200				
75	4,716	9	422	11,175				
76	7,532	14	683	11,028				
77	11,457	19	979	11,703				
78	16,704	24	1,405	11,889				
79	21,644	28	1,734	12,482				
80	20,480	32	1,901	10,733				
Average				11,427				7,957

a Experimental machines.
b The machines included in "others" were mainly Henderson harvesters (see note to Table 4.12).

Sources: Table 4.2, Table 4.10, Table 4.12.

Ferguson and 11,427 tons for the KTP-1 model. Hence, on the average, the Libertadora and the Massey-Ferguson models cut 40 and 47 per cent more respectively per *zafra* per unit than the KTP-1. In other words, the Libertadora and the Massey-Ferguson harvesters performed considerably better than the KTP-1 harvesters.

In Table 7.3 and Figure 7.2 the combine yield per day is shown for each of the three harvester models. During 1973-5, performance improved for all three models. The maximum capacity was reached in 1975 for the KTP-1, in 1976 for the Libertadora and in 1977 for the Massey-Ferguson. (Here the 1971 figure for the Massey-Ferguson and the 1972 figure for the Libertadora are excluded since they are based on small numbers of machines.) Thereafter performance deteriorated again for all three of them. From 1978 the Libertadora and the Massey-Ferguson machines performed better again. For the KTP-1 the trend was downward for the whole period from 1975 to 1979, but its performance improved somewhat between 1979 and 1980. Measured in terms of cane harvested per machine per harvest day, the Libertadora performed 37 per cent better than the KTP-1 and the Massey-Ferguson had 42 per cent higher capacity than the KTP-1 on the average. Hence, the Cuban/German and the Australian machines had a much higher capacity than the Cuban/Soviet one.

Table 7.3
Amount of Cane Harvested per Machine per Harvest Day
for each Model, 1972-80

	Length of zafra (days)	Libertadora (tons)	Massey-Ferguson (tons)	KTP-1 (tons)
1971	166	—	157.2	—
1972	153	152.4	100.7	—
1973	135	87.1	100.4	83.0
1974	128	96.6	101.7	87.5
1975	123	102.0	122.3	90.8
1976	130	127.7	122.5	84.8
1977	141	103.0	128.7	83.0
1978	168	99.8	95.2	70.8
1979	182	108.2	104.4	68.6
1980	149	109.4	105.9	72.0

Average: $\frac{986.2}{9} = 109.6$ $\frac{1139}{10} = 113.9$ $\frac{640.5}{8} = 80.1$

Sources: Table 7.1 and Table 7.2.

Discussion of Harvester Performance
In this section the performance differences between various harvester models will first be discussed. Thereafter we will turn to factors that may explain the changes in harvester performance over time irrespective of model.

Figure 7.2
Amount of Cane Harvested per Machine per Harvest Day
for each Harvester Model, 1971-80 (tons)

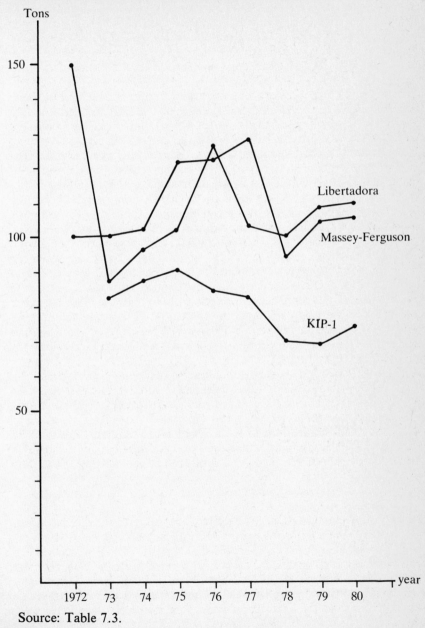

Source: Table 7.3.

The work of cane harvesters is considerably facilitated if cane fields are burnt before harvesting. In Jamaica burning was introduced simultaneously with mechanical loading, experimentally in 1957 and on a larger scale from the 1961 crop on. By 1969 nearly 70 per cent was burnt before harvest. In Cuba burning was not introduced in combination with mechanization of loading. It was initiated in the 1971 *zafra*. Thereafter it diffused quite rapidly and in the 1972 harvest, 70 per cent of the cane fields were burnt. In the latter half of the decade this proportion decreased again.

Apparently there was a strong resistance to burning in Cuba. Burning was introduced ten years earlier in Jamaica and several decades earlier in some other cane-producing countries. It is difficult to estimate the importance of the fact that burning started so late in Cuba. It may be noted, however, that the start and rapid diffusion of pre-harvest burning occurred simultaneously with the breakthrough of mechanical cutting in Cuba in the early 1970s. It could therefore be argued that one of the things that finally made the massive introduction of mechanical cutting possible was the burning. The combine harvesters available during the 1970s worked much more efficiently and with fewer breakdowns in burnt than in green cane. For example, when the KTP-1 combine harvesters were introduced in the Havana province, starting in 1972, all the cane that was harvested mechanically was burnt beforehand (Diaz Hernandez and Alvarez Portal 1981-55-7). It is therefore likely that the attempts to mechanize harvesting in the 1960s would have been more successful if this step had been taken earlier. It would have facilitated the operation of various machines and some of the Cuban harvesters could also have been designed specifically to cut burnt cane. In other words, the Cuban resistance to burning was probably quite important.

We also know, however, that burning has negative consequences. Because of these there is a renewed interest in harvesting green cane in many countries. At present there is a strong desire to cut green also in Cuba, so that the trash remains on the ground and conserves moisture, particularly in dry and non-irrigated areas. The Cubans also wish to use some of the green trash as a food supplement in their beef industry. In addition, there is an increase in the sugar yield per ton of cane of about 7 per cent cutting green (Hackett 1982). Therefore major efforts are currently being made in many countries to design combine harvesters which work efficiently also in green cane.

The capacity of a machine is always higher in burnt cane than in green cane. Therefore the superiority of the MF 201 in relation to the KTP-1 may be partly explained by the fact that the MF 201 was used only in burnt cane in contrast to the KTP-1 – and the Libertadora – which were used in green cane as well.[3] In addition, the MF 201 and the Libertadora 1400 have a higher capacity in cane fields with a higher yield per hectare than the KTP-1. Therefore the MF 201 and the Libertadora machines may have been selectively employed in higher-yield fields: the capacity of a machine often increases with a higher yield per hectare.[4] However, the fact that a machine can be efficiently used in high-yield fields is, of course, an important advantage as such.[5]

The two factors mentioned above can, however, account only for minor differences in the performance of the various harvester models. According to agricultural engineers in Cuba as well as in other countries, the major explanation lies in differences in the quality of the machines. Thus the main conclusion is that the actual performance of the MF 201 and the Libertadora 1400 was better mainly because they are more effective machines than the KTP-1. The main disadvantage with the KTP-1 is not, however, the capacity (in tons per hour) of the machine when actually operating. Instead, the main reason why the KTP-1 cuts less cane per day than the MF 201 and the Libertadora 1400 is that it suffers many more frequent breakdowns (Abreu 1981). Reliability of operation is the main problem.

To sum up, the difference in performance between the KTP-1 on the one hand and the Massey-Ferguson and the Libertadora on the other was around 40 per cent. The main reason for this difference was the properties of the machines. Differences in the characteristics pertaining to the environments in which the various harvester models are used probably account for only a minor part of the performance differences.

Table 7.1 showed that the yield per harvester per *zafra* irrespective of model was around 13,000 tons during the 1972-81 period. This is a respectable throughput compared to other Third World countries (Hagelberg 1983). However, compared to Australia it is quite low. There, it is not unusual for a contractor to cut 40,000 tons per year with one machine using an eight-hour day for 120 days (Hackett 1984).[6] Such large differences between industrialized and Third World countries may be explained by a number of factors. The most important ones are probably differences in the organization and efficiency of the transport system as well as differences in the time it takes to get spare parts when harvesters and sugar mills break down (Hackett 1984). After a broken harvester tyre the machine might be back at work after an hour in Australia. In a developing country it might take a week (Hackett 1984).

Figure 7.1 showed that the yield per combine harvester per harvest day irrespective of model increased from 1971 to 1975, decreased between 1975 and 1978 and increased somewhat thereafter. Since the capacity of combine harvesters is always considerably higher in cane burnt before harvesting than in green cane, the tendential increase in the yields per combine from 1971 to 1975 is probably related to the dramatically increased propensity to burn the cane before harvesting during the first half of the 1970s. Simultaneously, the decrease of burning during the second half of the decade is probably a partial explanation of the decline in yield per harvester during the 1975-8 period.[7]

As mentioned before, it is often argued that there is a positive correlation between cane yield per hectare and combine harvester yield. Figures on yield per hectare are presented in Table 4.2. It increased considerably between 1972 and 1973, was almost stable until 1976 and increased again during 1977-9. In 1980 it decreased dramatically because of the pest, but recovered again in 1981. The increase in yield per hectare probably contributed to the increase in yield per combine from 1972 to 1973. On the other hand, it should have had the same effect between 1977 and 1979, when the yield per combine was actually decreasing. The latter could have decreased even more if the yield per hectare had not increased. On the whole, therefore, there does not seem to have been a very strong correlation between changes in agricultural yield and changes in yield per combine harvester in Cuba during the 1970s.

Other factors which should lead to increased harvester productivity over time are improvements in field conditions and in operation, maintenance and repair skills, as well as in the organization of their use. On the other hand, the increasing average age of the harvesters should lead to decreasing productivity. This is particularly relevant for the Libertadora and the Massey-Ferguson since no units of these models were added to the total stock of harvesters from the mid-1970s. An increasing degree of mechanization should also mean that fields increasingly inappropriate for mechanization became mechanized. This may have been a matter of considerable importance in the late 1970s.

Because of the paucity of data, we cannot determine the relative importance of the various factors mentioned which influence the average productivity of harvesters. However, the single most important factor influencing the average productivity of harvesters was, most probably, the change in the composition of the harvester stock. Since we know the relative performance of various harvesters as well as the change in the structure of the stock of harvesters, this can be shown by means of some simple calculations which are presented below.

In 1973 43 harvesters out of 415, or 10 per cent, were of the KTP-1 model. In 1979 this proportion had increased to 1,734 out of 2,298, or 75.5 per cent (see Table 4.10). If we combine the 1973 proportions between the three different models in the stock of harvesters (Table 4.10) with the actual yields per combine of 1979 (Table 7.3), then the hypothetical average yield per combine harvester (irrespective of model) for 1979 can be calculated in the following way:

$$0.296 \times 108.2 + 0.6 \times 104.4 + 0.104 \times 68.6 =$$
$$32.0 + 62.6 + 7.1 = 101.7$$

Under these assumptions, the average amount of cane harvested per machine per harvest day, irrespective of model, would thus have been 101.7 tons. This is almost as high as the highest figure ever achieved – 105.7 tons in 1975 – and much higher than the actual record in 1979, which shows 77.6 tons. Alternatively stated, the average yield per combine harvester would have been 7.5 per cent higher in 1979 than in 1973 if the proportion between the three harvester models had been kept constant between 1973 and 1979. In reality the yield decreased by 18 per cent. To continue this hypothetical arguing ($101.8 \times 182 \times 2,298 =$) 42.6 million tons of cane, or 55 per cent of the total harvest, would have been harvested mechanically in 1979 under the above assumptions. In reality it was 32.3 million tons and 42 per cent, respectively.

As shown in Figure 7.1, the maximum yield per combine harvester per harvest day was reached in 1975. In Table 7.4 this year is taken as the point of departure for a calculation of the proportion of the decline in yield per harvester that can be explained by the change in the structure of the stock of harvesters. A hypothetical yield per harvester is calculated for 1975-80 under the assumption that the composition of the harvester stock is kept constant at the 1975 proportions. Table 7.4 shows that the actual yield per harvester decreased by 26.6 per cent for 1979 and 24.5 per cent for 1980 as compared with 1975. If the composition of the harvester stock had not changed, the figures would have been 14.9 per cent and 12.7 per cent respectively. Thus 44.0 per cent and 48.2 per cent respectively of the decrease in combine yield can be explained by the change in the composition in the harvester stock. Hence, this change of composition is most likely to be the single most important explanatory factor for the decrease in average combine yield for these years as compared to 1975. In summary, Table 7.4, as well as the previous comparison between 1973 and 1979, shows that the progressively increasing proportion of the KTP-1 harvesters in the machine park as a whole is the most important single factor explaining the change in average combine harvester performance in Cuba. The reason is the lower capacity of these machines as compared to the Libertadora and the MF 201.

With regard to Jamaica, we cannot present a discussion which corresponds to that concerning Cuba reported here and above. As we described earlier, however, experiments were carried out in Jamaica in the early 1970s with three different cane harvesting machines, all of them imported. The Cameco "Cost-Cutter", which is a whole-stalk harvester, was suitable only for a small proportion of the cane acreage in Jamaica. The MF 201 (self-propelled) and the Don Mizzi 740 (towed by a tractor) combine harvesters both proved capable of handling most of the cane grown in Jamaica. Hence the harvester model which contributed most to the breakthrough in combine harvesting in Cuba also performed well in Jamaica. The reasons for the failure to introduce the harvesters on a large scale in Jamaica were discussed on pp.94-5. None of the machines was, under the conditions prevailing in Jamaica in the early 1970s, competitive in relation to hand-cutting combined with mechanical loading. Therefore no one had an interest in introducing harvesters and thereby no social carrier of them could emerge.

Table 7.4
Hypothetical Combine Yield for each Harvester Model per Harvest Day in Cuba, 1975-80

	Libertadora	M-F	KTP-1		Hypo-thetical yield	% of 1975 yield	Actual yield	% of 1975 yield
1975	0.166 × 102.0 +	0.415 × 122.3 +	0.419 × 90.8	=	105.7	100.0	105.7	100.0
1976	0.166 × 127.7 +	0.415 × 122.5 +	0.419 × 84.8	=	107.6	101.8	103.1	97.5
1977	0.166 × 103.0 +	0.415 × 128.7 +	0.419 × 83.0	=	105.3	99.6	97.6	92.3
1978	0.166 × 99.8 +	0.415 × 95.2 +	0.419 × 70.8	=	85.8	81.2	78.5	74.3
1979	0.166 × 108.2 +	0.415 × 104.4 +	0.419 × 68.6	=	90.0	85.1	77.6	73.4
1980	0.166 × 109.4 +	0.415 × 105.9 +	0.419 × 72.0	=	92.3	87.3	79.8	75.5

Sources: Table 4.10, Table 7.1, Table 7.3

GENERATION OF TECHNOLOGICAL CAPABILITY

Technological capability can be defined as constituting the skills to operate, maintain, repair, design and produce capital goods. The first three of these elements are relevant for all sectors of industrial, agricultural and service production, where capital goods are *used*. They will be addressed below. The latter two are directly and exclusively related to *production* of capital goods, and will be discussed on pp.121-35. The issue of capability generation will be concluded on pp.135-46.

Use of Cane Harvesting Equipment

The development of an indigenous technical capability to use capital goods may be both a precondition for, and a consequence of, a certain choice of technique. In the case of sugar cane-cutting, technical capability was never an obstacle to the choice of machetes for cane-cutting. But at the same time the use of machetes does not lead to an improvement of the technical capability in the sector. The result is a more or less static situation in terms of skills and capabilities – with low productivity and high employment. For the choice and implementation of combine harvesters, the capability to operate, maintain and repair the machines is a necessary condition.[8]

In both Cuba and Jamaica the skills to use mechanical loaders have been created on a broad scale. In regard to combine harvesters, the corresponding skills have been created only in Cuba. In Jamaica, the choice of the machete implied the continued use of extremely low skilled labour engaged in cane-cutting. Practically no technical skills and capabilities were generated in relation to cane-cutting. In Cuba, thousands of harvester operators were trained and a nationwide system for the maintenance and repair of the harvesters was established. Productivity was also increased and employment drastically reduced. The creation of these skills is an investment in learning and may well be quite costly. However, such skill generation may also imply considerable benefits for the society as a whole.[9]

Design and Production of Cane Harvesting Equipment

Attempts to design and produce cane harvesters and loaders indigenously started in Cuba in the early 1960s. The first attempts failed, but in the late 1960s the Libertadora was designed by Cuban engineers and in the late 1970s the massive production of harvesters started in Cuba with Soviet assistance. In Jamaica practically no cane harvesting equipment is designed or produced. Below, I will discuss the various efforts to design and produce sugar cane harvesting machines in some detail. Before that, however, I will briefly mention a number of reasons for the establishment of indigenous capital goods production in Third World countries.

Some Reasons for Indigenous Production of Capital Goods

When investments are made in a developing country, all capital goods that are needed could in principle be imported.[10] In the literature on development and development strategies the capital goods industry is sometimes regarded as being crucial for developing countries. There are strong reasons why indigenous production of machinery and equipment is sometimes to be preferred to imports.[11]

First I want to mention a reason for the establishment of capital goods production in developing countries which is largely tautological but often ignored. It is frequently argued that the generation of a technological capability should be an important element in development strategies. As mentioned earlier, such capability consists of the skills required to use, design and manufacture capital goods. The latter two are often considered to be the most important ones. The only way to generate them is evidently to establish or develop an indigenous capital goods industry.

The basic function of the capital goods industry is to supply machinery, equipment and tools to the whole economy. Product innovations in the capital goods sector may lead to productivity increases in the rest of the economy, as well as in the capital goods sector itself, when new machines are designed and diffused throughout the economy. Recent examples are micro computers, numerically controlled machine tools, automatic weaving machines, continuous process dairy equipment and word processors, to name a few. The capital goods sector is an important link between research and development on the one hand and the productive system on the other. Therefore the capital goods industry plays a critical role in the innovative process in the economy.[12] If a country intends to reach the technological frontier in any sector, this link between R and D and the productive system is certainly a strong reason for the establishment of domestic capital goods production.

The fact that the capital goods sector constitutes a link between R and D and production is also important in another respect. Not all technologies can be acquired on the international market. Much custom design is carried out. That is, many industries require close contact with the producers of capital goods in order to specify and develop the appropriate production system or machine. While some of these needs can be met by foreign suppliers, it is sometimes impossible, or it may be prohibitively expensive, for developing countries to do so. Such custom design is particularly important in agriculture, where specific conditions in terms of topography, climate, soils, varieties grown, etc. demand local design or adaptation of machines.

From a slightly different angle, it might be argued that many developing countries' markets are different from those of the industrialized countries. Users of capital goods in the developing countries sometimes put much greater emphasis on price than on quality as compared with firms in the developed countries. This means that there may be a deliberate – and under certain circumstances also rational – downgrading of the quality of the machinery. Such downgrading or simplification of capital goods can also be rational if it makes possible indigenous production of the equipment.

Another fundamental reason is the sheer quantitative importance of capital goods in production and trade. In industrial countries such as the United States, the United Kingdom and Japan, the engineering sector accounts for 40 per cent or more of manufacturing output (RPI 1983:4).[13] In addition, the demand for capital goods often increases proportionately faster than the rate of economic growth. This implies that an economy which strives to grow at a given rate will, in the absence of a domestic capital goods industry, have to import increasing amounts of capital goods from abroad. This is sometimes not possible for developing countries because of the very serious balance of payments problems which many of them experience. Although it is certainly not self-evident that balance of payments problems should be solved through expansion of the capital goods industry, the size of the sector alone (in trade and global manufacturing) would lead one to believe that the industry might be an important instrument for mitigating the problems of foreign currency through import substitution and/or exports.

A more developed capital goods industry may also enable developing countries to import overseas technologies more successfully. A reasonably developed capital goods industry is likely to help make intelligent judgements about, and selections from, the overseas technologies which are potentially available for Third World countries. Furthermore, it is much easier to make the adaptations and adjustments that are often involved in importing foreign technologies if a domestic capability exists in the field.

Indigenous manufacturing of capital goods may very well be built up on the basis of foreign designs in the form of licences. However, the acquisition of technology in the form of licensing is frequently associated with export restrictions. Thus, a domestic design capability may be a prerequisite if a Third World country wants to export capital goods in addition to substitute imports.

Taken together, these arguments constitute a strong case why developing countries should also build up an autonomous capability in the capital goods industry if their develoment strategies are to be successful in the long run. However, there may certainly be large costs involved in establishing such a capability and it can of course not be achieved for all capital goods.[14] Below we will take a look at the actual record in the cases of Cuba and Jamaica.

The Various Techniques
In this section I will discuss various sugar cane harvesting techniques with respect to indigenous design and production capabilities. When relevant, I will also address technology imports to Cuba and Jamaica as well as problems associated with such transfers.

a) An Early Attempt in Cuba

The Ecea MC-1 cane-cutter was designed in 1962; 680 units were manufactured for the 1963 harvest. Both design and production were carried out exclusively by Cubans (pp.35-6).[15] This is an important explanation of the failure of this machine. Cuban engineers and technicians were at that time simply not sufficiently experienced to carry out such a task.

b) Mechanical Loaders

In 1963 a mechanical loader, designed and produced in Cuba, started to operate. However, the indigenous production of this machine was substituted by imports from the USSR of a grab-type loader (the PG 0.5 machine) in 1964. My sources do not indicate exactly why the production of loaders was terminated in Cuba. It could have been because of deficiencies of the machines as such, because the Cuban mechanical industry was inadequate, or for some other reason. It certainly has, however, important consequences for future technical skills and capabilities when indigenous design and manufacturing in a developing country is substituted by imports. As shown in Table 4.4, however, the transfer of cane-loading technology from the USSR was successful in the sense that almost 85 per cent – or 70 million tons – of the manually cut cane was mechanically lifted in 1970. However successful this transfer of technology was, it also led to a prolonged Cuban dependence on imports of mechanical cane-loaders from the Soviet Union, as shown in Table 7.5. So far neither design nor production of cane-loaders has been resumed in Cuba.

Table 7.5
Cuban Imports of Mechanical Cane-loaders from the USSR, 1971-82

Year	Number of units	Cost (million current pesos)
1971	1,153	1.897
1972	4	0.010
1973	1,123	1.709
1974	426	2.018
1975	2,110	7.815
1976	1,300	4.008
1977	301	2.337
1978	310	2.411
1979	912	3.116
1980	1,815	6.473
1981	953	5.591
1982	1,128	5.004
Total	*11,535*	*42.389*

Sources: AEC (1975: 171); AEC 1981: 202); AEC (1982: 352-3, 390-3).

In total 11,535 machines were imported during the 1971-82 period. The total cost was 42 million (current) pesos. It may also be observed that the cost per unit increased from 1,645 pesos in 1971 to 3,083 pesos in 1976 and further to 4,436 pesos in 1982.[16] The termination of production and the subsequent large import of loading equipment from the USSR is an indication of foregone skill formation in Cuba. On the other hand, it may be argued that it is – in the long run – wise to stress domestic production of combine harvesters rather than mechanical loaders. The reason is that loaders will not be needed when all cane is harvested by combines.

In Jamaica the degree of mechanical loading increased from zero in 1960 to 91 per cent in 1971. All loading equipment was imported, i.e. no indigenous design or production capability was created.[17] On p.66 above, evidence was presented which indicates that this conversion from manual to mechanical loading was profitable in the sense that harvesting costs decreased due to mechanization. Hence, it is an example of a successful transfer of technology – at least for the plantation owners. It should also be recalled that this transfer occurred earlier in Jamaica than in Cuba.

c) The Early Soviet Harvester and a Possible Alternative

We have already seen (pp.38-42) that the massive implementation of the combine harvesters KCT-1 and KT-1 in 1965-8 was a complete failure. For example, only 10 per cent of the 500 machines imported in 1965 were still in operation at the end of the same *zafra*. These machines were designed as well as produced in the Soviet Union. A general unfamiliarity with machines and lack of necessary maintenance of the harvesters were probably important reasons why so many of them became inoperative so quickly. The same is true for organizational problems and the fact that the fields were not prepared for mechanical harvesters. In addition, operators, technicians, as well as the government, must gradually have become aware of the fact that these machines could not possibly solve the problem of mechanization because of their inherent limitations and performance characteristics. And this naturally diminished the interest in handling and maintaining them properly.

It would be interesting to know whether the operational problems and the excessive rate of breakdown was caused by the properties of the Soviet machines as such, or if the problem was lack of knowledge about how to operate, maintain and repair them properly. If the fault was on the Cuban side, no alternative machine of a similar complexity would have been more reliable. If the problems originated in the machines themselves, some other – imported or locally produced – machine could have performed better than the Soviet ones. Probably it was some combination of the factors mentioned which caused the operational problems and the high rate of breakdowns. However, based upon the information presented earlier, as well as on various interviews in Cuba, it seems highly probable that the main source of the problems was the inherent deficiencies of the machines themselves.

However, it is not very surprising that this attempt to transfer technology failed. In the Soviet Union almost no sugar cane is grown, and there was no previous experience in the country of designing or producing cane harvesters or other machines capable of solving similar material handling problems. In spite of all that, the early Soviet harvesters were developed in less than three years. It is therefore often argued in Cuba that the Soviet Union should not be criticized for the failure. What *should* be noticed however, is the fact that political ties were allowed to determine from where technology was imported. Even if the machines were given to Cuba free of charge – which is not likely – it was probably a very costly enterprise for Cuba in a total sense and in terms of opportunities foregone. Imports of some other, quite expensive, machine could – as will be argued below – have been socially much more profitable if it had worked properly.

In other cane-producing countries, intensive attempts were also made to mechanize harvesting and many machines existed in various countries in the 1960s. However, it is often argued that because conditions in various areas are so different, no really efficient combine harvester that suited Cuban conditions existed in the world in the 1960s. But there was probably one exception: the Massey-Ferguson 515 which was a predecessor to the Massey-Ferguson 201 machine discussed on pp.49-51.

The first prototype of the MF 515 combine harvester was developed in Australia in 1956. Serial production started in 1960, when 24 machines were sold. In 1961, when 54 combines were sold, Massey-Ferguson began exporting the harvester (Gaunt 1964: 36; Spargo and Baxter 1975: 32). The MF 515 was a chopper harvester towed by a standard tractor, just like the KCT-1, but powered by its own engine. Mechanical harvesting started to gain momentum in Australia in 1960 and the most popular harvester in Australia was the MF 515. In the 1963 season, 144 of the 248 machines in use were MF 515s (Atkinson *et al.* 1965: 46-8).

In Australia, cane is produced both in Queensland and in New South Wales and the conditions in these two areas are quite different. The process of mechanization in Queensland moved fairly rapidly in the 1960s. The degree of mechanization increased from 2.7 per cent of the harvest in 1960 to 92 per cent (15.1 million tons) in 1970. In 1973, 99.6 per cent of the cane harvest in Queensland was processed by combine harvesters (Leffingwell 1974: 26).

Cuba never tried to import a single unit of the MF 515. However, in retrospect it seems as if there would have been good reasons for doing so. This machine could have been tested and used in the work to develop Cuban machines. Judging from its use in Australia, there are reasons for believing that the MF 515 would also have performed much better in Cuba than the KCT-1 and the KT-1. The fact that the characteristics of the cane and other conditions like soil and topography are very similar in Queensland and in Cuba is the basis for this argument, since it implies that machines designed for conditions in Queensland can be used in Cuba without major changes. And in Queensland, the degree of mechanization increased from 24 per cent in 1964 to 72 per cent in 1968 (Leffingwell 1974: 26), i.e. during the period when the Soviet machines failed in Cuba. One difference, however, was that the cane fields were burnt before harvesting in Queensland, but not in Cuba.

The argument above implies that it would probably have been more efficient to use the knowledge of one of the most experienced harvester producers in the world than to co-operate with the Soviet Union, a country which did not have any previous experience in the design and production of cane harvesters and which has virtually no sugar cane itself. The Cubans would probably have been more successful in the 1960s if they had introduced the MF 515 on a large scale as an alternative to the Soviet harvester.[18] The transfer of the Soviet machines failed, however, and the fact that the Australian technology was not transferred in the 1960s was possibly an important mistake which implied a large opportunity cost for Cuba by delaying the breakthrough of cutting mechanization by five to eight years. In this sense, Soviet technical assistance to Cuba probably constituted an obstacle to mechanization in the 1960s.

d) Cane Cleaning Stations

The dry cleaning stations were developed in the mid-1960s. The trials showed positive results, and in 1967 implementation on a large scale was initiated. Towards the end of the 1970s, the number in operation approached 500 units (see p.44). The stations themselves were designed by the Cubans as a specifically Cuban solution to the task of cleaning cane, taking into account that water is scarce in Cuba. The design was also adapted to the less developed character of the Cuban mechanical industry so that the stations could be fabricated in Cuba. In other words, dry cleaning stations are an example of a technique successfully developed and produced indigenously in a developing country and adapted to the specific conditions prevailing in that country.[19]

Although water is also scarce in most parts of Jamaica, cane washing plants were introduced from the early 1960s. Thus it could be argued that this imported technology – similar to the Hawaiian plants – was not very suitable for Jamaican conditions. If domestic production of cane cleaning devices had been feasible, they could possibly also have been adapted to local conditions, as in Cuba.[20]

e) The New Cuban Strategy from the Late 1960s

The almost complete failure to mechanize Cuban cane-cutting in the 1960s can be explained partly by the choice of Soviet harvesters. However, it must also be taken into account that mechanical cane-cutting is quite a complicated task and demands a highly complex machine. Cuba is still a developing country and had not, at that time, developed a sufficiently solid organizational and technological base upon which the mechanization efforts could be founded. In addition, during the 1960s attempts were made to develop an efficient harvester to cut green, unburnt cane. At that time such a machine had not been developed anywhere in the world. No efficient green cane harvester was available on the international market. In Australia and Hawaii – with long experience of mechanical harvesting – the cane fields were burnt before the cane was harvested mechanically. In other words, the Soviet and Cuban engineers had no working harvester on which to pattern their research and development efforts.[21]

One of the disadvantages with the early Soviet harvesters was that they could only be used in cane with a maximum inclination of 30° and with a yield below 50-60 tons per hectare. These machines could therefore only be employed in 30 per cent of the cane fields that existed in 1966. In 1967 it was announced by the political leadership that the goal should be to develop a machine which could be used in all kinds of cane, however entangled and interwoven it was, as well as in fields with a much higher yield per hectare.

Starting from this new conception, the design efforts continued. Three "families" of harvesters (Henderson, Libertadora and KTP) were developed, largely in Cuba. In addition a large number of Australian machines (MF 201) were imported during the first half of the 1970s. Previously the efforts were focused upon one idea/machine at a time. Accordingly, the strategy was different in the late 1960s and early 1970s in the sense that attempts were made with several ideas/machines simultaneously. Foreign machines were imported, and at the same time the efforts to design harvesters domestically continued. The performance of the imported machines and those developed locally could then be compared, the best machines identified and the increased knowledge about the characteristics of the foreign machines could stimulate the indigenous efforts. This openness and flexibility should be strongly stressed since it proved to be quite successful. The pluralistic approach described was, however, abandoned in the latter half of the 1970s, when all efforts were again concentrated on one family: the KTP Harvesters.

f) The Henderson Harvester
The Henderson harvester was a crude and simple machine which could cut and load any kind of cane with a fairly high productivity. It was designed in Cuba in such a way that it would be easy to construct domestically. A total of 248 units, in two versions, were also manufactured around 1970. However, these machines had no device for cleaning the cane, which was a major disadvantage compared to other machines which had been designed or imported simultaneously. Therefore, the Henderson machines were taken out of operation in 1972. Hence the attempts along this line were a failure.

g) The Libertadora Harvester
The Libertadora combine harvester is an example of a machine which was developed and basically designed by Cubans and then taken over, modified and produced on a large scale by a capitalist company in a West European country. Claas Maschinenfabrik has, for many years, been a major producer of grain harvesters. The following interpretation regarding the relations between the Cubans and the Germans in the process of design of the

machine was offered by the Claas company:

> The "CLAAS-Libertadora" was designed conceptually in Cuba but was
> engineered in Germany by CLAAS and all development work since then
> (1969-70) has been by CLAAS. Substantial improvements were made with
> the 1974/5 release of the CC 1400 as we now know the machine.
> (Stephenson and Loeser 1982)

According to Abreu, the Libertadora was conceived, designed and drawn
exclusively by Cuban specialists. No Germans took part in the development
and testing of the Libertadoras. They only participated in the construction
of the machines in their workshops and factories in Germany (Abreu
1981).

An outsider, but a knowledgeable observer, interpreted the relation in
the following way: "I think it more likely that the Cubans provided
conceptual inputs to the Libertadora but Claas executed the detail design in
which much grain harvesting technology is visible" (Hackett 1982). Hence,
the basic design was carried out by the Cubans and the detailed design by
the Germans. The Cuban contribution was of considerable importance in
this division of labour, since they provided the basic concept. It is therefore
an example of transfer of a technique from a developing socialist country to
an industrialized capitalist country. The Claas Maschinenfabrik started
serial production and, by 1978, had exported the harvester to more than 30
countries. In Argentina there were, for example, more than 80 machines in
1978 and in Venezuela around 30 (Leffingwell 1978: 125). According to
more recent figures from the company itself, the CC 1400 has been
exported to 44 countries since 1972. In addition to Cuba (169 units), these
sales include installations in Argentina (121 units), Florida (99 units),
Mexico (82 units), Puerto Rico (75 units), Venezuela (58 units) and the
Sudan (51 units) (Stephenson and Loeser 1982).

Complete production and sales figures are not available for publication,
but a safe estimate would be that between 700 and 800 machines had been
produced up to 1982. And, of course, all these machines have been
exported. The fact that no cane is grown in Germnay should be a
disadvantage to the Claas company as compared to, for example, the
Massey-Ferguson company, and also in comparison with Cuba. The
complete lack of a home market complicates marketing, and in the
development work there could be problems with testing and feedback from
customers. On the other hand, the two producers mentioned have a large
advantage over the Cubans since they are located in an industrially mature
environment. In contrast to the Cubans, they can draw on the specialist
help of various supply companies in such fields as hydraulics, metallurgy,
rubber, bearings, etc. A designer in an industrialized country gets important
inputs from these specialists who will also eventually supply components.
Such advantages are often not available to a designer or manufacturer in a
developing country.

Cuba was the single largest buyer of the Claas-Libertadora harvester during the 1972-82 period, although its import had been terminated in 1974. This should have been the basis for a considerable bargaining strength for the Cubans in negotiations with the German company.

The Libertadora harvester is capable of harvesting cane in fields with entangled and interwoven cane and with yields of more than 130 tons per hectare. The productivity was far superior to all previous machines used in Cuba (Direccion Nacional 1976: 14). Since all cane was still cut unburnt in Cuba during most of the process of development of the Libertadora, it was specifically designed for green cane. Hence, it was custom designed for the conditions prevailing in Cuba at that time. However, it can, of course, also be used in burnt cane. Among the machines used in Cuba today, the Libertadora is still the best one in green cane. It is also a common view among agricultural engineers in various countries that the Libertadora, compared to its competitors in the world market, is still the most productive combine harvester in green cane. The machine is also marketed by the Claas company as being particularly good in green cane.

Why did the Cubans then give the patent rights to West Germany? Cuba's general situation must be mentioned in this context. The US embargo and the international isolation were important factors since they created problems in acquiring information about and access to foreign machines. Another factor was the difficulty of harvesting the record *zafra* of 1970 which underlined the importance of rapid mechanization. But the basic underlying factor was that the Cubans simply could not at that time carry out detailed engineering nor produce such complicated pieces of equipment on a large scale (Fonseca 1981). I mentioned earlier that the KT-1 chassis was used for the Cuban Libertadora 800. This was because of deficiences in the mechanical industry. To mention just one further example, at this stage of its development, Cuba did not possess a good technical capability in the field of hydraulic components which the production of the Libertadora 1400 required.

An important lesson of the Libertadora story is that it may be easier for a developing country to design a machine indigenously than to produce it on a large scale. To design a machine and make a prototype requires half a dozen qualified engineers and technicians and a workshop with a limited number of skilled workers. To produce a couple of hundred units of complicated machines a developed mechanical industry is needed with sophisticated machine tools, etc. A technical capability is also required – in the form of large numbers of engineers, technicans and skilled workers – within many sub-fields like electrical components, hydraulics, etc. The requirements of organizational capability are also large in order to co-ordinate the manufacture (and importation) of thousands of components all the way through to their final assembly.

The Libertadora story is inconsistent with the general practice in developing countries. Normally foreign designs are bought in the form of licences and a production capability is built up indigenously. In this case, the design achievement could not be followed up by indigenous production.

The fact that the Claas company were interested in producing the Libertadora, as well as their production and sales record, certainly indicates that the Cuban engineers had managed to develop a machine of a high quality in comparison with others existing on the world market. We have already seen that the Libertadora performed much better in Cuba than the KTP-1. In green cane harvesting, the Libertadora was superior to the MF 201. Hence, the basic design of the Libertadora was a great Cuban technical success. However, Cuba has not profited economically from this success. The only economic benefit for the Cubans was a reduced price on harvesters bought from Claas in the early 1970s. In fact, the evidence strongly suggests that the Cuban technical success was simply not supported by sufficiently astute economic skills, i.e. the policy-makers were surprisingly naive. To relinquish the patent rights to the Germans was certainly bad business for Cuba – and meant a breakthrough in harvester production for the Claas company. As a mimumun, the Cubans could have licensed the Germans – as capitalist design companies without production facilities
do. Then Cuba would have received a licence fee and could have kept the patent rights in the long run. Another possible option would have been to have had the Libertadora produced in an industrialized socialist country. A third possibility would have been to secure comprehensive technical assistance from Claas – or Massey-Ferguson – in order to make possible production of the Libertadora in Cuba. Since the Cubans had a very strong bargaining position – thanks to the basic design concept and the huge domestic market for harvesters – this option would probably have been possible.

h) The Massey-Ferguson 201 Harvester
The design of the Libertadora harvester was a result of the Cuban efforts to mechanize cane harvesting from the early 1960s. From the mid-1960s, Cuba was also assisted by the Soviet Union in this task. But still the breakthrough in mechanical cane-cutting in Cuba was achieved primarily by the Massey-Ferguson 201, i.e. by a machine which was designed and produced in Austrialia. However, the Claas-Libertadora contributed to this breakthrough, as seen on p.51.

A total of 452 Massey-Ferguson sugar cane harvesters were imported into Cuba during the 1970-8 period. These included – in addition to the 201 model – 21 MF 102 models (a smaller machine, produced between 1970-1 and 1976-7). One 205 model was also imported as soon as it was developed by Massey-Ferguson in 1978.[22] The 205 model is a more advanced and efficient machine than the 201, but only marginally different in basic design. The 205 has only been used in the Cuban research and development activities, and was never imported on a large scale. Only KTP-1 harvesters have been added to the total Cuban stock of harvesters since the late 1970s.

Except for one unit of the 205 model, no Massey-Ferguson machines were imported by Cuba after 1976. Accordingly, neither the MF 105, which superseded the MF 102 in 1977-8, nor the MF 305, which replaced the MF 205 in 1978-9, have been taken to Cuba, even for trials or testing (Abreu 1982: Hackett 1982). This is quite surprising, as the MF 305 has, according to the company itself, much more capacity than any other Massey-Ferguson machine, particularly in green cane.[23] In 1982, Massey-Ferguson were at an advanced stage of development of a new machine designed particularly for green cane harvesting (Hackett 1982).

Massey-Ferguson's total sales of sugar cane harvesters during the 1969-80 period is shown in Table 7.6. Almost 21 per cent of the total number of harvesters produced were exported to Cuba, which represented the largest foreign market. As a whole, the Massey-Ferguson company produced 1,059 units of the 201 model before it was replaced by the 205 model in 1977-8. Cuba bought 430, i.e. more than 40 per cent of them. The second largest foreign customer for this model was Brazil, with 57 units, followed by Argentina (48), Taiwan (41) and the USA (31) (Hackett 1982).[24]

Table 7.6
Massey-Ferguson Sales of Sugar Cane Harvesters by Model and Market, 1969-80

	MF 201	MF 205	MF 102	MF 105	MF 305	Total
Cuba	430	1	21	0	0	452
Other exports	292	103	166	9	57	627
Australia	337	77	547	90	39	1,090
Total sales	1,059	181	734	99	96	2,169

Source: Hackett (1982).

The importance of the Cuban market for the Massey-Ferguson Company is shown even more directly in Table 7.7, where I have included only those years in which Cuba was really active in the world market. During the period 1969-74, 430 units of the MF 201 were sold to Cuba. This represented 67 per cent of all Massey-Ferguson exports and 49 per cent of total sales of this model during the period. The Cuban market was much more important than the home market for the company. In other words, the Cuban market was absolutely crucial for Massey-Ferguson. This should imply a very strong bargaining position for the Cubans. Whether it was exploited or not is unclear.

Table 7.7
Massey-Ferguson Sales of Sugar Cane Harvesters by Model
and Market, 1969-74

	MF 201	*MF 102*	*Total*
Cuba	430	1	*431*
Other exports	209	49	*258*
Australia	234	255	*489*
Total sales	*873*	*305*	*1,178*

Source: Hackett 1982.

Obviously the transfer of technique from Australia to Cuba was highly successful in the sense that the MF 201 machine produced the breakthrough in combine harvesting in Cuba.

i) The KTP-1 Harvester
The development of the KTP-1 was a result of Cuban–Soviet co-operation. On the basis of a Cuban prototype, and with the help of both Cuban and Soviet knowledge and experience, this machine was developed for Cuban use in both Cuba and the Soviet Union. Initially it was produced in the Soviet Union.

Again, the deficiencies of the Cuban mechanical industry were the main reason for the manufacture outside Cuba. However, the location of production of the KTP-1 was later moved from the Soviet Union to Holguin in Eastern Cuba. The factory and its equipment were supplied by the Soviet Union and Soviet specialists also assisted in the construction work. The preparations for building the factory started in 1972 and it was inaugurated in July 1977. During 1977, 30 units were produced. The record for the following years was: 165 units (1978), 360 units (1979), 501 units (1980), 605 units (1981) and 602 units (1982) (AEC 1982: 163; 60 Aniversario 1982: 1). By the end of 1982 a total of 2,263 KTP harvesters had been produced. By 1981 the factory had reached its potential capacity of 600 units a year, after some difficulties in the starting-up phase.[25] Simultaneous with the starting of the Holguin factory, the production of KTP-1 harvesters for Cuba in the Soviet Union was reduced and it was terminated in 1979.

The Holguin factory is now the biggest cane harvester factory in the world; it is about three times as large as the Massey-Ferguson one. The KTP-1 is the cane harvester model which exists in the largest quantity in the world.

In the beginning of 1981 there were still about 50 Soviet technicians and specialists in the Holguin factory to assist the Cubans in the use of the equipment. About 300 components used in the harvester were also still imported from the Soviet Union. These included – of course – complex elements like the engine and hydraulic, electrical and pneumatic parts, but

2,200 of the 2,500 components necessary to produce a KTP-1 combinada are manufactured in the factory (*Trabajadores* 1981). Hence, the factory certainly does not only assemble the harvesters.

The design and production of the KTP-1 harvesters must be considered a fairly successful joint venture between Cuba and the USSR although this harvester is certainly not among the most productive ones in the world. We saw earlier that the KTP-1 had a considerably lower capacity than the Libertadora and the Massey-Ferguson. The latter models cut about 40 per cent more per unit than the KTP-1. They were simply much better machines than the KTP-1, as I have already argued. This fact, in combination with the increasing proportion of KTP-1 harvesters in the Cuban machine park, was also suggested to be the most important single factor explaining the decline in average combine harvester performance in Cuba after 1975.

However, the fact that the KTP-1 machines have a considerably lower capacity in a technical sense is not necessarily very important from an economic point of view. To make an economic evaluation, the comparison must also take into account labour intensity, life expectancy, operation costs, maintenance costs, price of the different machines, etc. For reasons mentioned in the Preface I do not have access to all these data. Therefore an economic efficiency analysis cannot be pursued. One important fact is, however, that the MF 201 and the Libertadora 1400 have to be paid for exclusively in foreign convertible currency while much of the cost of the KTP-1 machines is in Cuban pesos and the rest in rubles. Since convertible currency is very scarce in Cuba, this fact may be sufficient to explain that only Cuban machines (KTP-1) are now being added to the total stock of harvesters in the continuing mechanization efforts, in spite of the fact that they have a much lower capacity. Hence, the exclusive choice of the KTP-1 harvesters from around 1975 may have mitigated the Cuban balance of payments problem.

It should also be mentioned that the objective, eventually to produce the KTP-1 in Cuba, influenced the design of the machine in a certain way. Its degree of complexity had to be limited in relation to harvesters produced in industrially and technologically advanced countries because of the deficiencies of the Cuban mechanical industry. Perhaps it can also be argued that it was wise not to use an overly complex and sophisticated machine, given the prevailing degree of development of the skill of operators, maintenance and repair crew, etc. in the 1970s. Therefore the low performance of the KTP-1 is probably a reflection of deliberate simplification and downgrading in the design of the machine. This argument is supported by the fact that the Cubans around 1970 had been able to design the Libertadora, which is considerably more sophisticated than the KTP-1. This deliberate downgrading may have been rational in the 1970s, but is probably not so any longer due to an increased capability to use – i.e. operate, maintain and repair – harvesters as well as to produce complex capital goods.

Now the Cuban strategy should be to design and produce harvesters with a capacity comparable to the leading international models. Such a strategy would also prepare the ground for exports of cane harvesters in the future. And the only way to learn to build better harvesters is to carry out research, development and manufacturing within the country. This is a necessary but not sufficient condition for quality upgrading.

j) Cane Harvesters in Jamaica

None of the cane harvesters which were imported and tried in Jamaica in the early 1970s was introduced commercially. The reasons for this failed attempt to transfer technology differed from machine to machine. In the case of the whole-stalk harvester – the Cameco "Cost-Cutter" – the machine as such was not suitable for the majority of the cane fields in Jamaica. However, both the MF 201 and the Don Mizzi 740 combine harvesters proved capable of handling the crop and field conditions prevailing in most parts of Jamaica. The main obstacle to their commercial introduction was instead to be found in the socio-economic characteristics of Jamaican society. Given the low wages for manual harvest work, these machines were simply not competitive with the existing harvesting techniques. They were not privately profitable for the plantation owners in the short run.

Capability Generation – a Discussion

We concluded earlier in this chapter that a technological capability to use, i.e. to operate, maintain and repair, mechanical loaders was created both in Cuba and Jamaica. As regards the use of cane harvesters, this was so only in the case of Cuba. When it comes to design and production of cane harvesting equipment, practically no indigenous technological capability has been built up in Jamaica. In the case of Cuba, the picture is more heterogeneous.

Although an attempt to design and produce mechanical loaders was made in the early 1960s, these machines were very soon substituted by imports. Today no capability exists in this field. As regards cane cleaning equipment, a certain design capability has been built up since an indigenous device was developed in Cuba. It has also been manufactured on a large scale within the country.

Cane-cutting machines are the most important and complex equipment used in cane harvesting. Design and production efforts started in Cuba in the early 1960s, but they failed. After almost a decade of strong efforts, however, the Libertadora and the KTP-1 were designed in Cuba, with some foreign assistance. The Liberatadora was produced in West Germany and the KTP-1 in the Soviet Union and later on in Cuba, i.e. a production capability was also eventually built up. Accordingly, mechanization of cane-cutting was associated with a considerable generation of certain technical skills and capabilities in Cuba which had practically no equivalent in Jamaica. A domestic technological capability has been built up not only as far as the operation, maintenance and repair of combine harvesting machines is concerned, but also for developing and manufacturing such equipment.

The Reasons for Local Capital Goods Production Reconsidered
A number of reasons were given earlier for the value of domestic production of capital goods in developing countries. In Cuba the production of cane harvesting machinery has certainly served as a link between research and development activities and the productive system. Product innovations have increased productivity in sugar cane harvesting. Two examples are the cane cleaning stations and the Libertadora harvester with its impressive performance even in green cane harvesting. Design and production of capital goods intended for cane harvesting has, in this way, played a catalytic role in the innovative process of the econony.

The cane cleaning stations in Cuba are an example of custom designed equipment. In Jamaica, on the other hand, the lack of a capital goods industry made custom design impossible and precious water is used for cane cleaning purposes.

The Libertadora harvester was also custom designed for the harvesting system prevailing in Cuba in the late 1960s, i.e. it was constructed for green cane harvesting. This made necessary such a high degree of complexity of the machine that it could not be manufactured in Cuba at that time. This of course shows that indigenous capital goods production is *not* needed for custom design as such. The Cubans could – in principle – have kept the patent rights and licensed production to companies in other countries. They could also have continued to improve the design along this line without local manufacturing.

As we know, this strategy was not followed. After having given the patent rights to the Claas company, the Cubans designed a machine which was less complex and of a lower quality. The design of the KTP-1 was deliberately simplified, in order to make possible local production of harvesters in Cuba.

If the capital goods industry in Cuba had been advanced enough to produce the Libertadora on a large scale, this change of strategy would not have been motivated. The downgrading would not have been justified and the Cubans could now be producing a much better harvester than the KTP-1. They could possibly even have been at, or very close to, the global technological frontier. Local capital goods production is, in principle, not necessary for (custom) design of high quality machines. However, in this case, the deficiences of the mechanical industry led to a deliberate downgrading of the design of harvesters produced – and used – in Cuba.

Provided that the Cuban production of cane harvesters from the late 1970s was reasonably efficient, it has mitigated the country's extreme balance of payments problem through the replacement of imports. So far Cuba has not tried to export cane harvesters. However, if they decide to do so, export restrictions tied to foreign licence agreements will not be an obstacle thanks to the indigenous design capability. Another problem is that the low performance of the KTP-1 may exclude large-scale exports. If the Cubans had kept the control of the Libertadora, exports would certainly have been much easier.

In spite of domestic efforts to design and produce cane harvesters, the selection of which foreign techniques to import was not very wise in the 1960s. For example, useless Soviet harvesters were imported instead of the Massey-Ferguson 515, which would probably have performed much better. This can probably be explained, in part, by political ties and lack of convertible currency – the latter, in its turn, partly necessitating the close ties to the USSR. However, after the failure with the early Soviet harvesters, the Cubans decided to import the Massey-Ferguson 201 from Australia in the early 1970s. This proved to be a successful choice which possibily reflects an improved capability to select among machines available on the world market. It was this Australian machine which – together with the Libertadora – produced the breakthrough in mechanical harvesting in Cuba. This does not imply that the Cuban efforts to create a design and production capability were completely in vain. What this experience does indicate, however, is that it is not an easy task to build up a machine industry in a developing country. It also indicates that there is a long time lag between the initiation of the efforts and large-scale results for the development of highly complex equipment. A decade was necessary before an efficient combine harvester could be designed in Cuba; but almost two decades were needed before large-scale manufacturing of (KTP-1) harvesters could be carried out in Cuba – still with Soviet assistance.

The Cuban experience also shows that it is important to make a distinction between design capability and manufacturing capability. The Cubans did design a highly efficient harvester – the Libertadora – which could not however be produced indigenously. Several other harvesters which could be produced, as well as designed, in Cuba did not work satisfactorily. If the Cubans designed a harvester which they could also produce, then it did not perform well enough. If they designed a machine which worked well, on the other hand, then it could not be produced on a large scale in Cuba. Hence, if the machine was adapted to the demands of the cane and the cane fields, it could not simultaneously be adapted to the capability of the mechanical industry.[26]

This dilemma indicates that the deficiences in the production capability of the Cuban mechanical industry were a much more severe bottleneck than indigenous design capability. This was certainly true up to 1977 when production of the KTP-1 started in Cuba. However, even after that, the deficiencies in production capability were probably an important part of the explanation for the low relative performance of the KTP-1, since the eventual objective to produce the KTP-1 in Cuba had made it necessary to adapt the previous design by decreasing the degree of complexity. And after all, by 1970 the Cubans had already been able to design a very efficient machine – the Libertadora.

Hence, the superiority of the foreign-produced combine harvesters in relation to the KTP-1 cannot primarily be explained by the existence of a better design capability in industrialized capitalist countries, like West Germany and Australia. Instead the main explanation is to be found in deficiencies in the mechanical industry in Cuba – and possibly also in the Soviet Union – as compared to the capitalist countries mentioned.

An important lesson from the Cuban case is thus that the relation between the mechanization efforts and the character of the mechanical industry is crucial. However, it was also a reciprocal relation. First, the undeveloped character of the mechanical industry was a severe bottleneck. Secondly, the effort to mechanize cane harvesting was instrumental in supporting the development of the mechanical industry. Thus the policy of mechanization of cane harvesting in Cuba certainly had repercussions on other sectors of the economy. In particular, it meant the development of an indigenous capability to design and produce cane harvesting machines. In other words, it supported the development of an indigenous production of capital goods. However, there are certain qualifications to the arguments, presented on pp.122-3 in regard to the reasons for building up domestic production of capital goods in developing countries. First, there are often large costs associated with the generation of a capital goods industry. Second, the capital good industry is extremely heterogeneous.[27]

The large social costs involved in building up a capital goods industry are reflected in either higher production costs or lower performance during the learning period of locally produced capital goods, as compared with those available on the world market. The performance differences between the KTP-1 on the one hand and the MF 201 and the Libertadora 1400 on the other may be a good example.

My guess would be that the lower performance of the KTP-1 (about 40 per cent) is not counterbalanced by a lower production cost of a similar size.[28] If this is correct, the building up of harvester production in Cuba implies foregone present consumption during the learning period, and as we have seen, the gestation period in this case is not yet completed.

The fact that there are normally large social costs associated with the building up of a capital goods industry is a very important aspect. To the extent that the creation of a local technological capability depends on having a domestic capital goods industry, its development also implies foregoing present consumption in the interest of future generations.

The extreme heterogeneity of the capital goods sector means that only exceptionally few, very large and highly developed countries can in practice produce the full range of capital goods they need. The combined effect of the heterogeneity and the high cost is that "technical dependency" on imported capital goods cannot be avoided by any developing country – or even by any, except very few, of the industrialized ones. The cost would be too high. Hence "technical dependency" is necessary in many or most technically advanced sectors in nearly all countries. Such integration with the world market for capital goods is useful and necessary since the economic gains are so large.

Still, some capability to design and produce capital goods should be developed by most countries for the reasons presented earlier. The crucial policy issue is therefore which types of capital goods specific countries should concentrate upon – or avoid – producing. A selection has to be made of those sectors in which a capability shall be built up.

The capital goods industry in the advanced industrial countries is continuously becoming more specialized in response to various sources of scale economies, static as well as dynamic. One critical effect of this growing specialization is that the costs of building a capital goods industry have probably increased over time.[29] Conversely, the costs of withdrawing from the world market have increased through a rise in the costs of domestically produced capital goods in comparison with world market prices. It is therefore more important today than, say, in the 1930s, when the Soviet Union developed its capital goods industry, to emphasize selectivity in the creation or strengthening of a local capital goods industry.[30]

The intention of such a specialization strategy is to determine which kinds of capital goods a certain country should concentrate upon producing and which it should continue to import. To deal with this problem in the specific context of Cuba and Jamaica would require an analysis of their capital goods sectors as a whole which is outside the scope of this study. The rest of this section illustrates, in a general way only, the complexity of this strategic choice. This illustration deals with the problem of specialization mainly from one angle, i.e. the question of generation of technological capability.

Based upon considerations associated with *the international context*, it can be argued that a developing country should avoid concentrating on sectors in which global technical change is very dynamic (such as microelectronics). In such sectors it would be difficult or impossible for most developing countries with a limited R and D infrastructure to keep up with companies and countries that are technologically in the lead. It could be argued that technically stagnant, "stable" industries should also be avoided, since it may be difficult to use such an industry as a springboard for developing the technological capability of the country further. This is particularly true if the international demand for the equipment in question can only be expected to grow slowly.

It is within the framework of this international environment that the developing countries have to formulate their technology policies. Global technological trends and tendencies are crucial when discussing which sectors or branches developing countries are, or may become, competitive in through the development of a dynamic comparative advantage.

Based upon considerations associated with *the national context in developing countries*, one possible line of argument would be to suggest that a country should, at least initially, concentrate on those capital goods for which there is a substantial domestic demand.[31] At a stage where import substitution is a dominant objective, the country can deliberately make itself temporarily independent of international competition by means of, for example, trade barriers, thereby possibly saving foreign exchange. At a later stage, however, it is possible that the export of capital goods will become an important objective. The internal demand could then hopefully be used as a springboard for exports, i.e. it could provide time for the country to build up a particular technical capability which can later provide the basis for a dynamic comparative advantage.[32]

Suppose, however, that the sectors selected on the basis of the international and national context respectively are not the same. Perhaps the world demand is growing very slowly for those capital goods for which there is a large internal demand. As regards exports, the country could then face a strategic problem. A way of approaching this problem would be to use the concept of the "technological family".[33] A technological family consists of a number of products (e.g. capital goods) which are technologically convergent, i.e. similar skills and technical capabilities are needed in their production. Obvious examples are valves and pumps or electric motors and generators. Less obvious perhaps is the former close technological relationship between traditional sewing machines and firearms.

For a country facing the kind of strategic problem mentioned above, an analysis in terms of technological families may possibly be helpful in identifying other, technologically related, capital goods which the country (almost) has the capability to produce and for which there is a large or growing world demand. A technological family approach might facilitate planning and decision-making by identifying the industry's potential diversifications and by providing insights into the technological relatedness of different production alternatives at an early stage of investment planning. In addition it is normally an advantage if the production system is as flexible as possible so that transferring to a new product – in the same or a related family – is easy and cheap. This is particularly important for small countries where many products are produced in small series.

Of course, other considerations may well come into play when selecting which capital goods to produce. For instance, a large domestic market may not necessarily be a prerequisite for the initiation or expansion of production of a particular capital good. For a number of products with low barriers to entry, an export-oriented strategy may well be implemented soon after the initiation of production.

A Note on Costs and Benefits under Capitalism and Socialism

So far no attempt has been made in this study to evaluate the different choices of technique in Cuba and Jamaica in terms of costs and benefits. Because of the unavailability of data this cannot be done very concretely. Since capability generation is also important in this context, however, it is appropriate to devote some attention to it. The following discussion will be pursued in quite a general way since the necessary information has not been made available to me, particularly for Cuba. For example, it has not been possible to provide a detailed comparison between costs and benefits of cane harvest mechanization over time because of the lack of information on prices and production costs for various machines.

Since cane-cutting was mechanized in Cuba but not in Jamaica one could believe that it was profitable in Cuba but would have been unprofitable in Jamaica. This is incorrect. Mechanization of cutting was unprofitable in both cases – at least in the short and medium term.

No mechanization of cutting was introduced in Jamaica, mainly because in trials it was shown to be privately unprofitable for plantation owners in the short run. However, in Chapter 6 I criticized the short term perspective in the evaluation of the trials with mechanical harvesters. It was argued that the outcome would probably have been more in favour of large-scale introduction of combine harvesters if the costs and benefits had been estimated in a longer time perspective.

The mechanization achieved in Cuba cannot be attributed to short-term profitability considerations either. On the contrary, the strong efforts to mechanize cutting in Cuba in the 1960s certainly imposed significant costs. For example as many as 680 units of the indigenously designed MC-1 harvester were produced in Cuba, and more than 1,000 machines were imported from the Soviet Union.[34] None of these models worked satisfactorily. Hence, during the first decade the costs were quite substantial and the material benefits were practically nil.[35] Accordingly, mechanization of cutting in Cuba was certainly not socially profitable in the short and medium run.

Whether mechanization was profitable in Cuba and would have been profitable in Jamaica in a longer time perspective is not easy to say. However, it is crucial to note that the answer to the question of profitability is closely related to time. Profitability cannot be estimated without specifying the time perspective. The fact that the variable of time is central in a process of technical change should not be surprising. Generally speaking all large-scale processes of technical change and the generation of technical skills and capabilities are a matter not of years, but of decades. In the context of developing countries this gestation period is normally even longer than for the industrialized countries.

Why then was the policy of mechanization in Cuba so intensively pursued? Did the Cuban government make a cost-benefit analysis indicating that mechanization would be profitable in a period of 15 or 25 years? Given the fact that large-scale processes of technical change take decades in developing countries, this would have been a correct procedure.[36]

Such a long-term cost-benefit analysis was not, to my knowledge, made in Cuba. Public statements by Cuban government officials in the 1960s made it clear that the decision-makers had an overly optimistic view of the costs and benefits of cane-cutting mechanization and of the time period necessary to achieve it, while they greatly underestimated the problems of mechanization. The strong Cuban interest in mechanization from the early 1960s was accordingly partly based upon an incorrect perception of the problems and possibilities of mechanization. A second explanatory factor of the intense interest of the state was, as we saw in Chapter 6, the shortage of harvest labour. A third relevant factor was a non-economic one: the socialist–humanist objective to abolish the tough, non-stimulating job of manual cane-cutting.

In an attempt to explain the differences in the mechanisms of choice and implementation of combine harvesters between the two countries, the differences in structural conditions and in the character of the relevant actors were discussed in Chapter 6. If failures on the scale experienced in Cuba had occurred in Jamaica, the plantation owners would have changed policy in time or gone bankrupt. Private companies of this size in a capitalist country can normally not survive comprehensive losses during such a long time period.

But in Cuba the socio-economic system was socialist and the character of the relevant actor was very different. The interest of the state in mechanization not only remained in spite of the failures; the state also had possibilities to continue the efforts. In other words, the state in a socialist country can sometimes do things which are impossible for a private company in a capitalist country since the structural constraints to which they have to adapt are quite different. For example, the state – in both socialist and capitalist countries – can run an unprofitable activity for a longer period of time than a private company. Given that comprehensive processes of technical change and the building up of a technological capability take decades before they can become profitable, they can accordingly more easily be implemented by a socialist state than by a private capitalist company. *If* such processes are socially profitable in the long run, socialism would seem to have, in this respect, an advantage over capitalism. A longer planning horizon can be applied in socialist countries, i.e. larger risks can be taken and greater losses can be afforded.

However, there are many problems involved in generalizing from specific cases to the level of socio-economic systems. For example, on the basis of the experiences in Cuba and Jamaica, it can certainly not be argued that socialist countries in general are more "innovative" than capitalist countries. For one thing, the hierarchical nature and structure of the socialist planning system functions as an obstacle to the generation and innovation of new techniques. This problem seems to be larger for mature and industrialized socialist countries than for developing ones. The reason is that gains in average productivity can no longer be attained in these countries by putting previously idle resources into production and transferring labour from sectors with low productivity (e.g. agriculture) to sectors with higher productivity (e.g. industry). Productivity has to be increased mainly through the development and implementation of new and more productive techniques in various sectors.[37]

The experience in Cuba certainly also reveals that there can be disadvantages with socialism as compared to capitalism in regard to the introduction of new techniques. An example is the failure of the massive introduction of the Cuban MC-1 and the Soviet combine harvesters in the

1960s. Mistakes are, of course, a natural part of attempts to introduce new techniques. However, there is a risk that the size – and thereby the cost – of the mistakes becomes larger in centralized socialist countries since a decision to implement a machine often involves a larger number of production units than a similar decision by one or two capitalist plantation owners. This is a negative side of the fact that larger risks can be taken under socialism.

The size of the mistakes could of course have been reduced if the models implemented had been tested more thoroughly before the decision was made to introduce them on a large scale. This was not done in Cuba in the 1960s, probably because mechanization was so urgently sought by the government.

It has already been mentioned that during the 1960s large costs were connected with the failed attempts in Cuba. It took about ten years before the first non-learning benefits could begin to be reaped from the breakthrough in mechanical cutting. A calculation of the profitability of mechanization of cane-cutting in Cuba would require reliable data for a large number of variables, including capital and operation costs of the various machines, their expected life time, etc. In addition certain spin-off consequences would have to be estimated, for example the economic value of the skills and capabilities generated in the process of mechanization.

This generation of technological capability is often not included as a benefit when profitabilities of various choices of technique are estimated, although such benefits can – in the long run – be very substantial in economic terms. However, the costs of generating technical skills and capabilities are normally included in such calculations. An important question then becomes: how should the value of the generation of technological skills and capabilities in Cuba be estimated? Such questions are particularly difficult to answer since it can be argued that the generation of skills is a long-term process which has by no means been "completed". And in one sense it will never be completed. Learning benefits will continue to result from it for a long time. Questions and problems like these certainly do not lessen the complexity of carrying out a comparison of the costs and benefits of mechanization.

A corollary question then becomes: what should the appropriate time perspective be for an evaluation of a process of agricultural mechanization – or lack of it? Should it be 10, 20 or 30 years? The outcome of the evaluation is highly dependent upon this choice. Given that the building up of technical skills and capabilities takes decades, my tentative answer would be 30 years rather than 10. In other words, comprehensive processes of technical change involve the distribution of income between generations. We could, of course – more or less arbitrarily – decide that the appropriate time perspective for an evaluation should be, for example, 20 or 25 years. Even then the unavailability of necessary data makes it impossible for me to calculate whether or not the process of mechanization was socially profitable in Cuba. I cannot estimate whether the costs and benefits of the mechanization of cane-cutting in Cuba balanced in 1980 or will balance in 1985. Perhaps someone within the Cuban administration would be in a better position in regard to availability of data. However, even then, a long-term cost-benefit analysis would have serious deficiencies for the following reasons.

In the case of Cuba, cane harvest mechanization was closely related to a structural transformation of the economy, e.g. through making possible comprehensive reallocations of labour and through supporting the development of an indigenous capital goods industry. In other words, it is not enough to calculate costs and benefits of cane harvest mechanization as such. The costs and benefits of the – closely related – process of building up production of capital goods intended for the sugar harvest should also be included in a global evaluation. In addition the technological capability to produce cane harvest equipment may diffuse to other capital goods and thereby serve as a basis for mechanization of other sectors of agriculture and also for producing equipment for Cuban industry.

Cane mechanization played the role of a "big push" in Cuba. In Jamaica no sector played a similar role. Such processes of structural change have been immanent elements in the processes of development of the now industrialized countries. An early example is the textile industry in England during the Industrial Revolution. The English textile industry and the sugar sector in Cuba can both be regarded as "leading sectors". The relation between these leading sectors and those parts of the mechanical industry which produce equipment for them is similar in important ways in the two cases of England and Cuba.[38]

If processes of long-term structural transformation are necessary elements in development processes, their significance is much larger than what a narrow analysis in terms of costs and benefits can reveal. Like processes of capability generation, they are never "completed". All relative costs and prices are also changed in the process. Therefore calculations of costs and benefits over long periods of time are extremely difficult to carry out.[39] They could, given that data is available, be carried out for shorter periods, but such calculations would be of limited value since it can be argued that development *is* long-term structural change. If a short-term cost-benefit analysis had been carried out in Cuba in 1961-2, it would have shown that mechanization of cane-cutting would be economically non-viable and should not be pursued. If, on this basis, mechanization had not taken place, the capability generation and other structural changes induced by mechanization would thereby not have occurred.[40]

Technical Capability, Technical Dependency and Technology Gap

I will below present some remarks on the relations between technical capability, technical dependency and technology gap in the field of cane harvesting equipment in Cuba and Jamaica respectively. Technical capability has been extensively discussed above and will here be confined to design and production skills. The technology gap is the difference between the capability in a certain country and the global technology frontier in the same field or for the same product. Both capability and gap may increase at the same time for a certain country, if the global technology frontier moves faster than the rate of capability generation in the country. Also technical dependency can increase simultaneously with technological capability.

The international debate has often related the relatively weak local production and development of capital goods in the great majority of developing countries to the vicious circle of sustained technical dependency. This dependency is associated with the uneven distribution of research and development resources in the world as well as with the differences in the efficiency between developed and developing countries in the use of these resources. It is argued that it is the fundamental lack of technical capability in the developing countries which necessitates the transfer of technology, particularly in the more advanced sectors of production. Hence the capital goods industry is very central if a developing country is to overcome its technical dependency. The arguments for building up a capital goods industry in developing countries, which were presented earlier are therefore simultaneously arguments for technical independence.

In the case of Jamaica practically no capability to design and produce cane harvesting machines has been generated. This means that the technical dependency in this field is absolute and that the technology gap is equal to the difference between zero capability and the global technological frontier for various kinds of cane harvesting equipment.

In the case of Cuba considerable capability for the design and production of cane harvesting equipment has been generated during the recent decades. In the field of cane cleaning the technological gap approaches zero and technical dependency is negligible. For mechanical loaders neither design nor production capability has been built up in Cuba. This means a large gap and considerable dependency. However, the significance of this is decreasing with the growth of combine harvesting which susbstitutes for mechanical loaders as well as manual cutters.

Starting in the early 1960s, a considerable capability in regard to design and production of mechanical cane-cutters has been generated. Around 1970 the technology gap was quite small in combine harvester design and towards the later 1970s production capability started to mature.

The research and development efforts in the field of cane harvesters have continued in Cuba. At the end of the 1970s an improved version of the KTP-1 – called KTP-2 – was tested with satisfactory results. Simultaneously research work on a third generation of KTP harvesters is being carried out. Six engineers, some technicians and 40 skilled workers are dedicated to this investigatory work, but a prototype does not yet exist (Rodriguez 1982). It may be questioned whether the Cubans will manage to keep up with other producers of combine harvesters, since the number of engineers involved in research and design is so small.

Serial production of the KTP-2 had not yet begun in 1984. This indicates quite a long time-lag between the generation of a prototype and its production on a large scale. This time-lag is probably explained by the comprehensive and complicated changes in the work and lay-out of the Holguin factory which are required for the production of the KTP-2. Again, production capability – or rather rigidity of the production system – seems to be a bottleneck.

The result is that the design of the combine harvester which is still produced in Cuba is now more than a decade old. And these KTP-1 machines have a considerably lower capacity than the foreign ones of the same generation. Simultaneously combine harvester producers in other countries continuously improve their designs. Thus an important objective for Cuba is still to develop and manufacture a harvester with a performance comparable to the foreign produced ones. In other words, there is still a technology gap between Cuba and producers of combine harvesters in industrialized countries. In terms of design it was small around 1970, but has widened since then. In regard to production the gap decreased considerably when the harvester factory in Holguin started to operate in 1977. However, recently it has increased again and will continue to do so unless Cuba manages to manufacture more sophisticated machines in the near future. Hence, there is a risk that the Cubans will continue to lag behind producers of harvesters in other countries in terms of the quality of the machines. Production of combine harvesters may in this way remain a permanent infant industry, which implies large costs to society in the long run.

We saw earlier in this chapter that several machines – Cuban as well as foreign – were tested and used simultaneously in the late 1960s and early 1970s. This strategy was quite successful. A breakthrough in mechanical harvesting was achieved and the design gap narrowed. The fact that this pluralistic approach was abandoned in the latter half of the 1970s may be an important explanation of the fact that the gap has started to increase again. A way out would then be to expose the domestic designers and producers more intensively to achievements in other countries. Technical journals, conferences and technical fairs are certainly not enough. Perhaps one useful supplement would be to enter some sort of co-operation agreement with one of the leading foreign producers. Due to the extraordinary bargaining power which Cuba has in this field, the terms of such an agreement could be quite advantageous.

EMPLOYMENT CONSEQUENCES OF THE CHOICE OF TECHNIQUE

In Chapter 6 it was argued that the employment situation is an important determinant of the choice of technique. The decreasing general rate of unemployment in Cuba during the 1960s combined with a serious sectorial shortage of labour for the sugar harvest led to a strong interest in mechanization among all actors in Cuba. The very high rate of unemployment in Jamaica was a basis for resistance to mechanization of harvesting among certain actors, notably the labour unions and the state. Therefore mechanization was much more of a conflict issue between actors in capitalist Jamaica than in socialist Cuba.

In this section we will consider the employment consequences of mechanization of sugar cane harvesting. A mechanical cane loader and a combine harvester are capable of replacing about 10 and 30 to 50 manual harvest workers respectively.[41] Therefore the consequences (in terms of quantity of employment) of mechanization of cane harvesting are substantial; the number of jobs affected is significant. The quality of employment, i.e. working conditions and qualification requirements of those employed, is also strongly affected by the choice of technique in this sector since the character of the jobs is quite different in manual and mechanical harvesting

Consequences of the choice of technique for the quantity and quality of employment will be dealt with in the following part of this chapter. A discussion of the interests and strategies of workers and unions under capitalism and socialism will then be presented on pp.153-7. The latter section will also include an empirically founded critique of the notion of "appropriate technology".

Quantity of Employment

Table 4.3 showed that the number of professional cane-cutters in Cuba decreased from almost 400,000 to approximately 80,000 between 1958 and 1970. The resulting shortage of harvest labour could not in the short run be met by mechanization and therefore large quantities of workers from other sectors of the economy were mobilized, resulting in inefficient harvesting and a very high opportunity cost (see p.42).

As an alternative to mechanization and mobilization, material incentives, a third possibility, might have mitigated the problem of harvest labour shortage. Wages and other renumerations of the workers could have been raised to stop the flight from cane harvesting. At least during most of the 1960s, when the general unemployment rate was still considerable, this could have been a viable method of keeping the supply of professional harvest workers higher and thereby partly solving the problem. However, this possibility of using material incentives was not practised in the 1960s or early 1970s, for ideological reasons. The dominant ideology in this period was to create "the new man" and use moral incentives rather than material ones. Thus, a means that would probably have been more efficient from an economic point of view was ruled out for ideological reasons. From the late 1970s onwards – when the ideology had changed – such material incentives were used to increase the efficiency of the harvest work. Manual harvest labour was paid according to task rates and the most productive ones could earn as much as an engineer. Automobiles and other shortage commodities were also distributed to productive cane harvest workers.

Cane-loading in the 1960s
We have seen that the attempts to mechanize cane-cutting in Cuba failed during the 1960s. In the case of loading, however, testing started in 1963 and a viable machine was available from 1964. In Jamaica the first experiments with mechanical loaders had already started in 1957 and in 1961 large-scale conversion to mechanical loading was initiated. In other words, testing started later in Cuba, but thereafter the process of mechanization went quicker than in Jamaica.

In Cuba the degree of mechanization of loading increased from 20 per cent in 1964 to almost 85 per cent in 1970. In 1966, 1970 and 1976 respectively, approximately 3,700, 5,460 and 6,000 mechanical loaders were in operation in Cuba. If a mechanical loader is operated by one man and replaces ten manual loaders, roughly 33,000, 49,000 and 54,000 workers were replaced in the years mentioned. Accordingly, the mechanization of loading considerably decreased the shortage of harvest labour. A shortage remained, however, and the mechanization of loading in Cuba did not lead to unemployment of professional harvest workers.

In Cuba the initiative to mechanize loading was taken by the state and its agencies and in Jamaica the WISCO company was the initiator. WISCO was the largest cane and sugar producer in Jamaica and a subsidiary of the British Tate & Lyle company. This of course reflects the differing array of actors in the sugar industries of socialist Cuba and capitalist Jamaica (see Figure 6.6). In Cuba there was a consensus of interest in mechanization of loading from approximately 1961, while in Jamaica small cane farmers and, in particular, workers and unions were opposed to mechanization.

The workers and unions in Jamaica had good reasons to oppose mechanization. First of all, the general unemployment rate in Jamaica was around 15 per cent of the labour force in the early 1960s. Secondly, the first large-scale conversion at Monymusk estate led to considerable displacement of workers. Those displaced had severe problems in finding alternative employment (see pp.64-6).

The two cases illustrate the difference in the socio-economic dynamics of mechanization in a labour-surplus economy and one characterized by a sectorial scarcity of labour and a decreasing general unemployment rate. In Cuba mechanization of loading in the 1960s partly and gradually mitigated the problem of scarcity of harvest labour and it created no major socio-economic problems. In Jamaica it created a lot of human suffering and social problems in addition to lowering harvesting costs for the estate owners and raising wages for those workers that could remain employed.

Cane-cutting in the 1970s
Since no large-scale mechanical cutting resulted from the trials with combine harvesters in Jamaica in the early 1970s, no displacement of harvest workers has been caused by such machines. Accordingly, more or less the same number of manual cutters are needed today as in earlier periods, although burning before harvesting as well as decreasing cane

production since 1966 may have reduced the number needed.

In Cuba 50 per cent of the sugar harvest in 1981 was cut by means of combine harvesters (see Table 4.4). This has liberated a large number of manual harvest workers for other sectors of the economy, as shown in Table 7.8. For example, the number of cane-cutters employed in peak periods of the sugar harvest decreased from 274,000 in 1971 to 175,600 in 1975. The quantity of cane harvested in both these years was approximately 52 million tons. In 1979 the number of cane-cutters had decreased further to 126,400, although the quantity of cane harvested was 73 million tons in that year. A major explanation for this decline in the number of cane-cutters was that the degree of mechanization of cutting increased from 3 per cent in 1971 to 25 per cent in 1975 and further to 42 per cent in 1979 (see Table 4.4). Other factors have however also affected employment in cane-cutting.

Before continuing discussing the data presented in Table 7.8, it must be stressed that column (2) shows the total number of cane-cutters employed in *peak* periods of the sugar harvest. Therefore these figures are not comparable to the ones in Table 4.3, which indicate the number of professional cane-cutters.

Column (2) in Table 7.8 does not show the total number of man-days executed by manual cane-cutters in the various *zafras* as I do not have access to such information. However, let us assume that there was a constant ratio between the total number of man-days executed and the number of cane-cutters employed in peak periods of the harvest in the various *zafras*. Then the calculations presented in column (8) can be regarded as an index of productivity of manual cane-cutters.[42] This index shows that the productivity of manual cane-cutters increased by 84 per cent between 1970 and 1979. Most of this increase occurred in the first half of the decade. The decreasing number of cane-cutters employed is certainly not explained exclusively by the increasing degree of mechanization. The rising productivity of manual cane-cutters is another important explanatory factor.

The following calculation is intended to show the approximate relative importance of mechanization and increased manual cane harvester productivity respectively, as factors explaining the decline in the number of manual cane-cutters needed. Let us assume that the productivity index (column 8 in Table 7.8) had not changed between 1971 and 1979, but remained 1.11 tons per manual cane-cutter per day.[43]

Under the assumption above, $1.11 \times 182 = 202.02$ tons of cane had been cut by each manual cane-cutter during the whole 1979 harvest. Then 382,635 (77,300,000/202.02) cane-cutters would have been needed during the harvest peak to cut the whole harvest manually. However, 42 per cent of the harvest was cut mechanically. To cut the remaining 44,800,000 tons manually 221,760 (44,800,000/202.02) cane-cutters would have been needed. 126,400 manual cane-cutters were actually employed. Thus 160,875 cutters were "replaced" by mechanization and 95,360 were

Table 7.8
Number of Manual Cane-cutters Employed and Amount of Cane Cut Manually in Cuba, 1970-79

(1) Year	(2) Number of cane-cutters employed in peak periods of harvest (thousands)	(3) Total amount of cane harvested (million tons)	(4) Cane cut manually (%)	(5) Amount of cane cut manually (3) × (4) (million tons)	(6) Amount of cane cut per cutter and zafra (5) / (2) (tons)	(7) Length of zafra (days)	(8) Index of amount of cane cut per cutter and day (6) / (7) (tons)
1970	350.0	81.5	99	80.7	230.6	217	1.06
1971	274.0	52.2	97	50.6	184.7	166	1.11
1972	210.5	44.3	93	41.2	195.7	153	1.28
1973	229.0	48.2	89	42.9	187.3	135	1.39
1974	200.3	50.4	82	41.3	206.2	128	1.61
1975	175.6	52.4	75	39.3	223.8	123	1.82
1976	153.3	53.8	68	36.6	238.7	130	1.84
1977	139.1	60.3	64	38.6	277.5	141	1.97
1978	153.9	69.6	62	43.1	280.0	168	1.67
1979	126.4	77.3	58	44.8	354.4	182	1.95

Sources: Column (2) Pollitt (1981: Table 8) (his source is "Memorias", Ministerio de la Agricultura, Havana, 1980); (3) Table 4.2; (4) Table 4.4; (7) Table 7.1.

"replaced" by the increasing productivity of the remaining cutters. Of the 256,235 cane-cutters "replaced", 62.8 per cent ($160,875 \times 100/256,235$) were "replaced" by mechanization; 37.2 per cent ($95,360 \times 100/256,235$) were "replaced" by increasing manual cane-cutter productivity. Hence, mechanization was the more important factor, but increased cane-cutter productivity was also of considerable importance in explaining the decline in the number of manual cane-cutters needed.

If we assume that one combine harvester replaces 40 harvest workers, then $3,000 \times 40 = 120,000$ workers were replaced by mechanization between 1970 and 1982. This should be compared to the figure 161,000 in the calculation above, which was based upon the number of cane-cutters employed in *peak* periods of the harvest. Hence, the number of cane-cutters which was replaced through the introduction of combine harvesters in Cuba can roughly be said to have been between 120,000 and 160,000 during the 1970s.

The size of the total Cuban labour force was 2.6 million in 1970 and 3.3 million in 1979 (Brundenius 1983: table 1). Hence job displacement because of combine harvesters represented between 4.5 and 6 per cent of the 1970 labour force.[44] The labour force in Cuban "Agriculture, Fishing and Forestry" in 1970 was 790,000 (Brundenius 1983: table 1). This means that the diffusion of combine harvesters could be said to have replaced between 15 and 20 per cent of the agricultural labour force in 1970. This is also reflected in a drastic decline in agricultural employment. It decreased to 716,000 workers in 1979, i.e. by 9.4 per cent as compared to 1970. Agricultural employment decreased from 30 per cent to 22 per cent of the total labour force between 1970 and 1979. In fact, "the sharp decrease in agricultural employment . . . is probably one of the most drastic structural changes in employment to have occurred in Latin America during the 1970s" (Brundenius 1983: 66).

Open unemployment in Cuba was 1.3 per cent in 1970 and gradually increased to more than 5 per cent in 1977-9, before dropping to 3.4 per cent in 1981. This coincided with the replacement of between 120,000 and 160,000 sugar harvest workers through combine harvesting. It could therefore be argued that the decline in the number of cane-cutters needed was causing the increased unemployment.

However, on closer examination one finds that the increase in unemployment in the 1970s coincided with the entrance of large numbers of women into the labour force. The female labour force more than doubled from 482,000 in 1970 to 1,108,000 in 1980 (Brundenius 1983: table 3). In addition, the labour force increased much faster than the population during the 1970s. Furthermore, women have a much higher rate of unemployment than men. For men it was 2.5 per cent in 1979 as compared with 12 per cent for women (Brundenius 1983: table 4). Since women have never worked as manual cane-cutters, and since the increase in unemployment was largely female unemployment, the increase in unemployment in Cuba during the 1970s cannot be considered to have been directly caused by the introduction of sugar cane combine harvesters. Of course, there may have been some substitution.

It could also be mentioned that employment in non-agricultural sectors increased considerably in Cuba during the 1970s. Between 1970 and 1979 employment in manufacturing and mining increased from 533,000 to 652,000, i.e. 119,000 jobs. In construction it increased from 157,000 to 256,000, i.e. 99,000. In services the increase was from 622,000 to 934,000. Hence 312,000 new service jobs were created, many of them in health and education (Brundenius 1984: table A1.1).

Previously it was mentioned that the productivity of manual cane-cutters increased by 84 per cent between 1970 and 1979. This may have been caused by a number of factors of varying importance. One may have been the increasing cane yield per hectare, particularly between 1972 and 1973 and in the late 1970s (see Table 4.2), since an increased yield per hectare normally increases the productivity of manual cutters. The gradual implementation of dry cleaning centres from the late 1960s onwards may also have contributed. Thanks to these, the manual cutters did not need to clean the cane stalks nor cut them into pieces. This increased their productivity considerably (see pp.42-4). Another possible factor is that the most productive cutters remained when the number of cutters decreased. The intensity of work may also have increased due to the new system of material incentives for cutters introduced in the late 1970s, and mentioned earlier in this section.

My guess is, however, that the introduction of pre-harvest burning was the most important factor, since burning of cane fields may as much as double the productivity of cane-cutters. Burning was also introduced in the 1971 *zafra* and diffused rapidly during the years following, i.e. it was simultaneous with the rapid increase in the productivity index of cane-cutters during the first half of the 1970s.

As argued earlier in this chapter, the breakthrough in mechanical cutting could have occurred earlier if burning had been introduced in the early 1960s. In addition manual cane-cutter productivity would probably have increased simultaneously. Hence, the fact that burning was introduced so late in Cuba was, in all likelihood, detrimental to the Cuban sugar harvest with severe consequences also for the rest of the economy.

On the other hand, the proportion of burning before harvesting decreased during the latter half of the 1970s. However, the potential negative impact on cane-cutter productivity was obviously counterbalanced by other factors, e.g. the new incentive system.

To summarize the discussion of manual cane-cutter productivity, it is obvious that there was a large potential for increasing it during the 1960s. If burning of cane fields and improved material incentives had been introduced in the first half of the 1960s, this potential could have been realized earlier and the negative consequences of the shortage of harvest labour during the following period would have been considerably mitigated.

Quality of Employment

The choice of technique also affects the quality of employment. Qualification requirements were dealt with earlier in the section on generation of technological capability. It was concluded that mechanization of cane-cutting led to a considerable generation of technical skills in Cuba which had practically no equivalent in Jamaica. These skills concerned operation, maintenance and repair of cane harvesting machines as well as their design and manufacture. Here I want merely to add a few comments on working conditions in sugar cane harvesting as a basis for the discussion of labour union strategies in the following section.

Manual cane-cutting and loading is an arduous and dirty task which needs almost no qualifications except physical strength and power of endurance. Mechanical cutting and loading, on the other hand, require skills to use – i.e. to operate, maintain and repair – equipment of a more or less complicated character. These tasks are also much less physically demanding than the manual work tasks. Hence mechanization and automation do not always lead to a dequalification of the workers and a degradation of work as is sometimes argued. Our example indicates that this is not true, at least not for mechanization of sugar-harvesting. Since almost no qualifications are needed in manual cane-cutting and loading, this task cannot become dequalified.

The Different Interests and Strategies of Workers and Unions in Capitalist Jamaica and Socialist Cuba

On the basis of the previous section, I will now – in a comparative manner – discuss the role, interests and strategies of the workers and unions in relation to choice of technique in sugar cane-cutting in Cuba and Jamaica. I will also relate this discussion to the notion, or rather ideology, of "appropriate technology", which has intensively been put forward in the field of technology in developing countries during the last decade – mainly by authors from industrialized countries. The discussion in this section partly has the character of a generalization from the two cases (countries) to the level of socio-economic system and is therefore somewhat speculative.

In Figure 6.3 we can see that the workers and their unions opposed mechanization of cane-cutting (and loading) in all situations where the structural environment was characterized by capitalism and large unemployment. But as a result of the structural changes accompanied by the revolution in Cuba, the workers left the heavy task of cane-cutting on a massive scale as soon as – or even before – alternative employment opportunities were created. The Cuban sugar workers and their union had no interest in opposing mechanization in the 1960s and 1970s. On the contrary, they had much to gain from it. There were no longer any social obstacles to mechanization in Cuba. In Jamaica the structure of the socio-economic system it still such that the workers and their unions must defend the machete and fight against mechanization to remain employed and fed. Obviously the same kind of actor has various interests in different structural environments.

During the last decade the concept of "appropriate technology" has been fashionable. The background is the huge unemployment in many developing countries. To solve or mitigate this problem it has been proposed that "appropriate", in the sense of more labour-intensive, techniques should be used instead of capital-intensive ones. I want to stress that I am here discussing "appropriate technology" only in the sense of (more) labour-intensive techniques, although the concept may mean very different things to various people.[45]

If the labour-intensive technique is simultaneously the more economically efficient one, it should of course be used. And this normally also happens if the decision-making actors function rationally. If such a technique is not implemented, the reason must be that there is no *social carrier* of the labour-intensive technique. If there is a conflict between labour intensity and efficiency, some advocates of appropriate technology still argue that the labour-intensive technique should be used. In other words, they prefer employment maximization *instead* of output maximization.

A combine harvester replaces 30 to 50 manual cane-cutters. Thus the difference in terms of labour intensity is quite large between the two techniques for cutting cane. Given the low wages in Jamaica around 1970, it was not profitable for the plantation owners to mechanize cutting. The machete combined with mechanical loading was more profitable in a private sense than combine harvesters in the short run. And in Cuba, mechanization was certainly not profitable – in any sense – during the first ten years of failed efforts. Thus the machete created much more employment and was more profitable than combine harvesters in the short run. In other words, the choice between the machete and the combine harvester is not a conflict case between employment (labour intensity) and profitability in the short run. Advocates of "appropriate technology" – in the sense specified above – would therefore favour the choice of the machete over combine harvesters, and they could consider their case strengthened by the fact that their strategy coincides with the interests of the workers and unions.

This strategy of appropriate technology can actually be considered a somewhat more theoretically elaborated version of the position spontaneously taken by the Jamaican workers and unions. Conversely the Jamaica workers follow in practice the strategy of appropriate technology.

So far, I have argued only in static terms. In the long run, i.e. in a dynamic perspective, the picture becomes much more complex and quite different. The following five considerations seem to be relevant in such a dynamic context.

1) If one assumes a wage considerably above subsistence level – as for example in Australia – it is clear that the machete is an inferior technique in

terms of economic efficiency and profitability.[46] Thus the continued profitability of the machete in Jamaica presupposes the permanance of a low wage level. In Chapter 3 it was mentioned that there is a trend towards increasing degrees of mechanization on a global scale. Given the competition on the world market, it can, in the long run, therefore be doubted that the machete will even be efficient enough to generate sufficient income to support the people engaged in cane-cutting. At the same time we know that, in the long run, increased productivity – and thereby real wages for the workers – is closely connected to technical progress.

2) To oppose mechanization in this case implies a defence of a technique requiring inhuman jobs which the workers reject even at the price of being unemployed. It gives no hope for the liberation of man from an extremely heavy, monotonous and boring job.

3) Simultaneously, the jobs created *through* the mechanization of cane-cutting, i.e. jobs as operators, repair crew, technicians, etc. are much more stimulating and require more skills than manual cane-cutting. Thus, mechanization in this case means a tremendous humanization of production and of social life in general. This has a value as such, although mechanization also creates a basis for increasing productivity and wages in the long run.

4) It would be ridiculous to try to stick to the machete in socialist Cuba, since people were not willing to carry out the manual cane-cutting when alternative sources of income became available.

5) In Cuba mechanization of cane-cutting means the beginning of a process of technical progress which will probably diffuse to other sectors of the economy. It is part of a process of structural change of the economy. In Jamaica the choice of the machete creates no basis for a future spiral of technical change. Hence, the strategy of "appropriate technology", as defined above, in this case implies a perpetuation of a technologically static situation.

For these five reasons absence of the mechanization of cutting will lead to disastrous results in the long run for the workers. It implies a continuation of underdevelopment both of the country and of the workers. The unions in capitalist Jamaica, and the advocates of appropriate technology in the sense indicated, are trapped by the socio-economic system. But they are trapped in very different ways.

The workers and unions in Jamaica are, for structural reasons, "forced" to defend the machete – an obsolete and inhuman technique offering no prospect for a better life. For them, there is a conflict of interest between employment and survival in the short run, and humanization of work and increased productivity – for a few of them – in the long run. However, if one is only seasonally employed and half fed there *is* only a short run. Their time horizon can be only one year or less. In other words, they are trapped by capitalism for material reasons. This is a modern equivalent to Luddism in England during the Industrial Revolution. In a socialist environment the workers are released from such a trap and there is no need for them to defend an inhuman technique. Thus, in the long run, or in socialist societies, the workers have very different interests as compared to their short-term interests under capitalism.

The strategy of appropriate technology does coincide with the interest of the workers, but only with the short-term interest of workers in capitalist countries with a large unemployment. In the long run, or in socialist societies, the workers have very different interests. Thus the advocates of the appropriate technology strategy are trapped by capitalism in a very different sense. They are simply unable to think in terms of other socio-economic systems than the liberal capitalist one. Their minds are trapped for ideological reasons since they implicitly consider this system as the only possible one and since they think of unemployment as exclusively technologically determined within this context. These are important hidden assumptions immanent in the ideology of "appropriate technology". They are always implicit but not always conscious. It could be argued that the notion of "appropriate technology" is an ideological or pseudo-theoretical expression of a modern form of Luddism.

The following quotation may be illuminating in this context:

> It took both time and experience before the workpeople learnt to distinguish between machinery and its employment by capital, and to direct their attacks, not against the material instruments of production, but against the mode in which they are used.
> (Marx 1967: 429)

Essentially the differing interests of the same actor (workers and unions) in various structural environments (capitalism and socialism) and between the short and the long term in capitalist countries, boils down to a problem of distribution of income. And the main means of distributing income is – in these cases – economic rewards from employment.

In Cuba the problem of distribution was gradually mitigated during the 1960s through a decrease in unemployment and through the implementation of a welfare system. Employment was offered to those previously unemployed, and to many of those employed in sugar cane agriculture through expansion of other sectors in the economy. Partly, this alternative employment was productive and partly it implied lower productivity in these sectors, i.e. disguised unemployment. But the problem of distribution was mitigated in the sense that practially everyone was given a reasonable income and some degree of social security. Accordingly, if the problem of distribution could be alleviated for example through employment expansion in other sectors – under capitalist or socialist conditions – the sugar workers and unions in Jamaica would have no interest in opposing the mechanization of cane-cutting. If the problem of distribution cannot be solved, the workers and unions will continue to oppose mechanization.

In a survey covering 35 cane growing regions, it has been shown that there is a strong correlation between the standard of living of agricultural workers and the degree of mechanization of sugar cane harvesting. Although the study says nothing about the causal relationship, it shows that a low degree of mechanization goes with a low standard of living and vice versa (Fauconnier 1983). This places workers and unions in an extremely difficult dilemma. If they are not successful in their resistance to mechanization – because of a weak position of power – it will have disastrous consequences for most of them in terms of increased unemployment in the short run. If they are successful, it will have disastrous effects for the workers in the long run – in terms of the permanence of a low, or even decreasing, real wage level as well as extremely heavy and monotonous work. Hence the prospects for cane harvest workers in Jamaica are not bright.

The most viable long-run strategy for the workers and unions is not to fight the machines as such, but to transform their struggle to the social and political level. This would, of course, include a fight for securing compensation in case some workers were replaced by machines. However, it must also include a struggle as regards the power over *how* to introduce and use the harvesters. The workers should fight for the power to control the pace of mechanization themselves. In this way they could make sure that mechanization is introduced only gradually and never faster than the pace at which a shortage of labour emerges. In this way not a single worker would be put out of work by the machines, but the workers would still benefit from the gradual mechanization in terms of higher wages and better working conditions. In a country such as Jamaica where the unions are very strong and much of the cane production is state controlled, such a power struggle should have better prospects than in many other capitalist cane-producing countries.

The problem discussed in this section certainly also has its parallels in industrialized countries with increasing structural unemployment, simultaneous with the introduction of increasing numbers of computers and robots. At the same time, however, the discussion here illustrates that unemployment is not principally technologically determined as those advocating "appropriate technology" seem to believe.[47] On the contrary, unemployment is – just like income distribution – first and foremost a socio-economic and political problem.

Notes

1. This is particularly so for the period 1973-9.
2. Possible reasons behind the changes in combine yield will be discussed later in the chapter.
3. However, we do not know to what extent the Libertadora and the KTP-1 were actually used in green cane during various years. Probably Libertadora was used in green cane to a larger extent than the KTP-1. The fact that only KTP-1 machines were used in the Havana province in the 1970s points in this direction

since almost all cane was burnt in this province (Abreu 1981).

4. Brian Pollitt directed my attention to these aspects in a letter dated 22 February 1983.

5. The argument above is, however, partly contradicted by the fact that the Libertadoras were used mainly in the Eastern provinces which have the lowest yield per hectare. On the other hand the province of Havana had the highest average yield per hectare and there only KTP-1 harvesters were used until 1982. It should also be mentioned that the capacity of a certain model often increases with increasing yield per hectare but after a certain point it starts decreasing again. For example, I have been told that the KTP-1 has difficulty in cutting cane fields with more than 100 tons per hectare. But this is also said to be true for the MF 201 (Abreu 1981).

6. Even if throughput in Cuba is respectable for developing countries, it is still very low as compared to Australia. In addition to being a problem, this must, however, be considered a *possibility*: it points to a potential for increasing the amount of cane cut mechanically without increasing the number of machines.

7. Pollitt also points to this factor as a partial reason for the decline in combine yields (Pollitt 1981: 6). However, this explanatory factor is not relevant for the Massey-Ferguson 201 model, since it is not used in green cane.

8. At the same time, such a choice serves as a generator of further technical capability which can also be used in other sectors of the economy.

9. Costs and benefits in relation to learning and skill generation will be discussed later in this chapter; see pp. 140-4.

10. Capital goods are here defined as ISIC group 38, excluding durable consumer goods such as home electronics and private automobiles.

11. A number of reasons why an autonomous capability in the capital goods industry is important for developing countries have been outlined in a description of the research programme within which the present study has been carried out. This section is, to a large extent, based upon that programme description (RPI 1983: 4-9).

12. Recent research also clearly demonstrates the positive relationship between innovative activity and economic performance.

13. The engineering sector includes, in addition to capital goods, durable consumer goods such as home electronics and private automobiles.

14. These qualifications to the arguments as regards the importance of building up a capital goods sector in developing countries will be discussed below: see pp. 136-40.

15. To what extent – if any – the production was based on import of components is not known to me.

16. All costs are in current pesos. For import data during the 1964-70 period, see Table 4.5.

17. Recently, local assembly under licence has started of the Broussard push-pile loader. However, the value added locally in Jamaica is quite small (Lee 1983).

18. This would, however, have required burning of the cane fields before harvesting.

19. It is an example of custom design as discussed earlier; the cane cleaning stations were adapted to natural conditions as well as to the prevailing capability of the Cuban capital goods industry.

20. Dry cleaning stations could, of course, also have been brought from Cuba.

21. It was not before 1971 that the systematic burning of cane fields was started in Cuba.

22. This unit was not included in Table 4.11.

23. It cuts green cane in Queensland, Australia, at about half the productivity compared to burnt cane (Hackett 1980). It should be recalled that the Claas-Libertadora – which Cuba practically gave away – is probably still the best machine in green cane.

24. Of the machines sold to the USA, 24 went to Texas and three or four each to Florida and Hawaii (Hackett 1984).

25. If 600 harvesters are produced per year, and the life expectancy is five years, then Cuba will have a constant machine park of 3,000 units in the future. Thus, the amount of cane harvested mechanically cannot increase from the present level, unless the yield per harvester increases. However, as we saw in note 6 above, a considerable potential for such an increase exists.

26. This generalization seems to be valid for all cane-cutting machinery until 1977, when indigenous production of the KTP-1 began. However, it is not valid for dry cleaning stations, for instance.

27. The rest of the following section is based on RPI (1983: 10-12 and 21-3).

28. However, when I asked about the cost of production in an interview with the management of the KTP-1 factory in Holguin, I was told that this figure was a secret. Without this information, it is impossible to make a comparison of the economic efficiency of various harvester models. However, the mere fact that the cost of production is kept secret creates the impression that the cost per unit is not sufficiently low to counterbalance the lower performance of the KTP-1.

29. In other words, it is likely that a relatively greater amount of present consumption needs to be sacrificed today, in order to build up a capital goods industry, than was the case in the past.

30. In addition, the Soviet Union is an exceptional case because of its size.

31. To take the Cuban case as an example, the choice of equipment for sugar cane agriculture and processing would be logical.

32. This reasoning is, of course, based upon the infant industry argument.

33. Hans Gustavsson, of the Technology and Development Group at the Research Policy Institute, is developing this concept into operationality within a project on the capital goods industry in Nicaragua.

34. A common world market price for a combine harvester in the 1960s was US $ 30,000. If the value of the Soviet machines was similar, their total cost would have been US $ 30 million.

35. The only benefit during this period was learning, but this gradual accumulation of skills did not start to pay off in a material sense until the 1970s.

36. However, I will argue below that it is extremely difficult to make such a long-term cost-benefit analysis in a satisfactory manner.

37. See Edquist and Edqvist (1979: 29) for a discussion of these issues.

38. However, it must be kept in mind that all historical analogies have limitations.

39. Costs, however, are somewhat easier to estimate than benefits.

40. Although development *is* long-term structural change, and generation of technical capability takes decades, one reason for carrying out short-term cost-benefit analyses remains. They may indicate the size of the losses in the short run. A decision can then be taken as to whether these can be accepted – with the expectation

that they will be balanced by long-term benefits.

41. However, these figures may vary considerably in different contexts.

42. However, it certainly does not measure productivity as such, which must have been considerably higher.

43. I have chosen not to use the 1970 figures, as this year was atypical and since the data are probably less reliable for this chaotic *zafra*.

44. In the industrialized countries, job reductions in industry due to the introduction of industrial robots are very much discussed. According to our estimate, the total stock of robots in the OECD countries taken together was 62,000 by the end of 1983. If one robot replaces two workers, the number of jobs displaced in all OECD countries is smaller than the number displaced by cane combine harvesters in only one small Third World country. Hence, the job displacement potential of robots is much smaller than that of harvesters. The estimate of the number of robots installed is taken from Edquist and Jacobsson (1984), which deals with the diffusion of electronically controlled capital goods in the engineering industry, i.e. numerically controlled machine tools, industrial robots, computer-aided design (CAD) systems and flexible manufacturing systems (FMS).

45. In Edquist and Edqvist (1979) various meanings of "appropriate technology" were discussed, and a critique of the concept was presented.

46. In Australia, there is general agreement that the real cost of cane harvesting has gone down as a result of mechanization (Hackett 1984).

47. In Palmer, Edquist and Jacobsson (1984) we discuss the relation between technical change and employment in greater depth. The problem was analysed at different levels of aggregation, such as machine level, firm level, industry level, national level and international level. One conclusion in that study was that unemployment is much more a political-economic problem than a technological one.

Part 4: Other Third World Countries

8. Some Implications for Other Third World Countries

I will devote this final part to a discussion of some implications of this study for Third World countries in general.[1] It is of course impossible to generalize – in a strict sense – from only two cases to the Third World as a whole. Parts of the following are, therefore, quite speculative, and for this reason I was initially reluctant to include this chapter. The argument that convinced me was that vague and intuitive ideas *may* be as valuable as scientifically solid and safe conclusions for various actors in Third World countries, when they are formulating strategies in relation to technical change. I will therefore simply present some ideas and arguments that have arisen during the work with the comparative case study which may be of relevance for other Third World countries. It should be borne in mind, however, that the following remarks are more relevant to relatively advanced Third World countries than to the poorest ones. Some of the ideas expressed have more the character of value judgements than empirically based results. Hopefully they can serve the purpose of stimulating a discussion. I would emphasize that what follows should not be read separately from the rest of this study, since it is closely related to the discussion in previous chapters.

On the basis of the economic history of the now developed countries, I would argue that one of the most striking characteristics of development is that it is a process of long-term structural change. The transition from economies based upon agriculture, through societies dominated by industrial production to service economies illustrates this. Technical change has always been an important inherent part of such processes of structural change. In a world characterized by an increasingly dynamic technological development, no country can afford to rely only on manual techniques like the machete. If advanced techniques are efficiently introduced and used in other countries competing in the same commodity markets, those countries lagging behind tend to lose out, and profits as well as real wages may decrease.[2] In order to increase productivity and the wealth of the people in the long run it is necessary to substitute people with machines in various sectors of production.

For these reasons Third World countries must introduce modern techniques – such as sugar cane combine harvesters at least in some

163

economic sectors. There are also strong reasons for some of them to introduce even more advanced techniques, such as those based on electronics, e.g. computer controlled machine tools. Sophisticated techniques should be seen as a means to overcome underdevelopment both of the country and of its working population. If modern techniques are not introduced in Third World countries, these countries will continue to be left behind and the vicious circle of underdevelopment will continue to operate. Advanced techniques are necessary to liberate mankind from the force of necessity. This is true for capitalist as well as socialist developing countries.

We can also see that modern techniques are being diffused to most Third World countries. The explicit objective of practically all Third World governments – in capitalist as well as socialist countries – is the introduction of modern techniques. However, the process of diffusion is not uniform; it has a variety of tempi and forms in different Third World countries and for various techniques.[3]

TECHNOLOGICAL CAPABILITY GENERATION

The generation of a technological capability is essential for all developing countries. Technological capability can be defined as the skills to operate, maintain, repair, design and produce capital goods. The ability to use (operate, maintain and repair) capital goods develops through practice in all sectors of production. When it comes to the elements of design and production, the establishment of a capital goods industry is necessary. Several reasons for indigenous production of capital goods were listed and discussed in Chapter 7 (pp.122-40) and will not be repeated here. The experience reported and the arguments presented earlier in this study clearly indicate that domestic design and production of capital goods is crucial for the generation of a technological capability as well as for the development process as a whole. Because of the significant long-run learning benefits, I would argue that almost all Third World countries should develop some capital goods production, even if the least developed countries must start with simple items and uncomplicated machines. On this basis they can then enter into production of more advanced capital goods.

However, not even large Third World countries should try to become self-sufficient with regard to the supply of capital goods. This means that technical dependency on imported capital goods cannot be avoided by any country, with the exception perhaps of the largest industrialized ones. The reasons are that the capital goods industry is extremely heterogeneous and it would, therefore, be too costly to establish a technological capability for producing all types of capital goods (see pp.138-9). In addition, technical change has led to greatly increasing economies of scale for many capital goods during recent decades. For these reasons an international specialization and integration with the world market for capital goods is necessary. Hence, dependence on imported goods is not necessarily a bad thing for Third World countries, since the alternative would be very high production costs and lower quality of products.[4] Therefore, all countries should produce some capital goods, but no country should try to produce all – or even most – of the capital goods items which the country requires. Third World countries should – like most industrialized ones – remain dependent for many capital goods, but not for all.

Countries like India and China have followed a strategy of self-reliance in the field of capital goods. In 1978, India, for example, had a self-sufficiency ratio of 86% with regard to engineering products (Edquist and Jacobsson 1982: 27). This is much higher than most industrialized countries with an industrial sector of a similar size, and I would argue that India has gone too far in this respect.[5] Self-reliance in the capital goods industry may have been a viable strategy for the Soviet Union in the 1930s and perhaps even for India in the 1950s. (In the Soviet case it may even have been the only possible strategy.) At present, however, the cost of not participating in the international specialization and division of labour in this sector has become too high. The only way out would be if Third World countries could establish joint firms for capital goods and thereby achieve specialization and capture economies of scale. If this is impossible, dependence – mainly on industrialized countries – is unavoidable in the capital goods sector.[6]

In this study we have seen that comprehensive processes of technological change and the building-up of a technical capability may take decades rather than years. In addition, each stage in the process is normally followed by another, i.e. the process is never "completed". (This is of course also true for development processes as a whole.) This implies that static short-term cost-benefit analysis is an insufficient or even misleading tool, since it cannot encompass long-term processes of structural change – which are the essence of development. A judgement based exclusively on a static cost-benefit analysis tends to be misleading, since it can capture the short-term costs but not the long-term benefits. Hence, decisions based on such analysis are shortsighted and imply high risk aversion. Still, static cost-benefit analysis is a standard tool in preinvestment evaluations of development projects, and it is often the sole basis for investment decisions.

If cost-benefit analysis is to be useful, it has to have a long-term and dynamic character. As we saw on pp.140-4, it is, however, extremely difficult to carry out such analyses *ex ante*. They are, therefore, almost never even attempted. In spite of the fact that development *is* long-term structural change, and that generation of technological capability often takes decades, one reason for carrying out static cost-benefit analyses remains valid. They can indicate the size of the costs or losses in the short run and thereby give an idea about the extent of the required financial investments and about how large the dynamic benefits must be if the project is to be pursued.

The decision to mechanize the sugar harvest in Cuba was probably highly instrumental in the Cuban process of structural change. For example, it led to a major reallocation of labour, and it contributed to the development of a domestic capital goods sector which is now also producing equipment for other economic sectors.[7] If a correct conventional (static) cost-benefit analysis of cane harvest mechanization had been carried out in Cuba in the early 1960s, it would have shown that the project would be unprofitable, since, in reality, it took at least 20 years before mechanization paid off. A decision based solely upon the analysis might then have resulted in the scrapping of the whole idea. The capability generation and other structural changes induced by mechanization would then not have occurred.[8]

Static cost-benefit analysis can capture only marginal changes, but what is needed for development are structural changes. Therefore, static cost-benefit analysis is misleading and dangerous as a basis for decisions if it is not supplemented by a dynamic analysis. The development process is continuous and it is basically wrong to talk about the end of such a process. How such structural changes can be started or triggered off is, however, a highly relevant and extremely important question.

TECHNOLOGY AND EMPLOYMENT

A common counter-argument to the introduction of advanced techniques – which are normally labour saving – in Third World countries, is that many of them are plagued by unemployment and underemployment. In this study, we have also seen that the problem of employment is crucial in the context of processes of technical change. The employment situation is an important determinant of technical change, or lack thereof (see Chapter 6). Technical change also has important employment consequences (see pp.146-57).

The main reason why workers and unions did not oppose mechanization in socialist Cuba was that unemployment decreased substantially after the revolution (see Table 4.1 and pp.148-52). This decrease was certainly *not* caused by changes in technology, but instead by the structural transformation of the socio-economic system. The need for education and health services certainly existed before the revolution, but they were not satisfied. After the revolution such services were gradually supplied to practically everyone. This provided a great amount of new employment in the service sector. Unemployed resources had been mobilized to satisfy basic human needs. The expansion of industrial production and housing construction also meant additional employment and thereby a decrease in the general rate of unemployment. Employment expansion in thise "new" sectors led to the shortage of cane harvest workers, and this shortage, in turn, made harvest mechanization necessary.[9] In Jamaica a persisting high general unemployment rate was the main reason for workers' and unions' resistance to cane harvest mechanization and partly explains the present lack of mechanized sugar cane-cutting.

When it comes to the consequences of technical change on employment and other variables, I have on page 155-7 argued that the absence of mechanization of cane-cutting will lead to disastrous results for the Jamaican workers in the long run. It contributes to the permanence of a low, or even decreasing, real wage as well as extremely heavy and monotonous work. It also contributed to the continuation of underdevelopment of the country.

We saw that mechanization of cane loading at the Monymusk estate in Jamaica in the early 1960s led to severe social problems for the some 4,000 workers made redundant (see pp.64-8). In Cuba, mechanical loaders replaced about 50,000 workers in the 1960s, and combine harvesters replaced between 120,000 and 160,000 workers during the 1970s (pp.148-52). Hence, there is certainly a close relationship between technical change and employment at the micro level: labour-saving technical changes result in less employment per unit of output and labour may be displaced. The uneven distribution and pace of technical change between various sectors of production continuously change the pattern of employment, both in capitalist and socialist countries.

When it comes to determinants of the level of employment and unemployment in a country as a whole, however, there are other, more important determinants. Hence, it is incorrect to equate the aggregated employment effects of labour-saving technical change at the micro level to an unemployment effect for the economy as a whole. It is not even possible to aggregate from the level of the machine to the level of the production unit, e.g. firm or farm. There may be compensatory effects operating. At the level of the firm, there may be substantial "automatic" compensatory effects due to increased competitiveness of the firm as a result of the technical change. Hence, total employment may remain the same – or even increase – due to increased volume of production – although employment per unit of output decreases. Of course the automatic compensation may be too small to make up for the increased labour productivity. It may even be zero. In such cases the number of workers employed by the firm decreases because of the technical change.[10]

At the level of the national economy the general economic policies of governments are of crucial importance. Most of the workers displaced by mechanization of cane loading in Jamaica could not be absorbed into other sectors of the economy. In Cuba, on the other hand, the 50,000 workers displaced by cane loaders in the 1960s were absorbed by the expansion of other sectors of the economy. This was closely associated with the radical structural transformation of the socio-economic system as a whole and the related change in development strategy. However, structural changes in the organization of a society do not necessarily have to take the form of a social revolution. Structural changes of more limited scope may also be highly important for the employment level. The state may widen the range of policy measures with which to steer the economy, co-operatives may be established, etc.[11]

The conclusion is that the level of (un)employment in a society is not primarily technologically determined. On the contrary, unemployment is first and foremost a political and socio-economic problem. It is still a fact, however, that labour-saving technical changes may displace labour at the level of the production units. Since I have argued that Third World countries should introduce advanced techniques to increase the productivity and wealth of their populations, the problem is how the workers displaced in the process can be re-employed in other production units, perhaps after appropriate re-education.

Theoretically the answer is simple. In all Third World countries – and in industrialized ones too, for that matter – there are unsatisfied basic human needs like housing, education and health care.[12] At the same time there are also potential or unutilized resources, including unemployed human labour, in most countries. In theory, these idle resources could be used to satisfy needs. It is a question of how the relations between material human needs on the one hand and production and distribution of goods and services on the other are organized and interact. This is to a great extent a socio-economic and political problem.

Politically and practically the problem may be extremely complicated to solve, since social and political changes are necessary. In Cuba needs were transformed into demand and satisfied. This simultaneously contributed to a decrease in unemployment in the 1960s.[13] In Jamaica – and most other Third World countries – the problems of widespread unemployment and basic needs satisfaction are still acute.[14]

It follows that the most viable long-term strategy for the workers and unions is to orient their struggle more to the socio-economic and political level and not to fight the machines as such. This does not mean that all advanced techniques should be introduced just because they are new. The advantages of introducing them – in terms of productivity, working conditions, etc. – must first be established. However, their introduction should certainly not be avoided merely because they save labour. Instead compensation mechanisims should be sought so that those displaced can be re-employed in other sectors. In addition, the investment ratio always has an upper limit. Because of resource limitations, advanced techniques cannot be introduced in all economic sectors simultaneously.[15] Selectivity is necessary, and priority should be given to those sectors where the difference between benefits and costs – in a dynamic sense – is greatest.

The workers should not fight against the introduction of advanced techniques, but fight, for example, for the conditional introduction of new techniques. They could demand economic compensation in cases where workers are displaced, but also power over the mode and pace of introduction of new techniques. Luddist machine-storming is an understandable reaction in specific situations but not a viable long-term strategy, since advanced techniques are necessary for higher real wages, and often also for better working conditions.

168

In spite of the fact that machine-storming is not a viable long-run strategy, workers and unions often oppose labour-saving technical changes in many countries, particularly capitalist ones. As we have seen this was the case in Jamaica as well as in pre-revolutionary Cuba. They are afraid of losing their jobs. They know that the deficiencies of the socio-economic system as well as the inability of government policy have led to high unemployment already, prior to the technical change. Hence, they certainly have good (short-term) reasons to assume that they will not be re-employed once they are displaced. This extremely difficult dilemma for the workers and unions was discussed at the end of Chapter 7. The workers *cannot* act in line with their long-term interest in a structural context of high unemployment. If one is only seasonally employed and half fed there *is* only a short-run. This is the basis for the fact that the resistance of workers and unions is an important obstacle to technical change in many countries where the unions really represent the (short-term) interests of the workers. Strong unions can also influence governments to prohibit the introduction of new techniques. This was the case in sugar cane-cutting in Jamaica in some periods and it is true also for certain economic sectors in some other Third World countries.

OBSTACLES TO TECHNICAL CHANGE

There are many other obstacles to technical change. The concept of social carriers of techniques – which was presented and used in Chapter 6 – indicates that six conditions (interest, organization, power, information, access and knowledge) must be fulfilled simultaneously if a technique is to be introduced. If all of them are fulfilled, the techniques *will* be introduced. This is true for all countries. If one or more of the conditions are not fulfilled, this constitutes an obstacle to technical change. Thereby the unfulfilled condition also constitutes a point of intervention in a policy aimed at introducing new techniques in a society.

The obstacles may be grouped in two main categories. They may be of a socio-economic and political nature (interest, organisation, power) or of a strictly technological character (information, access, knowledge).[16]

If obstacles are mainly of a social character, social changes are of course required. Such changes must often be of a comprehensive kind, since the conditions of interest and power of various actors are closely related to the structural features of the socio-economic system as a whole.[17] Social changes of a more limited scope may, however, sometimes be sufficient to overcome obstacles.

On the basis of the present study it may be argued that union resistance as a social obstacle to the introduction of advanced techniques is generally stronger in capitalist countries with high unemployment than in socialist countries with low open unemployment. For example, we have seen that there was no worker resistance to the mechanization of sugar cane harvesting in Cuba after the revolution. Instead there was a consensus among all actors that cane harvesting should be mechanized. In Jamaica workers and unions strongly opposed the introduction of sugar cane combine harvesters in order to save their jobs. It was a conflict issue. In many capitalist Third World countries it may be difficult to introduce labour-saving techniques, since there is no efficient socio-economic or political mechanism to take care of the workers displaced at the micro level. In addition, mechanization was facilitated in socialist Cuba since a longer planning horizon was applied by the state there as compared to the capitalists in Jamaica. Also, the fact that the implementation of techniques on a large scale often take decades, and that they are normally not profitable in the short and medium term facilitated mechanization in socialist Cuba as compared to capitalist Jamaica.[18] If the introduction of advanced techniques is a good thing, socialist Third World countries have an advantage over capitalist ones in this respect.[19]

This also means that conventional (static) cost-benefit analyses were insufficient as a basis for decision-making with regard to mechanization in both countries. In Cuba, such an analysis was probably not carried out at all. In Jamaica, union resistance and political lobbying seem to have been at least as important for the outcome as economic calculations made by managers. Contradictions between social classes and politically based decision-making are probably much more important determinants of technical change than managerial economic calculations also in many other Third World countries. What is rational for one actor or social class may be quite disadvantageous for another.

In a structural context where the main social obstacles (interest, organization and power) to the introduction of existing techniques have, on the whole, been overcome, technical change becomes more of a strictly technological problem. Cane-cutting in Cuba in the 1960s is an example of such a situation (see pp.82-7). What is then at issue is to identify the most suitable technique, secure access to it and build up skills and knowledge about how to operate, repair and maintain the equipment. The fulfillment of the technological conditions can – in contrast to the socio-economic and political ones – be secured partly by acquiring information, access and knowledge from the outside world through literature, trade, experts, consultants, etc.

These tasks may be quite substantial and complicated, particularly in Third World countries with a limited technological capability and R&D infrastructure. Therefore, severe mistakes may be made as we saw in Chapters 4 and 7. In Part 3 of this study I have – explicitly or implicitly – pointed to a number of important measures that could be taken in order to avoid such mistakes. Let me briefly rephrase some of them in a more general manner.

As a start the relevant actor with an interest in technical change and enough power to materialize that interest, should make a systematic attempt to identify, evaluate and compare many technical alternatives and the suppliers of them. The evaluation of technical alternatives should not be restricted by political considerations.[20] The evaluation should be technical as well as economic. Prior to the large-scale implementation of a technique, the leading candidates must also be thoroughly tested in practice. If someone had really compared the early Soviet cane harvesters with the Massey-Ferguson 515 he would probably have reached the conclusion that the latter was much better (see pp.125-7). Thereby both time (5-8 years) and money (millions of dollars) could have been saved. The economic value of this kind of investigation may often be very large.

With regard to own R&D and design, a pluralistic approach has many advantages. Various ideas, design concepts and prototypes should be pursued simultaneously and compete with each other.[21] Foreign solutions should be imported to fertilize indigenous design efforts. A conscious exposure to foreign ideas and their assimilation or imitation may be highly valuable. Isolation may lead to the "reinvention of the wheel" or to ignorance of technical breakthroughs made abroad. At the same time a close monitoring of achievements in other countries must not be allowed to replace completely independent R&D and design efforts. In the early stages of the development of a technological capability, information gathering is most crucial. The capacity to understand new techniques theoretically is, however, a precondition for the ability to modify them. And such adaptations to specific conditions are often necessary. Work with own basic design concepts is also important in Third World countries. However, it is of minor importance until the capabilities to monitor achievements in other countries and learn from them have been developed.[22]

In many developing countries contacts with foreign specialists are quite limited. They should instead be as extensive as possible and developed independently of political ties. They should involve people actually concerned with design, selection, testing, use and production of techniques, and not only high level decision-makers. A bureaucratic structure must be avoided. Creative activities like R&D cannot be planned in an inflexible manner, as we have seen from the experience of Eastern Europe in the 1960s and 1970s. The decision-making process should include an open debate on various alternatives. This requires diffusion of information to all involved actors. Secrecy is dangerous, and participatory democracy is of the utmost importance for creative thinking with regard to selection and development of various techniques. These suggestions may sound naive and self-evident, but it is still a fact that isolation, rigid hierarchies, secrecy and lack of participatory democracy are much more common than their opposites in most Third World countries.

The measures mentioned above are important in socialist as well as in capitalist countries. However, there is a risk that the size – and thereby the cost – of mistakes, become much larger in centralized socialist societies than in capitalist ones, where decisions are taken in a more decentralized manner. Because of this, the measures proposed are of greater importance in socialist countries.

The economic cost of these and other preparatory measures are quite minimal in relation to the costs of the mistakes that may result if they are not pursued. What I am arguing for is the necessity to make parallel trials on a small scale with several alternative techniques, as well as to study and analyse problems of choice, development and transfer of techniques in depth *before* big investments are made. Policy decisions must not be taken prematurely.

When, finally, a technique is to be implemented on a large scale, this should be planned in detail. The production system into which the new technique is to be integrated must often be changed substantially, people have to be educated, etc. Repair and maintenance facilities should also be established before large-scale implementation. Although it may be a truism, it is nevertheless important to stress that it is almost impossible to be too well prepared.

However, as I have repeatedly emphasized, technical change is never exclusively a technological problem. Techniques are always introduced in a socio-economic context. New problems of a social nature occur continuously. Technical change, therefore, cannot be handled only by engineers and technicians. Advanced techniques do not by themselves solve all problems, as is often believed in Third World countries, particularly socialist ones. The approach to technological change should, therefore, not be narrowly restricted to techniques as such, but be broad enough to include social, economic and cultural aspects. It is not enough that one has access to a "suitable" technique. The other five conditions defining a social carrier of techniques must also be fulfilled in order for implementation to take place. Incentives for workers, management, and other actors involved in the use of the technique are of crucial importance if the potential benefits of techniques are to be realized.[23] Material incentives are important, but democracy and grass-root involvement in decision-making are also crucial for the effective development and application of advanced techniques with the objective of liberating mankind.

Notes

1. Hence the main purpose of this final Part is not to summarize the main conclusions reached in this study nor to elucidate the policy implications of relevance for Cuba and Jamaica. The reader has certainly noted them as they have appeared in the text, particularly in Part 3.

2. As examples of profitable technical changes dealt with in this study we can mention sugar cane combine harvesters in Australia and mechanical cane loaders in Jamaica.

3. In another study, carried out with Staffan Jacobsson, I have investigated the diffusion in India and South Korea of four electronically based techniques used in the engineering industry. The techniques studied are numerically controlled machine tools (NCMTs), industrial robots, computer aided design (CAD) systems

and flexible manufacturing systems (FMS) NCMTs and CAD systems have been diffused fairly rapidly in both countries, while robots and FMS have so far been introduced to a very limited extent. For all four techniques the diffusion is faster in Korea than in India. See Edquist and Jacobsson (1985).

4. This begs the question *which* capital goods various Third World countries should produce themselves and which they should continue to import. A partial approach to this complicated problem was presented on pp.139-40.

5. This will be argued in more depth and detail in another project I am carrying out with Staffan Jacobsson, which deals with technical change and strategies of specialization in the capital goods industries of India and South Korea. See Edquist and Jacobsson (1982).

6. Another question is upon *whom* Third World countries should be dependent. It can be argued that dependency on medium-sized firms in small countries in Western Europe is preferable to dependency on large enterprises in the USA, Japan or the USSR. It may also be an advantage if the dependency is distributed among many firms based in several countries.

7. One example is the factory for various kinds of tractor implements with thousands of employees which has been established next to the cane harvester factory in Holguin.

8. Here it may be interesting to compare what a Vice-Minister of the Japanese Ministry of Trade and Industry (MITI) has to say: "The Ministry of International Trade and Industry decided to establish in Japan industries which require intensive employment of capital and technology, industries that in consideration of competitive cost of production should be the most inappropriate for Japan, industries such as steel, oil refining, petrochemicals, automobiles, aircraft, industrial machinery of all sorts, and electronics including electronic computers. From a short-run static viewpoint, encouragement of such industries would seem to conflict with economic rationalism. But, from a long-range viewpoint, these are precisely the industries where income elasticity of demand is high, technological progress is rapid, and labour productivity rises fast." (*The Industrial Policy of Japan*, Paris: OECD, 1972, quoted in Fransman 1984: 55-6). Obviously the Japanese correctly rejected the "short-run static viewpoint" with regard to many of the industries mentioned.

9. Hence the very strong state interest in the mechanization of the sugar harvest in Cuba was to a large extent due to a bottleneck of the economy. Bottlenecks like shortages of raw materials, labour or machinery seem to be a common reason for technical change in socialist countries. In capitalist contexts, technical change seems to be output oriented to a relatively larger extent; firms innovate to sell more and to be able to compete more successfully, i.e. to increase profits. (This note is based on a discussion with Martin Fransman, University of Edinburgh.)

10. This discussion is based upon Palmer, Edquist and Jacobbson (1984), where the problem of compensation is dealt with more systematically and in more detail.

11. Such possibilities are discussed in Palmer, Edquist and Jacobsson (1984), Chapter 3.

12. Note that I am talking about human needs and not about effective demand. To talk about effective demand is to imply that there is also some ghost called non-effective demand. The latter are needs which cannot influence production and distri-bution of commodities in a capitalist market economy. They remain unsatisfied.

13. All basic needs have certainly not yet been satisfied in Cuba. For example, there is still a severe housing problem.

14. The problem of unemployment can be solved also in capitalist developing countries – at least temporarily. The case of South Korea is one of these exceptions with a fairly low unemployment in the early 1980s.

15. This, of course, also limits the rate of labour displacement.

16. This distinction is made for analytical reasons and does not imply that technical changes can be seen only as a socio-economic problem or only as a technological problem. They are always both but the respective relative importance of them varies greatly between situations.

17. See pp.76-8 for a discussion of the relations between the six conditions defining a social carrier of techniques and the structural characteristics of the society.

18. It could be added that governments in capitalist countries can also, in practice, intervene and absorb part of the risks involved in technical change. In this way a longer planning horizon could have been applied in capitalist Jamaica.

19. This argument applies to the introduction of existing techniques in Third World countries, but certainly not to inventions and innovations of new techniques in socialist industrialized countries. In this respect the socialist countries are much more rigid than their capitalist counterparts. The centralized and hierarchical planning system is an important social obstacle to inventions and innovations in the developed socialist countries.

20. This is particularly important for socialist Third World countries since the Soviet Union is less dynamic in relation to developing and innovating new techniques than the leading capitalist industrialized countries.

21. This approach was successfully followed in Cuba around 1970, but abandoned in the late 1970s. See pp.128 and 146.

22. The early success with the Libertadora design in Cuba was an exception in this respect, see pp.128-31.

23. This is true for all techniques including manual ones. For example, the new system of material incentives in Cuba contributed to the doubling of the productivity of manual cane cutters during the 1970s, see pp.148-52.

Bibliography

Abreu, Lino E. (1973) "Apuntes para una historia de la cosecha mecanizada de la cana en Cuba", in *Revista ATAC* (Asociacion de Tecnicos Azucareros de Cuba), (La Habana, Julio/Agosto, 1973), pp.32-9.

Abreu, Lino E. (1975) "Apuntes para una historia de la cosecha mecanizada de la cana en Cuba (II parte)", in *Técnica Popular*, ano 1, vol.2 (30 diciembre 1975), pp.38-44. (Técnica Popular is published in Havana by the Ministry of the Metallurgical and Mechanical Industries).

Abreu, Lino E. (1976) "Apuntes para una historia de la cosecha mecanizada de la cana en Cuba" (III parte), in *Técnica Popular*, ano 1, no.3 (Enero-Marza 1976), pp.4-9.

Abreu, Lino E. (1981) Interview with Engineer Lino Abreu, Centro de Investigaciones de Construccion de Maquinaria/CICM in February 1981. Engineer Abreu has been working on the design of cane harvesters since the 1960s.

AEC (1975) *Comite Estatal de Estadisticas*, "Anuario Estadistico de Cuba 1975" (La Habana, 1976).

AEC (1977) *Comite Estatal de Estadisticas*, "Anuario Estadistico de Cuba 1977" (La Habana, 1978).

AEC (1979) *Comite Estatal de Estadisticas*, "Anuario Estadistico de Cuba 1979" (La Habana, 1980).

AEC (1981) *Comite Estatal de Estadisticas*, "Anuario Estadistico de Cuba 1981" (La Habana, 1982).

AEC (1982) *Comite Estatal de Estadisticas*, "Anuario Estadistico de Cuba 1982" (La Habana, 1984).

AIJCFA (The All-Island Jamaica Cane Farmers Association) (1981) *Fortieth Annual Report.*

AIJCFA (1982) *Forty-First Annual Report.*

Andérez, Manuel (1981) Interview in February 1981 with Engineer Manuel Andérez, Vice President of the Cuban Academy of Sciences.

Annual Report (1967) "Annual Report of the Field Development Sub-Committee for 1967'" in *Jamaican Association of Sugar Technologists (JAST) Journal*, vol.XXVIII (1967), p.101.

Atkinson, A.M., Quaid, G. and Deicke, R. (1965) "Mechanized Sugar Cane Harvesting in Australia", in *World Crops* (March 1965), pp.46-50.

Baark, E. (1981) "Studies on Technology and Science in India and China: Prospects and Methodology", in Baark, E. and Sigurdson, J. (eds.), *India-China Comparative Research – Technology and Science for Development* (London and Malmö, Curzon Press).

Barreda Sanchez, N. (1982) "Mecanizacion de la cana. Marcha de Gigantes", in *Cuba Azucar* (La Habana, Enero/Marzo), pp.42-5.

Betancourt, Armando F. (1970) "La mecanización de la cosecha canera en Cuba", in *Memoria de la 39 Conferencia ATAC*, 12 al 17 de Octubre de 1970 (La Habana, 1976), pp.27-81.

Blanchard, J.D. (1959) "Mechanical Loading and Trash Content of Cane", in *JAST Journal*, vol.XXII (1959), pp.51-3.

Blanchard, J.D. (1964) "Cane Washing at Monymusk", in *JAST Journal*, vol.XXV (1963/4), pp.78-82.

Briscoe, J.M. (1970) "MF 201 Trials in Mexico and Jamaica", in *Sugar y Azucar* (Sept 1970), pp.23-6 and 50.

Brundenius, Claes (1981) *Economic Growth, Basic Needs and Income Distribution in Revolutionary Cuba*. Research Policy Institute (University of Lund).

Brundenius, Claes (1983) "Some Notes on the Development of the Cuban Labour Force 1970-1980", in *Cuban Studies* (Center for Latin American Studies, University of Pittsburgh), vol.13, no.2 (Summer 1983), pp.65-77.

Brundenius, Claes (1984) *Revolutionary Cuba: The Challenge of Economic Growth with Equity* (Boulder, Colorado, Westview Press).

Brundenius, Claes (1985) "Cuba: Redistribution and Growth with Equity", Paper to be included in Halebsky, S. and Kirk, J. (eds.) *Cuba: Twenty-five Years of Revolution* (Praeger, New York).

Burgess, Reginald (1983) Interview with Reginald Burgess, Deputy Director at the Sugar Industry Research Institute, Mandeville, Jamaica.

Castro, F. (1976) "La Industria Azucarera Cubana" del Informe Central al Primer Congreso del Partido Comunista de Cuba, *Revista ATAC* (Marzo/Abril de 1976), pp.4-5.

Castro, F. (1977) "Esta Fabrica tiene un Significado especial: Cuenta nuestro pais ya con una modernisima industria capaz de producir magnificas combinadas" in *Revista ATAC* (Sept/Oct 1977), pp.11-20.

Central Planning Unit (1961) *A Study of Those Persons Displaced by Mechanization at Monymusk*, Jamaica Central Planning Unit, Paper no.2 (Kingston), mimeographed.

CERP (The Cuban Economic Research Project) (1965) *A Study on Cuba* (Coral Gables, Florida, University of Miami Press).

Chacon Reyes, Julio A. (1966) "History of Bulk Sugar in Cuba", in *Cuba Azucar* (Julio/Agosto 1966), pp.53-7.

Diaz Hernandez, L. and Alvarez Portal, R. (1981) "Los rendimientos de las combinadas caneras", in *Revista ATAC* (Enero/Febrero 1981), pp.47-65.

Direccion Nacional... (1976) Direccion Nacional de Cana del INRA,

Direccion de Cosecha de DINAME, Direccion de Desarrollo de DINAME y Centro de Investigacion y Desarrollo de Maquinaria Agropecuaria, "El Desarrollo de la Mecanizacion de la Cana de Azucar en Cuba", in *Revista ATAC* (Nov/Dic de 1976), pp.5-25.

Dominguez, Jorge I. (1978) *Cuba – Order and Revolution* (Cambridge, Mass., The Belknap Press of Harvard University Press).

Dpto . . . (1974) Departmento de Investigaciones Agro-Industriales del ICINAZ, "Hacia el Incremento de la Eficiencia y Productividad del Centro de Acopio", in *Revista ATAC* (Marzo/Junio de 1974), pp.61-5.

Edquist, Charles (1977) *Teknik, samhálle och energi* (Techniques, Society and Energy), (in Swedish) (Lund, Zenit/Bo Cavefors Bokförlag).

Edquist, Charles (1980) *Approaches to the Study of Social Aspects of Techniques – Summary of a Doctoral Thesis* (Lund, Research Policy Institute, University of Lund).

Edquist, Charles (1982a) *Technical Change in Sugar Cane Harvesting – A Comparison of Cuba and Jamaica (1958-1980)*, World Employment Programme Research, Working Paper no.96, Technology and Employment Programme (Geneva, International Labour Office).

Edquist, Charles (1982b) "Methodological Aspects of Comparing Technical Change – The Case of Sugar Cane Harvesting in Cuba and Jamaica 1958-1980", in Erik Baark (ed.), *Comparative Technological Change – Methodology and Theory* (Research Policy Institute, University of Lund).

Edquist, Charles (1983) "Mechanization of Sugar Cane Harvesting in Cuba", in *Cuban Studies* (Center for Latin American Studies, University of Pittsburgh), vol.13, no.2 (Summer 1983), pp.41-64.

Edquist, Charles (1984) *Technology and Work in Sugar Cane Harvesting in Capitalist Jamaica and Socialist Cuba 1959-1983*. Paper presented to the conference "Work in 1984 – Emancipation or Derogation", Karlstad, Sweden, June 1984. (To be published in Gustavsson, B-C., Karlsson, J.C., and Reftegard. C. (eds) *Work as Emancipation and Derogation* (London, Gower Publishing Co. Ltd., 1985.)

Edquist, Charles and Edquist, Olle (1979) *Social Carriers of Techniques for Development*, published as SAREC Report R3: 1979 by the Swedish Agency for Research Cooperation with Developing Countries, c/o SIDA, S-105 25 Stockholm, Sweden. (A somewhat abridged version under the same title, was published in *Journal of Peace Research*, vol.XVI, no.4 (1979). In Swedish the study has been published as Zenit Häften 5 (1980). (During 1985 it will be published in Indonesian.)

Edquist, Charles and Jacobsson, Staffan (1982) "Technical Change and Patterns of Specialization in the Capital Goods Industries of India and the Republic of Korea – a project description" (Research Policy Institute, University of Lund, Sweden) mimeo.

Edquist, Charles and Jacobsson, Staffan (1984) "Trends in the Diffusion of Electronics Technology in the Capital Goods Sector". Discussion

Paper No.161 (Research Policy Institute, University of Lund.) (To be published by UNCTAD, Geneva, 1985).

Edquist, Charles and Jacobsson, Staffan (1985) "Automation in the Engineering Industries of India and the Republic of Korea against the Background of the Experience in some OECD Countries" (Research Policy Institute, University of Lund, Sweden) mimeo.

Fauconnier, R. (1983) "Standard of Living and Degree of Mechanization of Sugar Cane Harvesting". Paper presented at the International Society of Sugar Cane Technologists, XVIII Congress, Cuba, mimeo.

Fletcher, Richard (1979) Interview in January 1979 with Minister of State, Richard Fletcher, Ministry of Finance, Jamaica. Mr Fletcher is a former chairman of the Sugar Industry Authority.

Fonseca, Luis (1981) Interview in February 1981 with engineer Luis Fonseca, Vice Minister in Ministerio de la Industria Sidero-Mecanica (SIME), Cuba.

Fransman, Martin (1984) "Conceptualizing Technical Change in the Third World in the 1980s: an Interpretive Survey" in *Journal of Development Studies*, July or October 1985 (forthcoming).

Gaunt, J.K. (1964) "Development of the Massey-Ferguson System of Mechanically Harvesting Sugar Cane", in *Proceedings of the Queensland Society of Sugar Cane Technologists*, Thirty-first Conference, Mackay, Queensland, April, pp.27-36.

Goldenberg (1960) *Report of the Commission of Enquiry on the Sugar Industry of Jamaica* ("Goldenberg Report"), mimeographed.

Gonzalez, Gilberto (1972) "Desarrollo de los centros de acopio de cana de azucar en Cuba", in *Cuba Azucar* (Abril/Junio 1972), pp.43.7.

Gonzalez Eguiluz, V. and Garcia Nunez, J. (1977) "Influencia de las Materias Extranas de la cana en el Recobrado" in *Revista ATAC* (Ene/Feb 1977), pp.11-21.

van Groenigen, J.C. (1970) "Evaluation of Mechanical Harvesters – 1970 crop", in *JAST Journal*, vol.XXXI (1970), pp.57-66.

van Groenigen, J.C. (1972) "Considerations in cleaner mechanical loading of cane", in *JAST Journal*, vol.XXXIII (1972), pp.96-102.

Hackett, Jack (1982) Letter of 23 March 1982, from Jack Hackett, Director of Technical Operations of the Massey-Ferguson Company, Victoria, Australia.

Hackett, Jack (1984) Letter of 5 January 1984 from Jack Hackett.

Hagelberg, G.B. (1983) Letter of 4 July 1983 from G.B. Hagelberg. Dr Hagelberg has been doing research on sugar production for a long time.

Higgins, W. (1980) "Worker Participation in Jamaican Sugar Production", in *Rural Development Participation Review* (Cornell University, Ithaca, New York), vol.1, no.2 (Winter 1980).

Jefferson, Owen (1972) *The Post-war Economic Development of Jamaica* (Kingston, Institute of Social and Economic Research, University of the West Indies, Jamaica).

Junta Central . . . (1970) *Junta Central de Planificacion*, Direccion Central de Estadistica, "Boletin Estadistico 1970" (La Habana).

Junta Central . . . (1972) *Junta Central de Planificacion*, Direccion Central de Estadistica, "Anuario Estadistico de Cuba 1972" (La Habana).

Lee, C.O. and van Groenigen, J.C. (1973) "Three Years of Mechanical Harvesting Study in Jamaica", in *Proceedings of the 1973 Meeting of West Indies Sugar Technologists* held in Barbados under the auspices of West Indies Sugar Association, May, pp.183-205.

Lee, C.O. (1983) Interview in January 1983 with Colin O. Lee, Agricultural Economist at the Sugar Industry Research Institute, Mandeville, Jamaica.

Leffingwell, Roy J. (1974) "Field Mechanization" in *Sugar y Azucar* (Sept 1974).

Leffingwell, Roy J. (1978) "Mecanizacion del Campo", in *Sugar y Azucar*, vol.73, no.5 (May 1978), pp.125-7.

MacEwan, Arthur (1981) *Revolution and Economic Development in Cuba* (London, The MacMillan Press Ltd).

Marx, Karl (1967) *Capital. A Critical Analysis of Capitalist Production*, vol.1 (New York, International Publishers).

Mecanizacion (1977) "Mecanizacion de la cana en Cuba", in *Cuba Azucar* (Enero/Marzo 1977), pp.7-15.

Mesa-Lago, Carmelo (1981) *The Economy of Socialist Cuba: A Two-Decade Appraisal* (Albuquerque, University of New Mexico Press).

Minster (1976) *The Sugar Industry Rehabilitation Programme*, prepared by Minster Agriculture, Belmont 13, Upper High Street, Thame, Oxfordshire OX9 3HL, England, July, mimeographed, on behalf of the Sugar Industry of Jamaica.

Mordecai, J. (1967) *Report of the Sugar Industry Enquiry Commission (1966)* (Jamaica, October). The Chairman of the Commission was John Mordecai.

Moreno Fraginals, Manuel (1978) *El Ingenio – Complejo Economico Social Cubano del Azucar*, tomo III (La Habana).

Morgan, W. (1962) *Economic Survey of the Sugar Plantation Industry* (Geneva, International Federation of Plantation, Agricultural and Allied Workers), mimeographed.

National Planning Agency (1978) *Economic and Social Survey, Jamaica 1978,* prepared by the National Planning Agency.

National Planning Agency (1980) *Economic and Social Survey, Jamaica 1980*.

Nelson, Lowry (1951), *Rural Cuba* (Minneapolis, University of Minnesota Press).

Nelson, Lowry (1972) *Cuba – The Measure of a Revolution* (Minneapolis, University of Minnesota Press).

O'Connor, James (1968) "Agrarian Reforms in Cuba, 1959-1963", in *Science and Society*, vol.XXXI, no.2 (Spring 1968).

Oviano, Ricardo (1973) "La Agricultura canera se transforma para multiplicar la produccion", in *Revista ATAC* (Julio/Agosto 1973), pp.3-19.

Page, Ralph G. (1981) *A Look at the Production of the Sugar Industry over the past Ten Years* (Mandeville, Jamaica, Sugar Industry Research Institute), mimeographed.

Palmer, Lesley; Edquist, Charles and Jacobsson, Staffan (1984) *Perspectives on Technical Change and Employment*, Discussion Paper No. 167 (University of Lund, Research Policy Institute).

Peralta, U.; Oviano, R.; Velarde, E.; Abreu, L. and Iglesias, C. (1980) "Los Medios de Mecanizacion Canera" in *Revista ATAC* (Enero/Febrero 1980), pp.55-64.

Pino Santos, Oscar (1980) Interview in April 1980 with Director Oscar Pino Santos, Centro de Investigaciones Economia Mundial (CIEM).

Pollitt, Brian (1981) *Revolution and the Mode of Production in the Sugar-Cane Sector of the Cuban Economy, 1959-1980: Some Preliminary Findings*, Occasional Paper no.35, Institute of Latin American Studies (University of Glasgow).

Pollitt, Brian (1982) Letter of 15 March 1982 from Brian H. Pollitt, Institute of Latin American Studies, The University of Glasgow, United Kingdom.

Posada, Eduardo David (1976) "Quince anos de revolucion en la produccion azucarera", in *Cuba Azucar* (Enero/Marzo 1976), pp.17-25.

Reunion ... (1974) "Reunion Nacional sobre la Cosecha de la Cana. Incrementan Macheteros y Operadores de Combinadas su Productividad en la zafra de 1974" in *Revista ATAC* (Marzo/Junio de 1974), pp.26-30.

Roberto, D. (1975) "El IV Encuentro de Jefes de Maquinaria de la Industria Azucarera" in *Revista ATAC* (Nov/Dic 1975), pp.35-7.

Roca, Sergio (1976) *Cuban Economic Policy and Ideology: The Ten Million ton Sugar Harvest* (Beverly Hills and London, Sage Publications).

Rodriguez, Juan (1982) Interview in February 1982 with Engineer Juan Rodriguez, Director, Instituto de Investigaciones de Mecanizacion Agropecuaria (IIMA), Havana.

RPI (Research Policy Institute) (1983) *Technology and Development – A Research Programme on Technological Change and Technology Policies with a Focus on the Capital Goods Sector in the Third World*, Research Policy Institute (University of Lund, Sweden, April).

Salomon Llanes, Roberto (1977) "La primera combinada KTP-1 producida en Cuba", in *Revista ATAC* (Sept/Oct 1977), pp.4-10.

Salomon Llanes, Roberto (1978) "El mayor y mas moderno sistema de exportacion de azucardel mundo", in *Revista ATAC* (Enero/Febrero 1978), pp.12-19.

Salomon Llanes, Roberto (1980) "El centro de acopio, un elemento valioso en la cosecha canera", *Revista ATAC* (Enero/Febrero 1980), pp.38-41.

Seaga Government (1981) "Seaga Government Terminates Sugar Workers Co-ops", in *Sugar World* (Published by GATT-Fly, Toronto, Canada), vol.IV, no.5 (December 1981).

Shaw, M.E.A. (1982) *Review of the 1982 Crop Year and Performance Trends since 1965* (Mandeville, Jamaica, Sugar Industry Research Institute), mimeo.

Shaw, M.E.A. (1983a) Interview in January 1983 with Mike Shaw, Director at the Sugar Industry Research Insitute, Mandeville, Jamaica.

Shaw, M.E.A. (1983b) Statement by Mike Shaw, Director of SIRI, at a seminar in January 1983 at the University of the West Indies, Kingston, when an earlier version of the present study was presented and discussed.

Shillingford, J.D. (1974) "Financial Potential and Welfare Implications of Sugar Cane Harvest Mechanization on Jamaican Plantations", PhD, Cornell University.

Sintesis . . . (1982) "Sintesis del Informe del Ministerio de la Industria Azucarera a la Asamblea Nacional del Poder Popular, Leido por Diocles Torralba", *Granma* (29 de Diciembre), p.2.

SMA (1970) "Mechanical Harvesting", in The Sugar Manufacturers Association (SMA) (of Jamaica) Limited, Research Department, *Annual Report 1970*, pp.35-47.

SMA (1971) "Mechanical Harvesting", in The Sugar Manufacturers Association (of Jamaica) Limited, Research Department, *Annual Report 1971*, pp.55-70.

SMA (1972) "Mechanical Harvesting", in The Sugar Manufacturers Association (of Jamaica) Limited, Research Department, *Annual Report 1972*, pp.36-45.

Spargo, R.F. and Baxter, S.W.D. (1975) "The Development of the Australian Chopped Sugar Cane Harvester", in *Sugar y Azucar* (Nov 1975), pp.31-68.

Stephenson and Loeser (1982) Letter of 25 March 1982, from Mr Stephenson and Mr Loeser of the Claas Maschinenfabrik, Harsewinkel, West Germany.

Suarez Gayol, Jesus and Henderson, Roberto (1966) "Centros de acopio; una perspectiva Halagüena", in *Cuba Azucar*, pp.15-23.

Sugar Industry Research Institute (1975) *Mechanization* (Mandeville), mimeographed.

Thesis (1978) *Thesis y Resoluciones. Primer Congreso del Partido Comunista de Cuba* (Ciudad de la Habana, Editorial de Ciencias Sociales).

Trabajadores (1981) 6 de Febrero (a Cuban daily paper).

US Department of Commerce (1956) *Investment in Cuba. Basic Information for United States Businessmen* (Washington, DC).

Vazquez, J. (1972a) "5 Preguntas de Zafra", Entrevista con Rafael

Francia Mestre, responsable nacional de canas del INRA, *Revista ATAC* (Enero/Febrero 1972), pp.16-20.

Vazquez, J. (1972b) "5 Preguntas de Zafra", Entrevista con Jose A. Borot, Director General de mecanizacion de la cana de azucar de la DINAME, *Revista ATAC* (Mayo/Junio 1972), pp.7-12.

Vazquez, J. (1975) "Ya son Campos Tipicos el 40% de las Areas Caneras Cubanas", Entrevista a Rafael Francia Mestre, Director General de la Agricultura Canera del INRA, por Jose Vazquez, *Revista ATAC* (Julio/Agosto de 1975), pp.22-33.

Vazquez, J. (1978a) "Produciran 10 Prototipos en 1978 de la Combinada KTP-2, que Cosecha con alta Productividad Cana Verde", Entrevista a Mario Cuesta, Director del CICMA, por Jose Vazquez, *Revista ATAC* (Enero/Febrero 1978), pp.4-11.

Vazquez, J. (1978b) "El Desarrollo de la Mecanizacion en las distintas fases de la Agricultura Canera es hoy una tarea Fundamental", Entrevista a Raul Trujillo, viceministro de la Agricultura Canera por Jose Vazquez, *Revista ATAC* (Nov/Dic 1978), pp.4-12.

Vazquez, J. (1979) "La Nueva Combinada Cubana KTP-2 Pasa con Exito las Pruebas de Explotacion", *Revista ATAC* (Mayo/Junio 1979), pp.4-10.

World Bank (1978a) *Staff Appraisal Report. Sugar Rehabilitation Project, Jamaica*, Document of the World Bank, Report no. 1732a-JM, 19 January.

World Bank (1978b) "Report and Recommendation of the President of the International Bank for Reconstruction and Development to the Executive Directors on a Proposed Loan to the Sugar Industry Authority with the Guarantee of Jamaica for a Sugar Rehabilitation Project", Document of the World Bank, Report no. p-2210-JM, 26 January.

2nd Congress . . . (1981) *2nd Congress of the Communist Party of Cuba. Documents and Speeches* (Havana, Political Publishers).

60 Aniversario (1982) "60 Aniversario de la Revolucion de Octubre factory has turned out 1661 KTP-1 cane harvesters since it opened in 1977", in *Granma Weekly Review*, 17 January.

LATIN AMERICAN AND CARIBBEAN TITLES FROM ZED BOOKS

Fidel Castro
THE WORLD CRISIS
Its Economic and Social Impact on the
Underdeveloped Countries
Hb and Pb

Donald Hodges and Ross Gandy
MEXICO 1910-1982: REFORM OR
REVOLUTION?
Hb and Pb

George Beckford and Michael Witter
SMALL GARDEN, BITTER WEED
The Political Economy of Struggle
and Change in Jamaica
Hb and Pb

Liisa North
BITTER GROUNDS
Roots of Revolt in El Salvador
Pb

Ronaldo Munck
POLITICS AND DEPENDENCY IN
THE THIRD WORLD
The Case of Latin America
Hb and Pb

George Beckford
PERSISTENT POVERTY
Underdevelopment in Plantation
Economies of the Third World
Pb

Tom Barry, Beth Wood and Deb
Preusch
DOLLARS AND DICTATORS
A Guide to Central America
Hb and Pb

George Black
TRIUMPH OF THE PEOPLE
The Sandinista Revolution in
Nicaragua
Hb and Pb

George Black
GARRISON GUATEMALA
Hb and Pb

Cedric Robinson
BLACK MARXISM
The Making of the Black Radical
Tradition
Hb and Pb

Teofilo Cabastrero
MINISTERS OF GOD, MINISTERS
OF THE PEOPLE
Hb and Pb

Chris Searle
WORDS UNCHAINED
Language and Revolution in Grenada
Hb and Pb

George Brizan
GRENADA: ISLAND OF
CONFLICT
From Amerindians to People's
Revolution 1498-1979
Hb and Pb

Maurice Bishop
IN NOBODY'S BACKYARD
Maurice Bishop's Speeches, 1979-
1983: A Memorial Volume
Hb and Pb

Carmelo Furci
THE CHILEAN COMMUNIST
PARTY AND THE ROAD TO
SOCIALISM
Hb and Pb

Latin American and Caribbean
Women's Collective
SLAVES OF SLAVES
The Challenge of Latin American
Women
Hb and Pb

Miranda Davies
THIRD WORLD — SECOND SEX
Women's Struggles and National
Liberation
Hb and Pb

Margaret Randall
SANDINO'S DAUGHTERS
Testimonies of Nicaraguan Women in
Struggle
Pb

Bonnie Mass
POPULATION TARGET
The Political Economy of Population
Control in Latin America
Pb

June Nash and Helen Icken Safa
(Editors)
SEX AND CLASS IN LATIN
AMERICA
Women's Perspectives on Politics,
Economics and the Family in the
Third World
Pb

David Stoll
FISHERS OF MEN OR FOUNDERS
OF EMPIRE
The Wycliffe Bible Translators in
Latin America
Hb and Pb

James Petras et al
CLASS, STATE AND POWER IN
THE THIRD WORLD
with Case Studies of Class Conflict in
Latin America
Hb

James Millette
SOCIETY AND POLITICS IN
COLONIAL TRINIDAD
Hb and Pb

Sue Branford and Oriel Glock
THE LAST FRONTIER
Fighting for Land in the Amazon
Hb and Pb

Michael Kaufman
JAMAICA UNDER MANLEY
The Failure of Social Democracy
Hb and Pb

Gabriela Yanes et al
MIRRORS OF WAR
Literature and Revolution in El
Salvador
Hb and Pb

Richard Harris and Carlos Vilas
(Editors)
NICARAGUA: THE REVOLUTION
UNDER THREAT
Hb and Pb

Enrique Medina
THE DUKE
Memories and Anti-memories of a
Participant in the Repression
Pb

Roxanne Dunbar Ortiz
INDIANS OF THE AMERICAS
Self-Determination and Human
Rights
Hb and Pb

Mario Hector
DEATH ROW
Hb and Pb

Charles Edquist
CAPITALISM, SOCIALISM AND
TECHNOLOGY
A Comparative Study of Cuba and
Jamaica
Hb and Pb

INTERNATIONAL RELATIONS/IMPERIALISM TITLES
FROM ZED BOOKS

Albert Szymanski
IS THE RED FLAG FLYING?
The Political Economy of the Soviet
Union Today
Hb and Pb

V.G. Kiernan
AMERICAN — THE NEW
IMPERIALISM:
From White Settlement to World
Hegemony
Hb

Satish Kumar
CIA AND THE THIRD WORLD:
A Study in Crypto-Diplomacy
Hb

Dan Nabudere
THE POLITICAL ECONOMY OF
IMPERIALISM
Hb and Pb

Yan Fitt et al
THE WORLD ECONOMIC CRISIS:
US Imperialism at Bay
Hb and Pb

Clyde Sanger
SAFE AND SOUND
Disarmament and Development in the
Eighties
Pb

Frederick Clairemonte and John
Cavanagh
THE WORLD IN THEIR WEB:
The Dynamics of Textile
Multinationals
(Preface by Samir Amin)
Hb and Pb

Henrick Secher Marcussen and Jens
Erik Torp
THE INTERNATIONALIZATION
OF CAPITAL:
Prospects for the Third World
Hb and Pb

Malcolm Caldwell
THE WEALTH OF SOME
NATIONS
Hb and Pb

Georgi Arbatov
COLD WAR OR DETENTE: THE
SOVIET VIEWPOINT
Hb and Pb

Rachel Heatley
POVERTY AND POWER:
The Case for a Political Approach to
Development
Pb

Ronald Graham
THE ALUMINIUM INDUSTRY
AND THE THIRD WORLD:
Multinational Corporations and
Underdevelopment .
Pb

Petter Nore and Terisa Turner
OIL AND CLASS STRUGGLE
Hb and Pb

Rehman Sobhan
THE CRISIS OF EXTERNAL
DEPENDENCE:
The Political Economy of Foreign Aid
to Bangladesh
Hb and Pb